Iamblichus on the Mysteries of the Egyptians, Chaldeans, and Assyrians

The Complete Text

Translated from the Greek by Thomas Taylor

Published by Pantianos Classics

ISBN-13: 978-1-78987-088-6

First published in 1895

Contents

Advertisement

The various translations and original works of Thomas Taylor, though still in request by the more zealous students of ancient philosophy and occult science, have now become so scarce and expensive that it is only within the power of comparatively wealthy collectors to obtain them. This is a matter for regret, inasmuch as it cannot be affirmed that his writings have been, or are likely to be superseded, or that they are without value. They can hardly be neglected without loss by those who desire to understand the systems of philosophy which satisfied the spiritual needs of the antique world. It is not possible, even for the most fervent believer in modern "progress," to dismiss the speculations of the ancient philosophers as antiquated notions which have had their day and no longer possess interest or value. The names of Socrates, Plato, and Aristotle can never grow dim with age, nor is it possible to conceive a time when men shall cease to study and reverence them. As the disciple, the translator, and the expounder of these and of other sages of antiquity, Thomas Taylor deserves to be held in honour and remembrance, and it would be a misfortune if his labours remained unknown because of the scarcity of his books. It is for this reason that the present reprint has been undertaken; and it is hoped that it will meet with such a measure of success as may encourage the republication of various other works by the same author. It has been printed in handsome style and published at a moderate price in order that it may be regarded as a desirable addition to the scholar's library, while yet it will not tax severely the means of the not too wealthy student. For the rest it is only necessary to say that this reprint is, in size, ' number of pages, type, and general get-up, an almost exact facsimile of the original edition, which was first printed in 1821. No alterations or additions have been made in or to the original text, as it is thought that those who care for Taylor's writings will prefer to have them in their integrity. Should it be found possible, however, to continue the series it is intended to prefix to a future volume an essay on Taylor, which will contain a biography of him, and a critical estimate of his writings.

May, 1895

Introduction

IT appears to me that there are two descriptions of persons by whom the present work must be considered to be of inestimable worth, the lovers of antiquity and the lovers of ancient philosophy and religion. To the former of these it must be invaluable, because it is replete with information derived from the wise men of the Chaldeans, the prophets of the Egyptians, the dogmas of the Assyrians, and the ancient pillars of Hermes; and to the latter, because of the doctrines contained in it, some of which originated from the Hermaic pillars, were known by Pythagoras and Plato, and were the sources of their philosophy; and others are profoundly theological, and unfold the mysteries of ancient religion with an admirable conciseness of diction, and an inimitable vigour and elegance of conception. To which also may be added, as the colophon of excellence, that it is the most copious, the clearest, and the most satisfactory defence extant of genuine ancient theology.

This theology, the sacred operations pertaining to which called *theurgy* are here developed, has for the most part, since the destruction of it, been surveyed only in its corruptions among barbarous nations, or during the decline and fall of the Roman empire, with which, overwhelmed with pollution, it gradually fell, and at length totally vanished from what is called the polished part of the globe. This will be evident to the intelligent reader from the following remarks, which are an epitome of what has been elsewhere more largely discussed by me on this subject, and which also demonstrate the religion of the Chaldeans, Egyptians, and Greeks to be no less scientific than sublime.

In the first place, this theology celebrates the immense principle of things as something superior even to being itself; as exempt from the whole of things, of which it is nevertheless ineffably the source; and does not, therefore, think fit to enumerate it with any triad [1] or order of beings. Indeed it even apologizes for giving the appellation of the most simple of our conceptions to that which is beyond all knowledge and all conception. It denominates this principle however, *the one* and *the good*; by the former of these names indicating its transcendent simplicity, and by the latter its subsistence as the object of desire to all beings. For all things desire good. At the same time, however, it asserts that these appellations are in reality nothing more than the parturitions of the soul, which, standing as it were in the vestibules of the adytum of deity, announce nothing pertaining to the ineffable, but only indicate her spontaneous tendencies towards it, and belong rather to the immediate offspring of the first God than to the first itself. Hence, as the result of this most venerable conception of the supreme, when it ventures not only to denominate it, though ineffable, but also to assert something of its relation to other things, it considers this as preeminently its peculiarity, that it is the *principle of principles*; it being necessary that the characteristic property of principle, after the same manner as other things, should not begin from multitude, but should be collected into one monad as a summit, and which is the principle of all principles.

The scientific reasoning from which this dogma is deduced is the following. As the principle of all things is *the one*, it is necessary that the progression of beings should be continued, and that no vacuum should intervene either in incorporeal or corporeal natures. It is also necessary that every thing which has a natural progression should proceed through similitude. In consequence of this, it is likewise necessary that every producing principle should generate a number of the same order with itself, *viz. nature*, a natural number; *soul*, one that is psychical (i.e. belonging to soul); and *intellect* an intellectual number. For if whatever possesses a power of generating, generates similars prior to dissimilars, every cause must deliver its own form and characteristic peculiarity to its progeny; and before it generates that which gives subsistence to progressions, far distant and separate from its nature, it must constitute things proximate to itself according to essence, and conjoined with it through similitude. It is, therefore, necessary from these premises, since there is one unity, the principle of the universe, that this unity should produce from itself, prior to every thing else, a multitude of natures characterized by unity, and a number the most of all things allied to its cause; and these natures are no other than the Gods.

According to this theology, therefore, from the immense principle of principles, in which all things causally subsist, absorbed in superessential light, and involved in unfathomable depths, a beauteous progeny of principles proceed, all largely partaking of the ineffable, all stamped with the occult characters of deity, all possessing an overflowing fulness of good. From these dazzling summits, these ineffable blossoms, these divine propagations, *being, life, intellect, soul, nature, and body* depend; *monads* suspended from *unities*, deified natures proceeding from deities. Each of these monads, too, is the leader of a series which extends from itself to the last of things, and which, while it proceeds from, at the same time abides in, and returns to, its leader. And all these principles, and all their progeny, are finally centred and rooted by their summits in the first great all-comprehending one. Thus all beings proceed from, and are comprehended in, the first being: all intellects emanate from one first intellect; all souls from one first soul; all natures blossom from one first nature; and all bodies proceed from the vital and luminous body of the world. And, lastly, all these great monads are comprehended in the first one, from which both they and all their depending series are unfolded into light. Hence this first one is truly the unity of unities, the monad of monads, the principle of principles, the God of Gods, one and all things, and yet one prior to all. No objections of any weight, no arguments but such as are sophistical, can be urged against this most sublime theory, which is so congenial to the unperverted conceptions of the human mind, that it can only be treated with ridicule and contempt in degraded, barren, and barbarous ages. Ignorance and impious fraud, however, have hitherto conspired to defame those inestimable works [2] in which this and many other grand and important dogmas can alone be found; and the theology of the ancients has been attacked with all the insane fury of ecclesiastical zeal, and all the imbecile flashes of mistaken wit, by men whose conceptions on the subject, like those of a man between sleeping and waking, have been *turbid* and *wild, phantastic* and *confused, preposterous and vain.*

Indeed, that after the great incomprehensible cause of all, a divine multitude subsists, cooperating with this cause in the production and government of the universe, has always been, and is still, admitted by all nations and all religions, however much they may differ in their opinions respecting the nature of the subordinate deities, and the veneration which is to be paid to them by man; and however barbarous the conceptions of some nations on this subject may be, when compared with those of others. Hence, says the elegant Maximus Tyrius, "You will see one according law and assertion in all the earth, that there is one God, the king and father of all things, and many Gods, sons of God, ruling together with him. This the Greek says, and the Barbarian says, the inhabitant of the continent, and he who dwells near the sea, the wise and the unwise. And if you proceed as far as to the utmost shores of the ocean, there also there are Gods, rising very near to some, and setting very near to others." [3]

The deification, however, of dead men, and the worshiping men as Gods, formed no part of this theology, when it is considered according to its genuine purity. Numerous instances of the truth of this might be adduced, but I shall mention for this purpose, as unexceptionable witnesses, the writings of Plato, the Golden Pythagoric Verses, [4] and the Treatise of Plutarch on Isis and Osiris. All the works of Plato, indeed, evince the truth of this position, but this is particularly manifest from his Laws. The Golden verses order that the immortal Gods be honoured first, as they are disposed by law; afterwards the illustrious Heroes, under which appellation the author of the verses comprehends also angels and daemons, properly so called; and in the last place, the terrestrial daemons, i.e. such good men as transcend in virtue the rest of mankind. But to honour the Gods as they are disposed by law, is, as Hierocles observes, to reverence them as they are arranged by their demiurgus and father; and this is to honour them as beings not only superior to man, but also to daemons and angels. Hence, to honour men, however excellent they may be, as Gods, is not to honour the Gods according to the rank in which they are placed by their Creator; for it is confounding the divine with the human nature, and is thus acting directly contrary to the Pythagoric precept. Plutarch too, in his above mentioned treatise, most forcibly and clearly shows the impiety of worshiping men as Gods. [5]

"So great an apprehension indeed," says Dr. Stillingfleet, [6] "had the Heathens of the necessity of *appropriate acts of divine worship*, that some of them have chosen to die, rather than to give them to what they did not believe to be God. We have a remarkable story to this purpose in Arrian and Curtius [7] concerning Callisthenes. Alexander arriving at that degree of vanity as to desire to have divine worship given him, and the matter being started out of design among the courtiers, either by Anaxarchus, as Arrian, or Cleo the Sicilian, as Curtius says; and the way of doing it proposed, *viz.* by incense and prostration; Callisthenes vehemently opposed it, *as that which would confound the difference of human and divine worship, which had been preserved inviolable among them.* The worship of the Gods had been kept up in temples, with altars, and images, and sacrifices, and hymns, and prostrations, and such like; *but it is by no means fitting, says he, for us to confound these things, either by lifting up men to the honours of the Gods, or depressing the Gods to the honours of men.* For if Alexander would not suffer any man to usurp his royal dignity by the votes of men; how much more justly may the Gods disdain for any man to take their honours to himself. And it appears by Plutarch, [8] that the Greeks thought it a mean and base thing for any of them, when sent on any embassy to the kings of Persia, to prostrate themselves before them, because this was only allowed among them in divine adoration. Therefore, says he, when Pelopidas and Ismenias were sent to Artaxerxes, Pelopidas did nothing unworthy, but Ismenias let fall his ring to the ground, and stooping for that, was thought to make his adoration; which was altogether as good a shift as the Jesuits advising the crucifix to be held in the mandarin's hands while they made their adorations in the Heathen temples in China.

Conon [9] also *refused to make his adoration, as a disgrace to his city*; and Isocrates [10] accuses the Persians for doing it, *because herein they showed that they despised the Gods rather than men, by prostituting their honours to their princes.* Herodotus mentions Sperchies and Bulis, who could not with the greatest violence be brought to give adoration to Xerxes, *because it was against the law of their country to give divine honour to men.* [11] And Valerius Maximus [12] says, "*the Athenians put Timagoras to death for doing it; so strong an apprehension had possessed them, that the manner of worship which they used to their Gods, should be preserved sacred and inviolable.*" The philosopher Sallust also, in his Treatise on the Gods and the World, says, "It is not unreasonable to suppose that impiety is a species of punishment, and that those who have had a knowledge of the Gods, and yet despised them, will in another life be deprived of this knowledge. And it is requisite to make the punishment of those who have honoured their kings as Gods to consist in being expelled from the Gods." [13]

When the ineffable transcendency of the first God, which was considered as the grand principle in the Heathen religion by the best theologists of all nations, and particularly by its most illustrious promulgators, Orpheus, Pythagoras, and Plato, was forgotten, this oblivion was doubtless the principal cause of dead men being deified by the Pagans. Had they properly directed their attention to this transcendency they would have perceived it to be so immense as to surpass eternity, infinity, self-subsistence, and even essence itself, and that these in reality belong to those venerable natures which are, as it were, first unfolded into light from the unfathomable depths of that truly mystic unknown, about which all knowledge is refunded into ignorance. For, as Simplicius justly observes, "It is requisite that he who ascends to the principle of things should investigate whether it is possible there can be any thing better than the supposed principle; and if something more excellent is found, the same inquiry should again be made respecting that, till we arrive at the highest conceptions, than which we have no longer any more venerable. Nor should we stop in our ascent till we find this to be the case. For there is no occasion to fear that our progression will be through an unsubstantial void, by conceiving something about the first principles which is greater and more transcendent than their nature. For it is not possible for our conceptions to take such a mighty leap as to equal, and much less to pass beyond, the dignity of the first principles of things." He adds, "This, therefore, is one and the best extension [of the soul] to [the highest] God, and is, as much as possible, irreprehensible; *viz.* to know firmly, that by ascribing to him the most venerable excellences we can conceive, and the most holy and primary names and things, we ascribe nothing to him which is suitable to his dignity. It is sufficient, however, to procure our pardon [for the attempt], that we can attribute to him nothing superior." [14] If it is not possible, therefore, to form any ideas equal to the dignity of the immediate progeny of the ineffable, i.e. of the first principles of things, how much less can our conceptions reach that thrice unknown darkness, in the reverential language of the Egyptians, [15] which is even beyond these? Had the Heathens, therefore, considered as they ought this transcendency of the supreme God, they would never have presumed to equalize the human with the divine nature, and consequently would never have worshiped men as Gods. Their theology, however, is not to be accused as the cause of this impiety, but their forgetfulness of the sublimest of its dogmas, and the confusion with which this oblivion was necessarily attended.

But to return to the present work. To some who are conversant with the writings of Porphyry, who know how high he ranks among the best of the Platonists, and that he was denominated by them, on account of his excellence, *the philosopher*, it may seem strange that he should have been so unskilled in theological mysteries, and so ignorant of the characteristics of the beings superior to man, as by his epistle to Anebo he may appear to have been. That he was not, however, in reality thus unskilful and ignorant, is evident from his admirable Treatise on Abstinence from Animal Food, and his Αφορμαι προς τα νοητα, Or Auxiliaries to Intelligibles. His apparent ignorance, therefore, must have been assumed for the purpose of obtaining a more perfect and copious solution of the doubts proposed in his Epistle, than he would otherwise have received. But at the same time that this is admitted, it must also be observed, that he was inferior to Iamblichus in theological science, who so greatly excelled in knowledge of this kind, that he was not surpassed by any one, and was equaled by few. Hence he was denominated by all succeeding Platonists *the divine*, in the same manner as Plato, "to whom," as the acute Emperor Julian remarks, "he was posterior in time only, but not in genius." [16]

The difficulties attending the translation of this work into English are necessarily great, not only from its sublimity and novelty, but also from the defects of the original. I have, however, endeavoured to make the translation as faithful and complete as possible; and have *occasionally* availed myself of the annotations of Gale, not being able to do so *continually*, because for the most part, where philosophy is concerned, he shows himself to be an inaccurate, impertinent, and garrulous smatterer.

[1] According to this theology, as I have elsewhere shown, in every order of things, a triad is the immediate progeny of a monad. Hence the intelligible triad proceeds immediately from the ineffable principle of things. Phanes, or intelligible intellect, who is the last of the intelligible order, is the monad, leader, and producing cause of a triad, which is denominated νοητος και νοεροσ, i. e. *intelligible, and at the same time intellectual.* In like manner the extremity of this order produces immediately from itself the intellectual triad, Saturn, Rhea, and Jupiter. Again, Jupiter, who is also the Demiurgus, is the monad of the supermundane triad. Apollo, who subsists at the extremity of the supermundane order, produces a triad of liberated Gods. (θεοι απολυτοι.) And the extremity of the liberated order becomes the monad of a triad of mundane Gods. This theory, too, which is the progeny of the most consummate science, is in perfect conformity with the Chaldean theology. And hence it is said in one of the Chaldean oracles, *"In every world a triad shines forth, of which a monad is the ruling principle."* (Παντα γαρ εν κοσμω λαμπει τριας ης μονας αρχει). I refer the reader, who is desirous of being fully convinced of all this, to my translation of Proclus on the Theology of Plato.

[2] *viz.* The Philosophical Works of Proclus, together with those of Plotinus, Porphyry, Iamblichus, Syrianus, Ammonius, Damascius, Olympiodorus, and Simplicius.

[3] Ενα οδοισαν εν πασα γη ομοφωνον νομον και λογον, οτι θεος εις παντων βασιλευς και πατηρ, και θεοι πολλοι, θεου παιδες, συναρχοντες θεοω. ταυτα και ο ελλην λεγει, και ο βαρβαρος λεγει, και ο ηπειρωτης και ο θαλαττοις, και ο σοφος και ο ασοφος. καν επι του ωκεανου ελθης τας ηϊονας, κακει θεοι, τοις μεν ανισχοντες αγχου μαλα, τοις δε καταδυομενοι.   Dissert, i. Edit. Princ.

[4] "Diogenes Laertius says of Pythagoras, that he *charged his disciples not to give equal degrees of honour to the Gods and heroes.* Herodotus (in Euterpe) says of the Greeks, *That they worshiped Hercules two ways, one as an immortal deify, and so they sacrificed to him; and another as a Hero, and so they celebrated his memory.* Isocrates (Encom. Helen.) distinguishes between the honours of heroes and Gods, when he speaks of Menelaus and Helena. But the distinction is no where more fully expressed than in the Greek inscription upon the statue of Regilla, wife to Herodes Atticus, as Salmasius thinks, which was set up in his temple at Triopium, and taken from the statue itself by Sirmondus; where it is said, *That she had neither the honour of a mortal nor yet that which was proper to the Gods.* Ουδε ιερα θνητοις, αταρ ουδε θεοισιν ομοια. It seems by the inscription of Herodes, and by the testament of Epicteta, extant in Greek in the *Collection of Inscriptions,* that it was in the power of particular families

xiv

to keep festival days in honour of some of their own family, and to give *heroical honours* to them. In that noble inscription at Venice, we find three (lays appointed every year to be kept, and a *confraternity* established for that purpose with the laws of it. The first day to be observed in honour of the Muses, and sacrifices to be offered to them as *deities*. The second and third days in honour of the *heroes* of the family; between which honour and that of deities, they showed the difference by the distance of time between them, and the preference given to the other. But whereinsoever the *difference* lay, that there was a *distinction* acknowledged among them appears by this passage of Valerius, in his excellent oration, extant in Dionvsius Halicarnass. Antiq. Rom. lib. ii. p. 696. *I call*, says he, *the Gods to witness, whose temples and altars our family has worshiped with common sacrifices; and neat after them, I call the Genii of our ancestors, to whom we give* δευτερας τιμασ, *the second honours next to the Gods*, (as Celsus calls those, τας προσηκουσας τιμασ, *the due honours that belong to the lower daemons.*) From which we take notice, that the Heathens did not confound all *degrees of divine worship*, giving to the lowest object the same which they supposed to be due to the *celestial deities*, or the *supreme God*. So that if the distinction of divine worship will excuse from idolatry, the Heathens were not to blame for it." See Stillingfleet's Answer to a book entitled Catholics no Idolaters, p. 510, 513, &c.

[5] See the extracts from Plutarch, in which this is shown, in the Introduction to my translation of Proclus on the Theology of Plato.

[6] Answer to Catholics no Idolaters. Lond. 1676. p. 211

[7] Arrian, de Exped. Alex. 1. iv. et Curt, lib. viii.

[8] Vit. Artaxerx. Aelian. Var. Hist. lib. i. c. 21,

[9] Justin. lib. vi.

[10] Panegyr.

[11] Lib. vii.

[12] Lib. vi. cap. iii.

[13] Και κολασεως δε ειδος ειναι αθειαν ουκ απεικος. τους γαρ γνοντας θεους, και καταφρονησαντας, ευλογον εν ετερω βιω και της γνωσεως σερεσθαι, και τους εαυτων βασιλεας ως θεους τιμησαντας, εδει την δικην αυτων τοιησαι των θεων εκπεσειν. Cap. xviii.

[14] Και χρη τον επι τας αρχας αναβαινοντα ζητειν, ει δυναμτον ειναι τι κρειττον της υποτεθεισης αρζηε κᾳν ευρεθη, παλιν επ' εκεινου ζητειν, εως αν εις τας ακροτατας εννοισα ελθωμεν, ων ουκετι σεμνοτερας εχομεν˙ και μη σησαι την αναβασιν. ουδε γαρ ευλαβητεον μη κενεμβατωμεν, μειζονα τινα και ψπερβαινοντα τας πρωτας αρχας περι αυτων εννοουντες. ου γαρ δυνατον τηλικουτον πηδημα πηδησαι τας ημετερας εννοισα, ως παρισωθηναι τη αξια των πρωτων αρχων, ου λεγω και υπερπτηναι. μια γαρ αυτη προς θεον ανατασις αροση, και ως δυνατον απταισος. και ων εννοομεν αγαθων τα σεμνοτατα, και αγιωτατα, και προτουργα, και ονοματα και πραγματα αυτω ανατιθεντας ειδεναι βεβαιως, οτι μεδεν ανατεθεικαμεν αξιων. αρκει δε ημιν εις συγγνωμην, το μεδεν εχειν υπερτερον. Simplic. in Epict. Enchir. p. 207. Lond. 1670. 8vo.

[15] Of the first principles, says Damascius in MS. περι αρχων, the Egyptians said nothing, but celebrated it as a darkness beyond all intellectual conception, a thrice unknown darkness. Πρωτην αρχην ανυμνηκασιν, σκοτος υπερ πασαν νοησιν, σκοτος αγνωσον τρις τουτοο επιφημιζοντες.

[16] For farther particulars respecting this most extraordinary man, see the introduction to my translation of his Life of Pythagoras, and my History of the Restoration of the Platonic Theology.

The Epistle of Porphyry to the Egyptian Anebo.

Porphyry to the Prophet Anebo greeting.

I COMMENCE my friendship towards you from the Gods and good daemons, and from those philosophic disquisitions, which have an affinity to these powers. And concerning these particulars indeed, much has been said by the Grecian philosophers; but, for the most part, the principles of their belief are derived from conjecture.

In the first place, therefore, it is granted that there are Gods. But I inquire what the peculiarities are of each of the more excellent genera, by which they are separated from each other; and whether we must say that the cause of the distinction between them is from their energies, or their passive motions, or from things that are consequent, or from their different arrangement with respect to bodies; as, for instance, from the arrangement of the Gods with reference to etherial, but of demons to aerial, and of souls to terrestrial, bodies?

I also ask, why, since [all] the Gods dwell in the heavens, theurgists only invoke the terrestrial and subterranean Gods? Likewise, how some of the Gods are said to be aquatic and aerial? And how different Gods are allotted different places, and the parts of bodies according to circumscription, though they have an infinite, impartible, and incomprehensible power? How there will be a union of them with each other, if they are separated by the divisible circumscriptions of parts, and by the difference of places and subject bodies?

How do theologists, or those who are wise in divine concerns, represent the Gods as passive, to whom on this account, it is said, erect phalli are exhibited, and obscene language is used? But if they are impassive, the invocations of the Gods will be in vain, which announce that they can appease the anger of the divinities, and procure a reconciliation with them; and still more, what are called the necessities of the Gods, will be in vain. For that which is impassive cannot be allured, nor compelled, nor necessitated. How, therefore, are many things, in sacred operations, performed to them as passive? Invocations, likewise, are made to the Gods as passive; so that not demons only are passive, but the Gods also, conformably to what Homer says,

" And flexible are e'en the Gods themselves." [1]

But if we assert with certain persons, that the Gods are pure intellects, but that daemons, being psychical, participate of intellect; in a still greater de-

16

gree will pure intellects be incapable of being allured, and will be unmingled with sensible natures. Supplications, however, are foreign to the purity of intellect, and therefore are not to be made to it. But the throbs which are offered [in sacred rites] are offered as to sensitive and psychical essences.

Are, therefore, the Gods separated from daemons, through the former being incorporeal, but the latter corporeal? If, however, the Gods are incorporeal alone, how will the sun and moon, and the visible celestials, be Gods?

How, likewise, are some of the Gods beneficent, but others malefic?

What is it that connects the Gods in the heavens that have bodies, with the incorporeal Gods?

What is it that distinguishes demons from the visible and invisible Gods, since the visible are connected with the invisible Gods?

In what do a daemon, hero, and soul, differ from each other? Is it in essence, or in power, or in energy?

What is the indication of a God, or angel, or archangel, or demon, or a certain archon, or soul being present? For to speak boastingly, and to exhibit a phantasm of a certain quality, is common to Gods and daemons, and to all the more excellent genera. So that the genus of Gods will in no respect be better than that of daemons.

Since the ignorance of, and deception about, divine natures is impiety and impurity, but a scientific knowledge of the Gods is holy and beneficial, the ignorance of things honourable and beautiful will be darkness, but the knowledge of them will be light. And the former, indeed, will fill men with all evils, through the want of erudition, and through audacity; but the latter will be the cause to them of every good. [I wish you, therefore, to unfold to me the truth respecting these particulars.] [2]

[And, in the first place, I wish you to explain to me distinctly] [3] what that is which is effected in divination? For we frequently obtain knowledge of future events through dreams, when we are asleep; not being, at that time, in a tumultuous ecstasy, for the body is then quiescent; but we do not apprehend what then takes place, in the same manner as when we are awake.

But many, through enthusiasm and divine inspiration, predict future events, and are then in so wakeful a state, as even to energize according to sense, and yet they are not conscious of the state they are in, or at least, not so much as they were before.

Some also of those who suffer a mental alienation, energize enthusiastically on hearing cymbals or drums, or a certain modulated sound, such as those who are Corybantically inspired, those who are possessed by Sabazius, and those who are inspired by the mother of the Gods. But some energize enthusiastically by drinking water, as the priest of Clarius, in Colophon; others, by being seated at the mouth of a cavern, as those who prophesy at Delphi; and others by imbibing the vapour from water, as the prophetesses in Branchidae. Some also become enthusiastic by standing on characters, as those that are filled from the intromission of spirits. Others, who are conscious what

17

they are doing in other respects, are divinely inspired according to the phantastic part; some, indeed, receiving darkness for a cooperator, others certain potions, but others incantations and compositions: and some energize, according to the imagination, through water; others in a wall, others in the open air, and others in the sun, or in some other of the celestial bodies. Some also establish the art of the investigation of futurity through the viscera, through birds, and through the stars.

I likewise ask concerning the mode of divination, what it is, and what the quality by which it is distinguished? All diviners, indeed, assert, that they obtain a foreknowledge of future events through Gods or daemons, and that it is not possible for any others to know that which is future, than those who are the lords of futurity. I doubt, therefore, whether divinity is so far subservient to men, as not to be averse to some becoming diviners from meal.

But, concerning the causes of divination, it is dubious whether a God, an angel, or a daemon, or sonic other power, is present in manifestations, or divinations, or certain other sacred energies, as is the case with those powers that are drawn down through you [priests] by the necessities with which invocation is attended.

Or does the soul assert and imagine these things, and are they, as some think, the passions of the soul, excited from small incentives?

Or is a certain mixed form of subsistence produced from our soul, and divine inspiration externally derived?

Hence it must be said, that the soul generates the power which has an imaginative perception of futurity, through motions of this kind, or that the things which are adduced from matter constitute daemons, through the powers that are inherent in them, and especially things adduced from the matter which is taken from animals.

For in sleep, when we are not employed about any thing, we sometimes obtain a knowledge of the future.

But that a passion of the soul is the cause of divination, is indicated by this, that the senses are occupied, that fumigations are introduced, and that invocations are employed; and likewise, that not all men, but those that are more simple and young, are more adapted to prediction.

The ecstasy, also, of the reasoning power is the cause of divination, as is likewise the mania which happens in diseases, or mental aberration, or a sober and vigilant condition, or suffusions of the body, or the imaginations excited by diseases, or an ambiguous state of mind, such as that which takes place between a sober condition and ecstasy, or the imaginations artificially procured by enchantment.

Nature, likewise, art, and the sympathy of things in the universe, as if they were the parts of one animal, contain premanifestations of certain things with reference to each other. And bodies are so prepared, that there is a presignification of some by others, which is clearly indicated by the works performed in predicting what is future. For those who invoke the divinities for this purpose, have about them stones and herbs, bind certain sacred bonds, which they also dissolve, open places that are shut, and change the deliberate intentions of the recipients, so as from being depraved to render them worthy, though they were before depraved. Nor are the artificers of efficacious images to be despised. For they observe the motion of the celestial bodies, and can tell from the concurrence of what star with a certain star or stars, predictions will be true or false; and also whether the things that are performed will be inanities, or significant and efficacious, though no divinity or daemon is drawn down by these images.

But there are some who suppose that there is a certain obedient genus of daemons, which is naturally fraudulent, omniform, and various, and which assumes the appearance of Gods and daemons, and the souls of the deceased; and that through these every thing which appears to be either good or evil is effected; for they are not able to contribute any thing to true goods, such as those of the soul, nor to have any knowledge of them, but they abuse, deride, and frequently impede those who are striving to be virtuous. They are likewise full of pride, and rejoice in vapours and sacrifices.

Jugglers likewise fraudulently attack us in many ways, through the ardour of the expectations which they raise.

It very much indeed perplexes me to understand how superior beings, when invoked, are commanded by those that invoke them, as if they were their inferiors; and they think it requisite that he who worships them should be just, but when they are called upon to act unjustly, they do not refuse so to act. Though the Gods, likewise, do not hear him who invokes them, if he is impure from venereal connexions, yet, at the same time, they do not refuse to lead any one to illegal venery.

[I am likewise dubious with respect to sacrifices, what utility or power they possess in the universe, and with the Gods, and on what account they are performed, appropriately indeed, to the powers who are honoured by them, but usefully to those by whom the gifts are offered.] [4]

Why also do the interpreters of prophecies and oracles think it requisite that they should abstain from animals, lest the Gods should be polluted by the vapours arising from them; and yet the Gods are especially allured by the vapours of animals?

Why is it requisite that the inspector [who presides over sacred rites] ought not to touch a dead body, though most sacred operations are performed through dead bodies? And why, which is much more absurd than this, are threats employed and false terrors, by any casual person, not to a daemon, or some departed soul, but to the sovereign Sun himself, or to the Moon, or some one of the celestial Gods, in order to compel these divinities to speak the truth? For does not he who says that he will burst the heavens, or unfold the secrets of Isis, or point out the arcanum in the adytum, or stop Baris, or scatter the members of Osiris to Typhon, [or that he will do something else of the like kind], [5] does not he who says this, by thus threatening

19

what he neither knows nor is able to effect, prove himself to be stupid in the extreme? And what abjectness does it not produce in those who, like very silly children, are possessed with such vain fear, and are terrified at such fictions? And yet Chaeremon, who was a sacred scribe, writes these things, as disseminated by the Egyptians. It is also said, that these, and things of the like kind, are of a most compulsive nature.

What also is the meaning of those mystic narrations which say that a certain divinity is unfolded into light from mire, that he is seated above the lotus, that he sails in a ship, and that he changes his forms every hour, according to the signs of the zodiac? For thus, they say, he presents himself to the view, and thus ignorantly adapt the peculiar passion of their own imagination to the God himself. But if these things are asserted symbolically, being symbols of the powers of this divinity, I request an interpretation of these symbols. For it is evident, that if these are similar to passions of the Sun, when he is eclipsed, they would be seen by all men who intently survey the God.

What also is the design of names that are without signification? and why, of such, are those that are barbaric preferred to our own? For if he who hears them looks to their signification, it is sufficient that the conception remains the same, whatever the words may be that are used. For he who is invoked is not of the Egyptian race; nor, if he was an Egyptian, does he use the Egyptian, or, in short, any human language. For either all these are the artificial contrivances of enchanters, and veils originating from our passions, which rumour ascribes to a divine nature; or we ignorantly frame conceptions of divinity, contrary to its real mode of subsistence.

I likewise wish you to unfold to me, what the Egyptians conceive the first cause to be; whether intellect, or above intellect? whether alone, or subsisting with some other or others? whether incorporeal, or corporeal; and whether it is the same with the Demiurgus, or prior to the Demiurgus? Likewise, whether all things are from one principle, or from many principles? whether the Egyptians have a knowledge of matter, or of primary corporeal qualities; and whether they admit matter to be unbegotten, or to be generated? For Chaeremon, indeed, and others, do not think there is any thing else prior to the visible worlds; but in the beginning of their writings on this subject, admit the existence of the Gods of the Egyptians, but of no others, except what are called the planets, the Gods that give completion to the zodiac, and such as rise together with these; and likewise, the sections into decans, and the horoscopes. They also admit the existence of what are called the powerful leaders, whose names are to be found in the calendars, together with their ministrant offices, their risings and settings, and their significations of future events. For Chaeremon saw that what those who say that the sun is the Demiurgus, and likewise what is asserted concerning Osiris and Isis, and all the sacred fables, may be resolved into the stars and the phases, occultations and risings of these, or into the increments or decrements of the moon, or into the course of the sun, or the nocturnal and diurnal hemisphere, or into the river [Nile]. And, in short, the Egyptians resolve all things into physical, and nothing into incorporeal and living essences. Most of them likewise suspend that which is in our power from the motion of the stars; and bind all things, though I know not how, with the indissoluble bonds of necessity, which they call fate. They also connect fate with the Gods; whom, nevertheless, they worship in temples and statues, and other things, as the only dissolvers of fate.

Concerning the peculiar daemon, it must be inquired how he is imparted by the lord of the geniture, and according to what kind of efflux, or life, or power, he descends from him to us? And also, whether he exists, or does not exist? And whether the invention of the lord of the geniture is impossible, or possible? For if it is possible he is happy, who having learned the scheme of his nativity, and knowing his proper daemon, becomes liberated from fate.

The canons, also, of genethliology [or prediction from the natal day] are innumerable and incomprehensible. And the knowledge of this mathematical science cannot be obtained; for there is much dissonance concerning it, and Choeremon and many others have written against it. But the discovery of the lord, or lords, of the geniture, if there are more than one in a nativity, is nearly granted by astrologers themselves to be unattainable, and yet they say that on this the knowledge of the proper daemon depends.

Farther still, I wish to know whether the peculiar daemon rules over some one of the parts in us? For it appears to certain persons, that daemons preside over the parts of our body, so that one is the guardian of health, another of the form of the body, and another of the corporeal habits, and that there is one daemon who presides in common over all these. And again, that one daemon presides over the body, another over the soul, and another over the intellect; and that some of them are good, but others bad.

I am also dubious whether this daemon is not a certain part of the soul, [such, for instance, as the intellectual part;] and if so, he will be happy who has wise intellect.

I see likewise, that there is a twofold worship of the peculiar daemon; the one being the worship as of two, but the other as of three. By all men, however, the daemon is called upon by a common invocation.

I farther ask, whether there is a certain other latent way to felicity, separate from the Gods? And I am dubious whether it is requisite to look to human opinions in divine divination and theurgy? And whether the soul does not devise great things from casual circumstances? Moreover, there are certain other methods which are conversant with the prediction of future events. And, perhaps, those who possess divine divination, foresee indeed what will happen, yet are not on this account happy; for they foresee future events, but do not know how to use this knowledge properly. I wish, therefore, that you would point out to me the path to felicity, and show me in what the essence of it consists. For with us [Greeks] there is much verbal contention about it, because we form a conjecture of good from human reasonings. But by those who have devised the means of associating with beings more excellent than man, if the investigation of this subject is omitted, wisdom will be professed by them in vain; as they will only disturb a divine intellect about the discovery of a fugitive slave, or the purchase of land, or, if it should so happen, about marriage, or merchandize. And if they do not omit this subject, but assert what is most true about other things, yet say nothing that is stable and worthy of belief about felicity, in consequence of employing themselves about things that are difficult, but useless to mankind; in this case, they will not be conversant either with Gods or good daemons, but with that daemon who is called fraudulent; or, if this is not admitted, the whole will be the invention of men, and the fiction of a mortal nature.

[1] Iliad, lib. x. v.
[2] Gale has omitted to give the original of the sentence contained in the brackets; the translation of which I have added from the answer of Iamblichus to this epistle.
[3] Here also the original is omitted by Gale, and the translation of it is given by me from the text of Iamblichus.
[4] The paragraph within the brackets is omitted in the original; but I have supplied it from the following answer of Iamblichus to this Epistle. This omission is not noticed by Gale.
[5] Here likewise the words within the brackets, which are omitted in the original, are added from Iamblichus; but the omission is not noticed by Gale.

The Answer of the Preceptor Abammon To the Epistle of Porphyry to Anebo

And A **Solution of The Doubts Contained in It.** [1]

Section I.

Chap. I.

HERMES, the God who presides over language, was formerly very properly considered as common to all priests; and the power who presides over the true science concerning the Gods is one and the same in the whole of things. Hence our ancestors dedicated the inventions of their wisdom to this deity, inscribing all their own writings with the name of Hermes. If, therefore, we participate of a portion of this God, adapted and commensurate to our powers, you do well to propose your theological doubts to the priests, as friends, and to make these doubts known to them. I also very properly conceiving that the epistle sent to my disciple Anebo was written to me, shall give you a true answer to your inquiries. For it would not be becoming, that Pythagoras and Plato, Democritus and Eudoxus, and many other of the ancient Greeks, should have obtained appropriate instruction from the sacred scribes of their time, but that you who are our contemporary, and think conformably to those ancients, should be frustrated of your wish by those who are now living, and who are called common preceptors. I, therefore, thus betake myself to the present discussion; and do you, if you please, conceive that the same person to whom you sent the letter returns you an answer. Of, if it should seem fit to you, admit it to be me who discourses with you in writing, or some other prophet of the Egyptians, for this is of no consequence. Or, which I think is still better, dismiss the consideration whether the speaker is an inferior or a superior character, but direct your attention to what is said, so as readily to excite your mind to survey whether what is asserted is true or false.

In the first place, therefore, we shall divide the genera of the proposed problems, in order that we may know the quantity and quality of them. And, in the -next place, we shall show from what theologies the doubts are assumed, and according to what sciences they are investigated. For some things that are badly confused, require a certain distinction; others are conversant with the cause through which they subsist, and are apprehended; others, which we propose according to a certain contrariety, draw our decision on both sides; and some things require from us the whole development of mystic doctrines. Such, therefore, being the nature of the subjects of discussion, they are assumed from many places, and from different sciences. For some things introduce animadversions from what the wise men of the Chaldeans have delivered; others produce objections from what the prophets of the Egyptians teach; and there are some that, adhering to the theory of philosophers, make inquiries conformably to them. There are now likewise some, that from other opinions, which do not deserve to be mentioned, elicite a certain dubitation; and others originate from the common conceptions of mankind. These things, therefore, are of themselves variously disposed, and are multiformly connected with each other. Hence, through all these causes, a certain discussion is requisite for the management of them in a becoming manner.

[1] The following testimony of an anonymous Greek writer, prefixed to the manuscript of this treatise, which Gale published, proves that this work was written by Iamblichus: Ιστεον οτι ο φιλοσοφος Προκλος υπομνηματιζων τας του μεγολου Πλωτινου εννεαδας, λεγυει οτι ο αντιγραφων εις την προκειμενην του Πορφυριου επισολην, α θεσπεσιος εσιν Ιαμβλιχος˙ και δια το της υποθεσεως οικειον και ακαλουον, υποκρινεται προσωπον Αιγψπτιου τινος Αβαμωνος˙ αλλα και το της λεξεως κομματικον και αφορισικον, και το των εννοιων πραγματικον, και γλαφυρον, και ενθουν, μαρτψρει τον Προκλον καλως και κριναντα, και ισορησαντα. i.e. "It is requisite to know that the philosopher Proclus, in his Commentary on the Enneads of

23

the great Plotinus, says that it is the divine Iamblichus who answers the prefixed Epistle of Porphyry, and who assumes the person of a certain Egyptian of the name of Abammon, through the affinity and congruity of the hypothesis. And, indeed, the conciseness and definiteness of the diction, and the efficacious, elegant, and divine nature of the conceptions, testify that the decision of Proclus is just." That this, indeed, was the opinion of Proclus, is evident from a passage in his Commentaries on the Timaeus of Plato, which has escaped the notice of Gale, and which the reader will find in a note on the fourth chapter of the eighth section of the following translation.

Chap. II.

WE shall, therefore, deliver to you the peculiar dogmas of the Assyrians; and also clearly develop to you our own opinions; collecting some things from the infinite writings of the ancients, but others from those particulars which were comprehended by the ancients in one treatise, and pertain to the whole knowledge of divine natures. If also you should propose any philosophic inquiry, we shall discuss it for you, according to the ancient pillars of Hermes, which Plato and Pythagoras knew before, and from thence constituted their philosophy. But such things as exhibit foreign inquiries, or which are contradictory and contentious, we shall assist mildly and aptly, or we shall demonstrate their absurdity. Such, likewise, as proceed conformably [1] to common conceptions, we shall endeavour to discuss in a way perfectly known and clear. And things, indeed, which require the experience of divine operations to an accurate knowledge of them, we shall explain, as far as this is possible to be effected by words alone; but such as are full of intellectual theory, we shall develop with a view to the purification of the soul. But indications of this theory worthy of notice may be mentioned, by which it is possible for you, and those who resemble you, to be conducted by intellect to the essence of [real] beings. And with respect to such things as become known by a reasoning process, we shall leave no one of these without a perfect demonstration. But in all things we shall give to each that which is appropriate. And such questions, indeed, as are theological, we shall answer theologically; such as are theurgic, theurgically; but such as are philosophical, we shall, in conjunction with you, philosophically explore. Of these, also, such as extend to first causes, we shall unfold into light, by following them conformably to first principles. But such as pertain to morals, or to ends, we shall fitly discuss, according to the ethical mode. And, in a similar manner, we shall examine other things methodically and appropriately. Let us, therefore, now betake ourselves to your inquiries.

[1] In the original κατα τας κοινας εννοισασ, which Gales erroneously translates *contra communes opiniones*.

Chap. III.

IN the first place, therefore, you say, "*it must be granted that there are Gods.*" Thus to speak, however, is not right on this subject. For an innate knowledge of the Gods is coexistent with our very essence; and this knowledge is superior to all judgment and deliberate choice, and subsists prior to reason and demonstration. It is also counited from the beginning with its proper cause, and is consubsistent with the essential tendency of the soul to *the good*. If, indeed, it be requisite to speak the truth, the contact with divinity is not knowledge. For knowledge is in a certain respect separated [from its object] by *otherness*. [1] But prior to the knowledge, which as one thing knows another, is the uniform connexion with divinity, and which is suspended from the Gods, is spontaneous and inseparable from them. Hence, it is not proper to grant this, as if it might not be granted, nor to admit it as ambiguous (for it is always unically established in energy); nor are we worthy thus to explore it, as if we had sufficient authority to approve or reject it. For we are comprehended in it, or rather we are filled by it, and we possess that very thin; which we are, [or by which our essence is characterized] in knowing the Gods.

I shall likewise say the same thing to you, concerning the more excellent genera that follow the Gods, I mean daemons, heroes, and undefiled souls. [2] For it is necessary to understand respecting these, that there is always in them one definite reason of essence, and to remove from them the indefiniteness and instability of the human condition. It is likewise requisite to separate from them that inclination to one side of an argument rather than another, arising from the equilibrium of a reasoning process. For a thing of this kind is foreign from the principles of reason and life, and rather tends to secondary natures, and to such things as pertain to the power and contrariety of generation. But it is necessary that the more excellent genera should be apprehended uniformly.

The connascent perception, therefore, of the perpetual attendance of the Gods, will be assimilated to them. Hence, as they have an existence which is always invariably the same, thus also the human soul is conjoined to them by knowledge, according to a sameness of subsistence; by no means pursuing through conjecture, or opinion, or a syllogistic process, all which originate in time, an essence which is above all these, but through the pure and blameless intellections which the soul received from eternity from the Gods, becoming united to them. You, however, seem to think, that there is the same knowledge of divine natures as of any thing else, and that one thing, rather than another, may be granted from opposites, in the same manner as it is usual to do in dialectic discussions. There is, however, no similitude whatever between the two kinds of knowledge. For the knowledge of divine natures is different from that of other things, and is separated from all opposition. It likewise neither subsists in being now granted, or in becoming to be, but was from eternity, uniformly consubsistent with the soul. And thus much I say to you concerning the first principle in us, from which it is necessary those should begin who speak or hear any thing about the natures that are superior to us.

[1] Damascius περι αρχων says, " that *difference* not *existing*, there will not be knowledge." And, "that the contact as of one with one is above knowledge." Likewise, "that the intellectual perception of the first intelligible is without any difference or distinction. ετεροτητος ην ουσης, μηδε γνωσις εσαι. Et συναφη ως ενος προς εν, υπερ γνωσιν. Alibi, αδιακριτος η του πρωτου νοητου νοησις.
[2] Between souls that always abide on high with purity, such as the souls of *essential* heroes, and those that descend into the regions of mortality, and are defiled with vice, such as the souls of the greater part of mankind, the class of *undefiled* souls subsists. These descend into the realms of generation, partly from that necessity by which all human souls are, at times, drawn down to the earth, and partly for the benevolent purpose of benefiting those of an inferior class. But they descend without being defiled with vice. They are also called heroes, κατα σχεσιν, i.e. according to *habitude*, in order to distinguish them from *essential* heroes. And, in the Pythagoric Golden Verses, they are denominated the *terrestrial* heroes.

Chap. IV.

WITH respect to your inquiry, *"what the peculiarities are in each of the more excellent genera, by which they are separated from each other?"* if you understand by peculiarities the specific differences under the same genus, which are distinguished by opposite qualities, as the rational and irrational under animal; we by no means admit peculiarities of this kind, iii things which neither have one common essence, nor an equal contradistinction, nor receive a composition from something common, which is indefinite, and defines the peculiarity. But if you apprehend the peculiarity to be, as in prior and secondary natures, differing in their whole essence and whole genus, a certain simple condition of being, definite in itself; in this case, your conception of peculiarities will be reasonable. For these peculiarities of things, which have an eternal subsistence, are simple, and entirely exempt. The inquiry, however, proceeds imperfectly. For it was necessary, in the first place, to inquire what the peculiarities are of the more excellent genera, according to essence; in the next place, what they are according to power; and thus afterwards, what they are according to energy. But, as your question now stands, with respect to the peculiarities by which these genera are separated, you alone speak of the peculiarities of energies. Hence you inquire concerning the difference in the last things pertaining to them; but you leave uninvestigated such things as are first, and most honourable in them, and which are the elements of their difference. In the same place, also, something is added concerning *"efficacious and passive motions,"* which is a division by no

26

means adapted to the difference of the more excellent genera. For the contrariety of action and passion is not inherent in any one of them; but their energies are unrestrained, immutable, and without habitude to their opposites. Hence, neither must we admit in them motions of such a kind as arise from action and passion. For neither do we admit in the soul a self-motion, which consists of the mover and that which is moved; but we conceive that it is a certain simple essential motion, subsisting from itself, [1] and not possessing a habitude to another thing, and exempt from acting on, and suffering from, itself. Who, therefore, can endure that the peculiarities of the genera superior to the soul, should be distinguished according to active or passive motions?

That also which is added by you, *"or of accidents,"* is foreign from these genera. For in composites, and things which exist together with, or in others, or are comprehended by others, some things are conceived to be precedaneous, but others consequent; and some as essences, but others, as afterwards acceding to essences. For there is a certain coarrangement of them, and incongruity and interval intervenes. But, in the more excellent genera, all things must be conceived in τῳ ειναι, i.e. *in merely existing*; and wholes have a precedaneous subsistence, are separate by themselves, and have not their hypostasis from, or in others; so that there is not any thing in them which is accidental. Hence the peculiarity of them is not characterized from accidents.

At the end, likewise, of your inquiry, you introduce a distinction according to nature. For your question asks, *"How essences are known by energies, by physical motions, and by accidents?"* The very contrary, however, to all this takes place. For if energies and motions were constitutive of essences, they would be the lords of the difference which is between them. But if essences generate energies, the former being separate prior to the latter, will impart to motions, energies, and accidents, that by which they differ from each other. This, therefore, subsists contrarily to what you suppose, for the purpose of discovering the peculiarity which you now investigate.

In short, whether you think that there is one genus of the Gods, one of daemons, and in a similar manner of heroes, and souls essentially incorporeal; or whether you admit that these are severally many, you inquire what the difference of them is according to peculiarities. For if you apprehend that each of these is one [and the same genus] the whole arrangement of scientific theology is confounded. But if, as truth requires, you admit that they are generically distinguished, and that there is not in them one common essential definition, but that those of them which are prior, are exempt from those that are inferior, it is not possible to discover their common boundaries. And even if this were possible, this very thing would destroy their peculiarities. In this way, therefore, the object of investigation cannot be found. He, however, he who directs his attention to the analogous sameness which exists in superior natures, as, for instance, in the many genera of the Gods, and again in daemons and heroes, and, in the last place, in souls, will be able to define their peculiarities. Hence through this, it is demonstrated by us what the rectitude is of the present inquiry, and what its [accurate] distinction, and also in what manner it is impossible, and in what manner it is possible, for it to subsist.

[1] For αυτην εαυτοις ουσαν in this place, it is necessary to read αυτην εαυτης ουσαν.

Chap. V.

IN the next place, let us direct our attention to the solution of your inquiries. There is, therefore, *the good itself* which is beyond essence, and there is that good which subsists according to essence; I mean the essence which is most ancient and most honourable, and by itself incorporeal. And this is the illustrious peculiarity of the Gods, which exists in all the genera that subsist about them, preserving their appropriate distribution and order, and not being divulsed from it, and at the same time being inherent with invariable sameness in all the Gods, and their perpetual attendants.

In souls, however, which rule over bodies, and precedaneously pay attention to them, and which, prior to generation, have by themselves a perpetual arrangement, essential good is not present, nor the cause of good, which is prior to essence; but to these a certain participation [1] and habit, proceeding from essential good, accedes; just as we see that the participation of beauty and virtue is very different [in these souls] from that which we behold in men. For the latter is ambiguous, and accedes to composite natures as something adventitious. But the former has an immutable and never failing establishment in souls, and neither itself ever departs from itself, nor can be taken away by any thing else. Such, therefore, being the beginning and end in the divine genera, conceive two media between these extreme boundaries, *viz.* the order of heroes, which has an arrangement more elevated than that of souls, in power and virtue, in beauty and magnitude, and in all the goods which subsist about souls, and which, though it entirely transcends the psychical order, yet, at the same time, is proximately conjoined to it, through the alliance of a similar formed life. But the other medium, which is suspended from the Gods, though it is far inferior to them, is that of daemons, which is not of a primarily operative nature, but is subservient to, and follows the beneficent will of the Gods. It likewise unfolds into energy the invisible good of the Gods, being itself assimilated to it, and gives completion to its fabrications conformably to it. For it renders that which is ineffable in the good of the Gods effable, illuminates that which is formless in forms, and produces into visible reasons [or productive forms] that which in divine good is above all reason. Receiving also a connascent participation of things beautiful, it imparts and transfers it, in unenvying abundance, to the genera posterior to itself. These middle genera, therefore, give completion to the common bond of the Gods and souls, and cause the connexion of them to be indissoluble.

They also bind together the one continuity of things from on high as far as to the end; make the communion of wholes to be inseparable; cause all things to have the best, and a commensurate mixture; in a certain respect, equally transmit the progression from more excellent to inferior natures, and the elevation from things posterior to such as are prior; insert in more imperfect beings order and measures of the communication -which descends from more excellent natures, and of that by which it is received; and make all things to be familiar and coadapted to all, supernally receiving the causes of all these from the Gods.

You must not, therefore, think that this division is the peculiarity of powers or energies, or of essence; nor assuming it separately, must you survey it in one of these. But by extending it in common through all the genera, you will give perfection to the answer concerning the peculiarities of Gods, daemons, and heroes, and also of those in souls which are now the subjects of your inquiry.

Again, however, according to another mode of considering the subject, it is necessary to ascribe to the Gods the whole of that which is united, of whatever kind it may be; that which is firmly established in itself, and which is the cause of impartible essences; the immoveable, which also is to be considered as the cause of all motion, and which transcends the whole of things, and has nothing in common with them; and the unmingled and the separate, understood in common in essence, power and energy, and every thing else of this kind. But that which is now separated into multitude, and is able to impart itself to other things, and which receives from others bound in itself, and is sufficient in the distributions of partible natures, so as to give completion to them; which also participates of the primarily operative and vivific, having communion with all real and generated beings; receives a commixture from all things, imparts a contemperation to all things from itself, and extends these peculiarities through all the powers, essences, and energies, in itself; all this we shall truly ascribe to souls, by asserting that it is naturally implanted in them.

[1] For εποχη here, I read μετοχη.

Chap. VI.

WHAT, therefore, shall we say concerning the media? I think, indeed, that from what has been before said, they will be manifest to every one; for these give completion to the indivisible connexion of the extremes. Nevertheless, it is necessary to be more explicit. I consider, therefore, the daemoniacal tribe to be multiplied, but, unitedly, to be comingled, but in an unmingled manner, and to comprehend all other things of a subordinate nature, according to the idea of that which is more excellent. But again, the tribe of heroes supernally presides over a more obvious division and multitude, and likewise over motion, commixture, and things allied to these. It also receives gifts of a more excellent nature, concealed as it were inwardly; I mean union, purity, a firm establishment, impartible sameness, and a transcendency above other things. For one of these middle genera is proximate to the first, but the other to the last, of the extremes. But it reasonably follows, according to continuity of alliance, that the medium which begins from the most excellent natures, should proceed to such as are less excellent; but that the medium which primarily produces a contact with the last of things, should also in a certain respect communicate with the natures that transcend it. From these media, also, the completion may be seen of the first and last genera, and this entirely connascent, in a similar manner, in existence, in power, and in energy. As we have, therefore, in these two ways, perfectly completed the division of the four genera, we shall deem it sufficient in the others, to exhibit the extreme peculiarities alone, for the sake of conciseness, and because what remains, i.e. the comprehension of the media, is in a certain respect evident. But the media themselves, as being known from the extremes, we shall omit; making a definition of the extremes in the shortest way, as follows.

Chap. VII.

OF the extremes, therefore, one is supreme, transcendent, and perfect; but the other is last in dignity, deficient, and more imperfect. And the former, indeed, is capable of accomplishing all things at once, uniformly in an instant; but the latter is neither able to effect all things, nor at once, nor suddenly, nor impartibly. The former also generates and governs all things, without being inclined towards them; but the latter is naturally disposed to verge, and be converted to the things which it generates and governs. And the former, indeed, as primordial and cause, precedes all things in power; but the latter, being suspended from the will of the Gods, as from a cause, is from eternity consubsistent with it. The former, likewise, according to one vigorous acme, comprehends the ends of all energies and essences; but the latter passes from some things to others, and proceeds from the imperfect to the perfect. Farther still, to the former that which is highest and that which is incomprehensible pertain, and also that which is better than all measure, and is in such a manner formless, as not to be circumscribed by any form; but the latter is vanquished by inclination, habitude, and propensity; and is detained by appetites directed to that which is less excellent, and by familiarity with secondary natures. Hence, in the last place, it is formalized by all various measures derived from them. Intellect, therefore, which is the leader and king of all beings, and which is the demiurgic art of the universe, is always present with the Gods with invariable sameness, perfectly, and without indigence, being purely established in itself, according to one energy. But soul participates of a partible and multiform intellect, having its attention directed to the government of the whole. It also providentially attends to inanimate natures, becoming at different times ingenerated in different forms.

From the same causes, therefore, order and beauty itself are consubsistent with the more excellent genera; or, if some one had rather admit it, the cause of these is consubsistent with them. But with soul, the participation of intellectual order and divine beauty is always present. And with the former, indeed, the measure of wholes, or the cause of this, perpetually concurs. But soul is terminated by the divine boundary, and participates of this in a partible manner. To the former, also, empire over all beings, through the power and domination of cause, may be reasonably ascribed. But soul has certain distinct boundaries, as far as to which it is able to have dominion. Such, therefore, being the different peculiarities in the extremes, it will not be difficult to understand what we have now said, and to perceive the middle peculiarities of daemons and heroes, which are allied to each of the extremes, possessing a similitude to each, departing from both to the medium, and embracing a concordant communion comingled from them, and connected with it in appropriate measures. Such, therefore, must be conceived to be the peculiarities of the first divine genera.

Chap. VIII.

BUT neither must we admit that cause of the distinction of these genera which you subjoin, viz. *"that it is an corrangement with reference to different bodies; as, for instance, of Gods to etherial bodies, but of demons to aerial bodies, and of souls to such as are terrene."* For such an arrangement as this, which resembles that of Socrates to a tribe, when he is a senator, is unworthy of the divine genera, because all of them are essentially unrestrained and free. To which may be added, that it is dreadfully absurd to ascribe to bodies a principal power of giving a specific distinction to the first causes of themselves. For bodies are in servile subjection to these causes, and are ministrant to generation. And farther still, the genera of the more excellent natures are not in bodies, but the former externally rule over the latter. Hence they are not changed in conjunction with bodies. Again, they impart from themselves to bodies every such good as they are able to receive, but they themselves receive nothing from bodies; so that neither will they derive from them certain peculiarities. For if they were as the habits of bodies, or as material forms, or were in some other way corporeal-formed, it would, perhaps, be possible for them to be changed together with the differences of bodies. But if they are separate from bodies, and essentially preexist unmingled with them, what reasonable distinction, produced from bodies, can be transferred to them? To which also may be added, that this assertion of yours makes bodies to be more excellent than the divine genera, since the former afford a seat to superior causes, and insert in them peculiarities essentially. He, therefore, who coarranges allotments, distributions, and consociations of governors with the governed, will evidently assign a principal authority to more excellent natures. For, because the presiding powers are such [as we have shown them to be], on this account they have such an allotment, and give to it an essential specific distinction, but they are not assimilated to the nature of their receptacles.

It is necessary, therefore, to admit a thing of this kind in partial souls. For such as is the life which the soul received, prior to its insertion in a human body, and such as the form which it readily exerted; such also is the organical body which it has suspended from itself, and such the consequent corresponding nature, which receives the more perfect life of the soul. But with respect to more excellent natures, and which, as wholes, comprehend the principle [of parts] in these, inferior are produced in superior natures; bodies, in incorporeal essences; things fabricated, in the fabricators; and, being circularly comprehended in, are directed and governed by, them. Hence, the circulations of the celestial bodies, being primarily inserted in the celestial circulations of the etherial soul, are perpetually inherent in them; and the souls of the worlds [i.e. of the spheres], being extended to their intellect, are perfectly comprehended by it, and are primarily generated in it. Intellect, also, both that which is partial and that which is universal, is in a similar manner comprehended in the genera that are more excellent than intellect. Since, therefore, second are always converted to first natures, and superior are the leaders of inferior essences, as being the paradigms of them, hence essence and form accede to subordinate from superior natures, and things posterior are primarily produced in such as are more excellent; so that order and measure are derived from primary to secondary beings, and the latter possess that which they are from the former. But the contrary must not be admitted, *viz.* that peculiarities emanate from things less excellent to the natures which precede them.

Hence, through these things such a corporeal formed division as you introduce, is demonstrated to be false. It is, indeed, especially necessary not to propose any thin;; of this kind; but if this should appear to you to be requisite, yet you must not think, that what is false deserves to be discussed. For such a discussion does not exhibit a copiousness of arguments; but he wearies himself in vain, who, proposing things that are false, endeavours afterwards to subvert them, as things that are not true. For how is it possible that an essence, which is of itself incorporeal, and which has nothing in common with the bodies that participate of it, should be distinguished from other things by corporeal qualities? How can that which is not locally present with bodies, be separated by corporeal places? And how can that which is not inclosed by the partible circumscriptions of subjects, be partibly detained by the parts of the world? What, also, is that which can prevent the Gods from being every where? And what can restrain their power from extending as far as to the celestial arch? For to effect this, must be the work of a more powerful cause, which is able to inclose and circumscribe them in certain parts. But truly existing being, and which is essentially incorporeal, is every where, where ever it may wish to be. And that which is divine, and which transcends all things, would [if what you say were admitted] be transcended by the perfection of the whole world, and, as a certain part, would be comprehended by it. Hence, it would be inferior to corporeal magnitude. I do not, however, see after what manner these sensible natures could be produced and specifically distinguished, if there was no divine fabrication, and if no participation of divine forms, extended through the whole world.

In short, this opinion wholly subverts sacred institutions, and the theurgic communion of the Gods with men; since it exterminates from the earth the presence of the more excellent genera. For it says nothing else than that divine dwell remote from earthly natures, and that this our place of abode is deserted by them. According to this assertion, therefore, neither can we, that are priests, learn any thing from the Gods, nor do you rightly inquire of us, as knowing more than others, since we shall differ in no respect from other men.

No one, however, of these assertions is sane. For neither are the Gods detained in certain parts of the world, nor are terrene natures destitute of their providential attention. But the divinities are characterized by this, that they are not comprehended by any thing, and that they comprehend all things in themselves. But terrestrial natures possess their existence in the *pleromas* [1] of the Gods; and when they become adapted to divine participation, then prior to their own proper essence, they immediately possess the Gods, which [latently] preexisted in it.

Through these things, therefore, we have shown that the whole of this division is false; that the method [employed by you] of investigating peculiarities is irrational; and that to suppose the government of the Gods is fixed in a certain place, is by no means to apprehend the whole essence and power which is in them. It would have been proper, therefore, to have omitted the opposite inquiry made by you, about this distribution of more excellent natures, as not contradicting in any respect true conceptions. Because, however, it is necessary rather to direct the attention to true science, but not to dispute with men, on this account, we also shall adapt the present inquiry to a certain rational and theological apprehension.

[1] *viz.* In the plenitudes, or *total* perfections, of the Gods.

Chap. IX.

I CONSIDER you, therefore, as asking, for it is your inquiry, *"Why, since the Gods dwell the heavens alone, there are invocations by the theurgists of terrestrial and subterranean Gods?"* For what you assert in the beginning is not true, that the Gods circumvolve in the heavens alone: since all things are full of them. You also inquire, *"How some of the Gods are said to be aerial, and different Gods are allotted different places, and circumscribed portions of bodies, though they possess infinite, impartible, and incomprehensible power? And how, likewise, there will be a union of them with each other, as they are separated by divisible circumscriptions of parts, and by difference of places and subject bodies?"* Of all these, therefore, and an infinite number of other similar questions, one and the best solution will be obtained by surveying the mode of divine allotment.

A divine nature, therefore, whether it is allotted certain parts of the universe, such as heaven or earth, or sacred cities and regions, or certain groves, or sacred statues, externally [1] illuminates all these, in the same manner as the sun externally irradiates all things with his rays. Hence, as light comprehends the things which are illuminated by it, thus also the power of the Gods externally comprehends its participants. As, likewise, the solar light is present with the air in an unmingled manner; but this is manifest from no light being left in the air, when once that which illuminated it has departed, though heat is still present with it, when that which heated it is entirely withdrawn; thus also the light of the Gods illuminates separately, and being firmly established in itself, wholly proceeds through all beings. Moreover, the light which is the object of sensible perception, is one, continuous, and every where the same, whole; so that it is not possible for any part of it to be separate and cut off from the whole, nor to be inclosed in a circle, nor at any time to depart from its illuminating source. After the same manner, therefore, the whole world being partible, is divided about the one and impartible light of the Gods. But this light is every where one and the same whole, and is impartibly present with all things that are able to participate of it; through an all perfect power fills all things, and by a certain causal comprehension, incloses and terminates the whole of things in itself, and is every where united to itself, and conjoins ends to beginnings. This too, all heaven and the world imitating, revolve with a circular motion, are united to themselves, and lead the elements which are carried round in a circle. Hence the world causes all things to be in each other, and to tend to each other, makes the end of one thing to coalesce with the beginning of another, as, for instance, earth with heaven, and produces one connexion and concord of wholes with wholes.

Will not, therefore, he who surveys this conspicuous statue of the Gods, thus united to itself, be ashamed to have a different opinion of the Gods, who are the causes of it, so as to introduce among them sections, and separations, and corporeal-formed circumscriptions? I, indeed, should think, that every one would be thus disposed. For if there is no ratio, no habitude of symmetry, no communion of essence, nor a connexion either in capacity or in energy, between that which is adorned and the adorning cause; if this be the case, there will neither be found in the world a certain extension according to interval, nor local comprehension, nor partible interception, nor any other such like connascent equalization in the presence of the Gods [with mundane natures]. For in things which are of a kindred nature, according to essence and power, or which are, in a certain respect, of the same species, or homogeneous, a certain comprehension, or conservation, may be discovered. But in such things as are entirely exempt from all mundane wholes, what opposing circumstance, or transition through all things, or partible circumscription, or local comprehension, or any thing else of this kind can justly be perceived? I think, therefore, that the several participants of the divinities are of such a nature, that some partake of them ethereally, others aerially, and others aquatically; which also, the art of divine works perceiving, employs adaptations and invocations, conformable to such a division. And thus much concerning the distribution of the more excellent genera into the world.

[1] i.e. Without habitude, proximity, or alliance to the things which it illuminates.

Chap. X.

AFTER these things, you again subjoin another division for yourself, "*in which you separate the essences of the more excellent genera by the difference of passive and impassive.*" But neither do I admit this division. For no one of the more excellent genera is passive, nor yet impassive in such a way as to be contradistinguished from that which is passive; nor is naturally adapted to receive passions, but liberated from them through virtue, or some other worthy condition of being. But because they are entirely exempt from the contrariety of action and passion; and because they are not at all adapted to suffer, and have essentially an immutable firmness, on this account I place the impassive and the immutable in all the divine genera.

For consider, if you are willing, the last of divine natures, a soul purely liberated from bodies. What does such a soul want with the generation which is in pleasure, or the restitution which is in it to a natural condition, since such a soul is above nature, and lives an unbegotten life? Why, also, should it participate of the pain which leads to corruption and dissolves the harmony of the body, since it is beyond all body, and the nature which is divided about body, and is entirely separate from the harmony which descends from the soul into the body? But neither is it in want of the passions which precede sensation: for neither is it detained in body, nor inclosed by it, so as to require corporeal organs, in order to apprehend certain other bodies which are external to these organs. And, in short, being impartible, and abiding in one and the same form, and also being essentially incorporeal, and having no communication with a generated and passive body, it cannot suffer any thin-either according to division, or according to a change in quality, nor can have any thing which is allied to any kind of mutation or passion.

But neither does the [rational] soul, when it accedes to body, either itself suffer, or the reasons which it imparts to the body. For these *reasons* are *forms*, and being simple and uniform, they receive no perturbation in themselves, and no departure from their proper mode of subsistence. That which remains, therefore [or the participant of the rational soul], becomes the cause of suffering to the composite. Cause, however, is not the same with its effect. Hence, as soul is the first origin of generable and corruptible composite animals, but is itself by itself ingenerable and incorruptible; thus, also, though the participants of the soul suffer, and do not wholly [i.e. truly] possess life and existence, but are complicated with the indefiniteness and diversity of matter, yet the soul is itself by itself immutable, as being essentially more excellent than that which suffers, and not as possessing impassivity, in a certain deliberate choice, which verges both to the impassive and the passive, nor as receiving an adscititious immutability in the participation of habit or power.

Since, therefore, we have demonstrated that it is impossible for even the last genus of the more excellent order of beings, *viz.* the soul, to participate of suffering, how can it be proper to adapt this participation to demons and heroes, who are perpetual, and the attendants of the Gods, and who always invariably preserve the same divine order, and never desert it? For we know this indeed, that passion is something disorderly, confused, and unstable, never having any proper authority of its own, but being devoted to that by which it is detained, and to which it is subservient for the purposes of generation. This, therefore, rather pertains to some other genus, than to that which always exists, and is suspended from the Gods, and which, in conjunction with them, observes the same order, and accomplishes the same period. Hence daemons are impassive, and all the more excellent genera which follow them [and the Gods]

Chap. XI.

"*H*ow therefore," you ask, "*are many things performed to them in sacred operations, as if they were passive?*" I reply, that this is asserted through an ignorance of sacerdotal mysticism. For of the things which are perpetually effected in sacred rites, some have a certain arcane cause, and which is more excellent than reason; others are consecrated from eternity to the superior genera, as symbols; others preserve a certain other image, just as nature, which is effective of invisible reasons, expresses certain visible formations; others are adduced for the sake of honour, or have for their end some kind of similitude, or familiarity and alliance; and some procure what is useful to us, or in a certain respect purify and liberate our human passions, or avert some other of those dire circumstances which happen to us. It must not, however, be on this account granted, that a certain portion of sacred institutions is employed in the service of Gods or daemons, as if they were passive. For an essence which is by itself perpetual and incorporeal, is not naturally adapted to receive a certain mutation from bodies.

Nor, even though we should admit that this essence is especially in want of such things, will it require the aid of men to a sacred worship of this kind; since it is itself filled from itself, and from the nature of the world, and the perfection which is in generation; and, if it be lawful so to speak, prior to being in want it receives the self-sufficient, through the never failing wholeness of the world and its own proper plenitude, and because all the more excellent genera are full of appropriate good. Let this, therefore, be a lenitive for us in common, concerning the worship of the undefiled genera, as being appropriately coadapted to the beings that are more excellent than we, and because pure things are introduced to pure, and impassive things to impassive, natures.

But directing our attention to particulars, we say that the erection of the *phalli* is a certain sign of prolific power, which, through this, is called forth to the generative energy of the world. On which account, also, many phalli are consecrated in the spring, because then the whole world receives from the Gods the power which is productive of all generation. But I am of opinion, that the obscene language which then takes place, affords an indication of the privation of good about matter, and of the deformity which is in material subjects, prior to their being adorned. For these being indigent of ornament, by so much the more aspire after it, as they in a greater degree despise their own deformity. Again therefore, they pursue the causes of forms, and of what is beautiful and good, recognizing baseness from base language. And thus, indeed, the thing itself, *viz.* turpitude, is averted, but the knowledge of it is rendered manifest through words, and those that employ them transfer their desire to that which is contrary to baseness.

Another reason, also, of these things may be assigned. The powers of the human passions that are in us, when they are entirely restrained, become more vehement; but when they are called forth into energy, gradually and commensurately, they rejoice in being moderately [1] gratified, are satisfied; and from hence, becoming purified, they are rendered tractable, and are vanquished without violence. On this account, in comedy and tragedy, by surveying the passions of others, we stop our own passions, cause them to be more moderate, and are purified from them. In sacred ceremonies, likewise, by certain spectacles and auditions of things base, we become liberated from the injury which happens from the works effected by them. [2] Things of this kind, therefore, are introduced for the sake of our soul, and of the diminution of the evils which adhere to it through generation, and of a solution and liberation from its bonds. On this account, also, they are very properly called by Heraclitus remedies, as healing things of a dreadful nature, and saving souls from the calamities with which the realms of generation are replete.

[1] What is here asserted by Iamblichus is perfectly true, and confirmed by experience, *viz.* that the passions, when *moderately* gratified, are vanquished without vio-

lence. But (Gale, not understanding this, says, " Hoc adeo verum est, ac si dixisset, ignem extingues, oleum addendo camino." For a moderate gratification of the passions does not resemble the pouring of oil on fire; since this similitude is only applicable to them when they are *immoderately* indulged.

[2] See my Dissertation on the Eleusinian and Bacchic Mysteries.

Chap. XII.

Y OU also say, *"that invocations are directed to the Gods as to beings that are passive, so that not only daemons are passive, but likewise the Gods."* This, however, is not the case. For the illumination which takes place through invocations, is spontaneously visible and self perfect; is very remote from all downward attraction; proceeds into visibility through divine energy and perfection, and as much surpasses our voluntary motion as the divine will of *the good*transcends a deliberately chosen life. Through this will, therefore, the Gods, being benevolent and propitious, impart their light to theurgists in unenvying abundance, calling upwards their souls to themselves, procuring them a union with themselves, and accustoming them, while they are yet in body, to be separated from bodies, and to be led round to their eternal and intelligible principle.

But it is evident, from the effects themselves, that what we now say is the salvation of the soul. For the soul in contemplating blessed spectacles, acquires another life, energizes according to another energy, and is then rightly considered as no longer ranking in the order of man. Frequently, likewise, abandoning her own life, she exchanges it for the most blessed energy of the Gods. If, therefore, the ascent through invocations imparts to the priests purification from passions, a liberation from generation, and a union with a divine principle, how is it possible to connect with it any thing of passion? For an invocation of this kind does not draw down the impassive and pure Gods, to that which is passive and impure; but, on the contrary, it renders us, who have become passive through generation, pure and immutable.

Neither do the invocations which implore the Gods to *incline* to us, conjoin the priests to them through passion; but procure for them the communion of an indissoluble connexion, through the friendship which binds all things together. Hence, it does not, as the name seems to imply, incline the intellect of the Gods to men; but, according to the decision of truth, renders the will of man adapted to the participation of the Gods, elevates it to them, and coharmonizes the former with the latter, through the most appropriate persuasion. On this account also, such names of the Gods as are adapted to sacred concerns, and other divine symbols, are able, as they are of an anagogic or elevating nature, to connect invocations with the Gods themselves.

Chap. XIII.

MOREOVER, *"the pacifications of anger"* will become manifest, if we understand what the anger of the Gods is.[1] This, therefore, is not, as it appears to be to some, a certain ancient and inveterate rage, but an abandonment of the beneficent care of the Gods, from which we turn ourselves away, withdrawing, as it were, from meridian light, hiding ourselves in darkness, and depriving ourselves of the beneficent gift of the Gods.

Hence *pacification* is able to convert us to the participation of divinity and the providential care of the Gods, from which we were divulsed, and to bind together, commensurately, participants and the participated natures. So far, therefore, is pacification from accomplishing its work through passion, that it separates us from the passive and tumultuous abandonment of the Gods.

But *"the oblation of victims,"* when some evil is present in places about the earth, procures a remedy for the evil, and secures us from the incursion of any mutation or passion. Hence, whether a thing of this kind is effected through Gods or daemons, it invokes these as the expellers of evil, and [our true] saviours, and through them exterminates all the injury which may accede from the calamities. Those powers, also, who avert genesurgic [2] and physical punishments, do not expel them through passions. And if some one should think that the suppression of the guardian care of the Gods, introduces a certain spontaneous injury, in this case the persuasion arising from *pacification* recalls the benevolence of the more excellent genera, to a providential attention to our affairs, and takes away our privation of good, being itself perfectly pure and immutable.

[1] In the original, Και δη, και "αι της μηνιδος εξιλασεις" εσενται σοφεις, εαν την μηνιν των δεων καταμαθωμν, which Gale, most erroneously translates as follows:" Sed et ratio possit reddi *supplicationum, quibus divinam iram procuramus,* si recte intelligamus, qualis sit deorum ira"

[2] *viz.* Punishments produced by the realms of generation, or the sublunary region.

Chap. XIV.

FARTHER still, with respect to *"what are called the necessities of the Gods,"* the whole truth of this is, that necessities are peculiar to, and subsist in such a way as accords with the nature of, the Gods. [1] Hence they do not subsist as if they were externally derived, or were the effect of violence, but after such a manner as the good ought to be from necessity, so the Gods entirely exist, and are by no means otherwise disposed. This necessity, therefore, is mingled with beneficent will, and is the friend of love; through an order adapted to the Gods, possesses identity and immutability; and because it is contained in one boundary, abides in this, and never departs from it.

Hence, through all these particulars, the contrary to what you infer takes place. For it happens that a divine nature is incapable of being allured, is impassive and uncompelled, if there are in reality such powers in theurgy, as we have demonstrated there are.

[1] It is well observed by Proclus, "that divine necessity concurs with the divine will." Θεια αναγκη συστρεχει τη θυια βουλησει. Procl. in Tim. lib. i.

Chap. XV.

AFTER this, you pass on to another division into contraries, *viz.* the division of Gods with reference to daemons. For you say, *"that the Gods are pure intellects;"* but you propose this opinion as an hypothesis, or you narrate it as a dogma adopted by certain persons. And you infer, *"that demons are psychical essences participating of intellect."* Neither, therefore, am I ignorant that this is the opinion of many philosophers; but to you, I do not think it is proper to conceal what appears to me to be the truth. For all such opinions are full of confusion; since they wander from daemons to souls, which also participate of intellect; and from the Gods to an immaterial intellect in energy, which the Gods entirely excel by a priority of nature. Why, therefore, is it requisite to attribute to them these peculiarities, which are by no means appropriate? And thus much concerning this division, for it would be superfluous to make any further mention of it. But it is requisite that your doubts respecting this distinction should be properly considered, as the discussion of them pertains to the sacerdotal province.

Farther still, having said *"that pure intellects are inflexible, [i.e. not to be changed or altered] and unmingled with, sensibles,"* you doubt, *"whether it is requisite to pray to them."* But I think it is necessary to pray to no others than these. For that in us which is divine, intellectual, [1] and one, or intelligible, if you are willing so to call it, is most clearly excited in prayer; and, when excited, vehemently seeks that which is similar to itself, and becomes copulated to perfection itself. But if it should appear to you to be incredible, that an incorporeal nature can be capable of hearing sounds, and it should be urged by you, that for this purpose the sense of hearing is requisite, that it may apprehend what is said by us in prayer; you willingly forget the excellency of primary causes, which consists in both knowing and comprehending in themselves at once the whole of things. The Gods, therefore, do not receive prayers in themselves, through any corporeal powers or organs, but rather contain in themselves the energies of pious invocations; and especially of such as, through sacred ceremonies, are established in, and united to, the Gods. For then, in reality, a divine nature is present with itself, and does not communicate with the intellectual conceptions in prayer, as different from its own.

"Supplications, however," you say, *"are too foreign to the purity of intellect to be offered to the Gods."* But this is by no means the case. For on this very account, because we fall short of the Gods in power, purity, and every thing else, we shall act in the most opportune manner, by invoking them with the most vehement supplications. For the consciousness of our own nothingness, when we compare ourselves with the Gods, causes us to betake ourselves spontaneously to suppliant prayer. But from supplication, we are in a short time led to the object of supplication, acquire its similitude from intimate converse, and gradually obtain divine perfection, instead of our own imbecility and imperfection.

If, indeed, it is considered that sacred prayers are sent to men from the Gods themselves, that they are certain symbols of the divinities, and that they are only known to the Gods, with whom, in a certain respect, they possess the same power,-how can it any longer be justly apprehended, that a supplication of this kind is sensible, and not divine and intellectual? Or what passion can accede to a thing of this kind, the purity of which the most worthy human manners cannot easily equal?

You say, however, *"that the things which are offered in supplications are offered as to sensitive and psychical natures."* And, indeed, if the offerings consisted of corporeal and composite powers alone, or of such things as are merely subservient to corporeal organs, your assertion would be true. But as the offerings participate of incorporeal forms, of certain reasons, and more simple measures, the aptitude of them is to be surveyed according to this alone. And if a certain alliance, or similitude, is present, which is either proximate or remote, it is sufficient to effect the contact of which we are now speaking. *For there is not any thing which in the smallest degree is adapted to the Gods, to which the Gods arc not immediately present, and with which they are not conjoined.* The connexion, therefore, of supplications with the Gods, is not as with sensitive or psychical natures, but as with divine forms, and with the Gods themselves [as Gods, i.e. as superessential hyparxes]. So that we have sufficiently spoken in opposition to this division.

[1] For νοητον here, it is obviously necessary to read νοερον.

Chap. XVI.

THE difference which separates *"Gods from daemons by the corporeal and incorporeal,"* is the next thing that follows in what you have written; this being much more common than the former difference, and yet it is so far from expressing the peculiarities of their essence, that it does not afford a conjectural knowledge of them, nor of any accidents which pertain to them. For neither is it possible from these things to apprehend whether they are animals or not, and whether they are deprived of life, or are not at all in want of it. Farther still, neither is it easy to conjecture how these names are predicated, whether in common, or of many different things. For if in common, it is absurd that a line and time, God and demons, fire and water, should be under the same incorporeal genus. But if of many things, what reason is there when you speak of the incorporeal, that you should rather manifest by its Gods than points; or when you speak of the corporeal, that you should not be thought to speak of the earth rather than of daemons? For neither is this very thing defined, whether Gods and daemons have bodies, or are carried in bodies, as in a vehicle, or use them, or comprehend them, or are alone the same [1] with body. But, perhaps, it is not proper to examine this distinction very minutely. For you do not propose it as your own decision, but you exhibit it as the opinion of others.

[1] For τουτο here, it is necessary to read ταυτο

Chap. XVII.

WE will exchange, therefore, this division for the doubt which may be adduced by you against the present opinion. *"For,"* it may be said by you, *"how, conformably to what we assert, can the sun and moon, and the visible natures in the heavens, be Gods, if the Gods are alone incorporeal?"* To this we reply, that the celestial divinities are not comprehended by bodies, but contain bodies in their divine lives and energies; that they are not themselves converted to body, but they have a body which is converted to its divine cause; and that body does not impede their intellectual and incorporeal perfection, nor occasion them any molestation by its intervention. Hence it does not require an abundant attention, but follows the divinities spontaneously, and after a certain manner, self-motively, not being in want of manual direction; but, through an anagogic tendency, being itself uniformly coelevated by itself, to the one of the Gods.

It may also, if requisite, be said that a celestial body is most allied to the incorporeal essence of the Gods. For as the latter is one, so the former is simple; as the latter is impartible, so the former is indivisible; [1] and as that is immutable, so this is unchanged in quality. If, likewise, it is admitted that the energies of the Gods are uniform, a celestial body also, has one circulation. To which may be added, that it imitates the sameness of the Gods, by a perpetual motion, which is invariably the same, and which subsists according to one reason and one order. It also imitates a divine life, by the life which is connascent with etherial bodies. Hence, this celestial body does not consist of things contrary and different, as is the case with our body; nor does the soul of the celestial Gods coalesce with the body into one animal from two things; but the celestial animals of the Gods are entirely similar and counited, and are throughout wholes, uniform, and incomposite. For things of a more excellent nature are always transcendent in them, after the same manner; and things of an inferior nature are suspended from the dominion of such as are

42

prior, yet so as never to draw down this dominion to themselves. But all these are congregated into one coarrangement and perfection; and, after a certain manner, all things in the celestial Gods are incorporeal, and wholly Gods; because the divine form which is in them predominates, and inserts every where throughout one total essence. Thus, therefore, the visible celestials are all of them Gods, and after a certain manner incorporeal.

[1] For as a celestial body consists of light so pure and simple, that, compared with a terrestrial body, it may be said to be immaterial; hence, like the light of the sun, it cannot be divided, or in other words, one part of it cannot be separated from another.

Chap. XVIII.

YOUR next inquiry doubts, *"how some of the Gods are beneficent, but others malefic."* This opinion, therefore, is assumed from the predictors of nativities. It is, however, entirely remote from the truth. For all the Gods are good, and invariably the causes of good; and all of them are uniformly convolved to one good, according to the beautiful and good alone. The bodies, likewise, which are subject to them possess immense powers; some of which are firmly established in the divine bodies themselves, but others proceed from them into the nature of the world, and into the world itself, descending in an orderly manner through the whole of generation, and extending without impediment as far as to things which have a partial subsistence.

With respect to the powers, therefore, which remain in the heavens in the divine bodies themselves, there can be no doubt that all of them are similar. Hence, it remains that we should discuss those powers which are thence transmitted to us, and are mingled with generation. These, therefore, descend with invariable sameness for the salvation of the universe, and connectedly contain the whole of generation after the same manner. They are likewise impassive and immutable, though they proceed into that which is mutable and passive. For generation being multiform, and consisting of different things, receives *the one* of the Gods, and that in them which is without difference, with hostility and partibility, conformably to its own contrariety and division. It also receives that which is impassive, passively; and, in short, participates of them according to its own proper nature, and not according to their power. As, therefore, that which is generated [or has a subsistence in becoming to be,] participates of being generatively, and body participates of the incorporeal, corporeally; thus, also, the physical and material substances which are in generation, participate of the immaterial aud etherial bodies, which are above nature and generation, in a confused and disorderly manner. Hence they are absurd who attribute colour, figure, and contact to intelligible forms, because the participants of them are things of this kind; as likewise are those who ascribe depravity to the celestial bodies, because their participants sometimes produce evils. For the participation from the first could not be a thing of this kind, unless the recipient had some mutation. But if that which is participated is received as in another and different thing, this other thing in terrene natures is evil and disorderly. The participation, therefore, becomes the cause of the abundant difference in secondary natures, and also the commixture of material substances with immaterial eflluxions; and besides these, another cause is this, that what is imparted in one way, is received in another by terrestrial substances. Thus, for instance, the efflux of Saturn is constipative, but that of Mars is motive; but the passive genesiurgic receptacle in material substances receives the former according to congelation and refrigeration, but the latter according to an inflammation which transcends mediocrity. Do not, therefore, the corruption and privation of symmetry arise from an aberration which is effective of difference, and which is material and passive? Hence the imbecility of material and terrene places, not being able to receive the genuine power and most pure life of the ethereal natures, transfers its own passion to first causes. Just as if some one having a diseased body, and not being able to bear the vivific heat of the sun, should falsely dare to say, in consequence of looking to his own maladies, that the sun is not useful to health or life.

A certain thing of this kind also may take place in the harmony and crasis of the universe: for the same things may be the salvation of the whole, through the perfection of the things inherent and the recipients; but may be noxious to the parts, through their partible privation of symmetry. In the motion, therefore, of the universe, all the circulations preserve the whole world invariably the same; but some one of the parts is frequently injured by another part, which we see is sometimes the case in a dance.

Again, therefore, corruptibility and mutability are passions connascent with partial natures. But it is not proper to ascribe these to wholes and first causes, either as if they existed in them, or as if they proceeded to terrestrial substances from them. Hence, through these things it is demonstrated, that neither the celestial Gods, nor their gifts, are effective of evil.

Chap. XIX.

In the next place, therefore, we shall answer your question, *"What it is which conjoins the Gods that have a body in the heavens with the incorporeal Gods."* What this is, therefore, is evident from what has been before said. For if these Gods, as incorporeal, intelligible, and united, ride in the celestial spheres, they have their principles in the intelligible world, and intellectually perceiving the divine forms of themselves, they govern all heaven according to one infinite energy. And if they are present with the heavens in a separate manner, and lead the perpetual circulations of them by their will alone, they are themselves unmingled with a sensible nature, and exist together with the intelligible Gods.

It will be better, however, to answer you more particularly, as follows: I say, therefore, that the visible statues of the Gods originate from divine intelligible paradigms, and are generated about them. But being thus generated, they are entirely established in them, and being also extended to, [1] they possess an image which derives its completion from them. These images likewise fabricate another order; sublunary natures are in continuity with them, according to one union; and the divine intellectual forms, which are present with the visible bodies of the Gods, exist prior to them in a separate manner. But the unmingled and supercelestial intelligible paradigms of them, abide by themselves in unity, and are at once all things, according to the eternal transcendency of themselves.

There is, therefore, one common indivisible bond of them according to intellectual energies; and there is also this bond according to the common participations of forms, since there is nothing which intercepts these, nor any thing which comes between them. For indeed, an immaterial and incorporeal essence itself, being neither separated by places, nor by subjects, nor defined by the divisible circumscriptions of parts, immediately concurs, and is connascent with sameness. The progression also, from, and the regression of all things to, *the one*, and the entire domination of *the one*, congregates the communion of the mundane Gods with the Gods that preexist in the intelligible world.

Farther still, the intellectual conversion of secondary to primary natures, and the gift of the same essence and power imparted by the primary to the secondary Gods, connects the synod of them in indissoluble union. For in things of different essences, such as soul and body, and also in those of a dissimilar species, such as material forms, and those which are in any other way separated from each other, the connascent adventitious union is derived from supernal causes, and is lost in certain definite periods of time. But by how much the higher we ascend, and elevate ourselves to the sameness both in form and essence, of first natures, and proceed from parts to wholes, by so much the more shall we discover the union which has an eternal existence, and survey the essence, which has a precedaneous and more principal subsistence, and possesses about, and in itself, difference and multitude. [2]

Since, however, the order of all the Gods is profoundly united, and the first and second genera of them, and all the multitude which is spontaneously produced about them, are consubsistent in unity, and also every thing which is in them is one,-hence the beginning, middles, and ends in them are consubsistent according to *the one itself*; so that in these, it is not proper to inquire, whence *the one* accedes to all of them. For the very existence in them, whatever it may be, is *this one* [3] of their nature. And secondary genera, indeed, remain with invariable sameness in *the one* of such as are primary; but the primary impart from themselves union to the secondary genera, and all of them possess in each other the communion of an indissoluble connexion.

From this cause, therefore, the perfectly incorporeal Gods are united to the sensible Gods that have bodies. For the visible Gods also are external to bodies, and on this account are in the intelligible world; and the intelligible Gods, through their infinite union, comprehend in themselves the visible Gods; and both are established according to a common union and one energy. In a similar manner, also, this is the illustrious prerogative of the cause and orderly distribution of the Gods, on which account the same union of all the divinities extends from on high, as far as to the end of the divine order. But if this deserves to be doubted, the contrary would be wonderful, *viz*, that there should not be this union of the visible and intelligible Gods. And thus much concerning the contact with, and establishment of, the sensible in the intelligible Gods.

[1] For προς αυτην in this place, I read προς αυτα.
[2] The nature of *the one*, as it is all-receptive, and all-productive (πανδεχης και παντοφυης) exhibits in itself a certain representation and indication of multitude; for it is all things prior to all.
[3] For the Gods are essentialized in *the one*; or, as Damascius observes, speaking Chaldaically, in the paternal peculiarity. For in every God there is father, power, and intellect; *father* being the same as hyparxis and *the one*.

Chap. XX.

AFTER this, you again resume the same inquiries, of which what has been already said may be considered as a sufficient solution. Since, however, it is necessary, according to the proverb, frequently to speak of and consider things that are beautiful, neither shall we pass over these particulars, as if they had been now sufficiently answered, but by repeatedly discussing them we may, perhaps, obtain from all of them a certain perfect and great scientific good. For you doubt *"what it is which distinguishes daemons from the visible and invisible Gods, since the visible are conjoined with the invisible divinities."* But I, beginning from this as the first thing, shall demonstrate what it is in which they differ. For, because the visible are united to the intelligible Gods, and have the same idea with them, but daemons are far distant from them, according to essence, and scarcely adumbrate them through similitude, on this account they are separated from the visible Gods; and they differ from the invisible Gods, according to the difference itself of the invisible. [1] For daemons, indeed, are invisible, and by no means to be apprehended by sense; but the Gods transcend rational knowledge and material intelligence. And, because they are unknown and unapparent to these, they are thus denominated; but are said to be invisible in a way very different from that in which this is asserted of daemons. What, therefore, have the invisible Gods, so far as they are invisible, more excellent than the visible Gods? Nothing. For that which is divine, wherever it may be, and whatever allotment it may possess, has the same power and dominion over all the natures that are arranged under it. Moreover, though the invisible Gods should become visible, yet they rule over invisible daemons. For neither the place, which is the recipient of divinity, nor a certain part of the world, produces any mutation in the dominion of the Gods. But the whole essence of the Gods remains everywhere the same, indivisible and immutable, which all subordinate beings similarly venerate, in the order assigned them by nature.

By the assistance also of this reasoning, we may discover another difference between Gods and daemons. For both the visible and invisible Gods, indeed, comprehend in themselves the whole government of whatever is contained in all heaven and the world, and in the total invisible powers in the universe. But those powers that are allotted a daemoniacal prefecture, distributing certain divisible portions of the world, govern these, and have themselves a partible form of essence and power. They are, likewise, in a certain respect, connascent with, and inseparable from, the subjects of their government. But the Gods, though they may ride in bodies, are entirely separated from them. The providential attention, therefore, to bodies, produces no diminution in those to whom body is subservient: for it is connectedly contained by a more excellent nature, is converted to it, and is not the cause of any impediment to it. But the adhering to a genesiurgic nature, and the being divided about it, necessarily give to daemons a more subordinate condition. In short, that which is divine is of a ruling nature, and presides over the different orders of beings; but that which is daemoniacal is of a ministrant nature, and receives whatever the Gods may announce, promptly employing manual operation, as it were, in things which the Gods intellectually perceive, wish, and command. The Gods, therefore, are liberated from the powers which verge to generation; but daemons are not entirely purified from these. And thus much concerning this distinction; and we trust, that from the former and the present exposition, the difference between Gods and daemons will become more known.

[1] *viz.* According to the difference which there is between the invisibility of Gods and the invisibility of daemons.

Chap. XXI.

THE division, however, of *the passive from the impassive,* which you adopt, may perhaps be rejected by some one, as not adapted to either of the more excellent genera, through the causes which we have before enumerated; and it also deserves to be subverted, because it is inferred that these genera are passive, from what is performed in religious ceremonies. For what sacred institution, what religious cultivation, which is conformable to sacerdotal laws, is effected through passion, or produces a certain completion of passions? Is not each of these legislatively ordained from the first, conformably to the sacred laws of the Gods, and intellectually? Each also imitates both the intelligible and celestial order of the Gods; and contains the eternal measures of beings, and those admirable signatures which are sent hither from the Demiurgus and father of wholes, by which things of an ineffable nature are unfolded into light through arcane symbols, things formless are vanquished by forms, things more excellent than every image are expressed through images, and all things are accomplished through a divine cause alone, which is in so great a degree separated from passions, that reason is not able to come into contact with it.

This, therefore, is nearly the cause of our aberration to a multitude of conceptions. For men being in reality unable to apprehend the reasons of sacred institutions, but conceiving that they are able, are wholly hurried away by their own human passions, and form a conjecture of divine concerns from things pertaining to themselves. In so doing, however, they err in a twofold respect; because they fall from divine natures; and because, being frustrated of these, they draw them down to human passions. But it is requisite not to apprehend after the same manner, things which are performed both to Gods and men, such as genuflexions, adorations, gifts, and first fruits, but to establish the one apart from the other, conformably to the difference between things more and things less honourable; and to reverence the former, indeed, as divine, but to despise the latter as human, and as performed to men. It is proper, likewise, to consider, that the latter produce passions, both in the performer and those to whom they are performed; for they are human and corporeal formed; but to honour the energy of the former in a very high degree, as being performed through immutable admiration, and a venerable condition of mind, because they are referred to the Gods.

Section II.

Chap. I.

IT is also necessary to demonstrate to you, in what daemons, heroes, and souls differ from each other, and whether this difference is according to essence, or according to power, or according to energy. I say, therefore, that demons are produced according to the generative and demiurgic powers of the Gods, in the most remote termination of progression, and ultimate distribution into parts. But heroes are produced according to the reasons [or effective principles] of life in divine natures; and from these, the first and perfect measures of souls receive their termination and distribution into parts.

Since, however, the nature of daemons and heroes is thus generated from different causes, it is also necessary that the essence of the one should be different from that of the other. Hence, the essence of daemons is effective,

48

and perfective of mundane natures, and gives completion to the superintendence of generated individuals. But the essence of heroes is vital and rational, and is the leader of souls. And, with respect to the powers of each, those of daemons must be defined to be prolific, inspective of nature, and of the bond by which souls are united to bodies. But it is requisite to attribute to heroes vivific powers, which are the leaders of men, and are liberated from generation.

Chap. II.

IT follows, therefore, that in the next place we should define the energies of them. And those of daemons, indeed, must be surveyed as occupied about the world, and more widely extended in their effects; but those of heroes as less extended, and as converted to the order of souls. Hence, these being thus distinguished, soul succeeds, which proceeds as far as to the end of the divine orders; and, being allotted from these two genera certain portions of powers, is redundant with partible additions, and other prerogatives derived from itself. It also produces at different times different forms and reasons and manners, which originate from different sources; and, according to each part of the world, employs various lives and ideas; becoming connascent with, and likewise receding from, whatever natures it pleases; being assimilated to all things, and at the same time, through difference, being separated from them; drawing forth reasons allied to real beings and generated natures; and connecting itself with the Gods, according to other harmonies of essences and powers, than those by which daemons and heroes are united to the divinities. It likewise possesses the eternity of a similar life and energy in a less degree than daemons and heroes; yet, through the beneficent will of the Gods, and the illumination imparted by them, it frequently proceeds higher, and is elevated to a greater, i.e. to the angelic order; when it no longer remains in the boundaries of soul, but the whole of it is perfected into an angelic soul and an undefiled life. Hence, also, soul appears to comprehend in itself all-various essences and reasons, and forms or species of every kind. If, however, it be requisite to speak the truth, soul is always defined according to one certain thing, but adapting itself to precedaneous causes, it is at different times conjoined to different causes.

So great, therefore, being the difference between the energies of daemons, heroes, and souls throughout, it is no longer proper to doubt, what it is which separates them from each other; but they are to be distinguished by the peculiar nature of each. And so far as they are able to form one conjunction, so far the communion of them must be surveyed. For thus it will be possible truly to comprehend and define separately the conception which ought to be formed of them.

Chap. III.

LET US, however, now proceed to the appearances of the Gods and their perpetual attendants, and show what the difference is in their appearance. For you inquire, *"by what indication the presence of a God, or an angel, or an archangel, or a daemon, or a certain archon [i.e. ruler], or a soul, may be known."* In one word, therefore, I conclude that their appearances accord with their essences, powers, and energies. For such as they are, such also do they appear to those that invoke them, and they exhibit energies and ideas consentaneous to themselves, and proper indications of themselves. But that we may descend to particulars, the phasmata, or luminous appearances, of the Gods are uniform; those of daemons are various; those of angels are more simple than those of daemons, but are subordinate to those of the Gods; those of archangels approximate in a greater degree to divine causes; but those of archons, if these powers appear to you to be the cosmocrators, [1] who govern the sublunary element, will be more various, but adorned in order; but if they are the powers that preside over matter, they will indeed be more various, and more imperfect, than those of the archons [properly so called]; and those of souls will appear to be all-various. And the phasmata, indeed, of the Gods will be seen shining with salutary light; those of archangels will be terrible, and at the same time mild; those of angels will be more mild; those of daemons will be dreadful; those of heroes (which you have omitted in your inquiry, but to which we shall give an answer for the sake of truth) are milder than those of daemons; but those of archons, if their dominion pertains to the world, produce astonishment, but if they are material, they are noxious and painful to the spectators; and those of souls are similar to the heroic phasmata, except that they are inferior to them.

Again, therefore, the phasmata of the Gods are entirely immutable, according to magnitude, morphe, [2] and figure, and according to, to all things pertaining to them; those of archangels approximate to those of the Gods, but fall short of the sameness of them; those of angels are subordinate to these, but are immutable; and those of demons are at different times seen in a different form, and appear at one time great, but at another small, yet are still recognized to be the phasmata of daemons. Moreover, those of such archons as are leaders are immutable; but those of such as are material are multiformly changed; those of heroes are similar to those of daemons; and those of souls imitate in no small degree the daemoniacal mutation. Farther still, order and quiet pertain to the Gods; but with archangels, there is an efficacy of order and quiet. -With angels, the adorned and the tranquil are present, but not unattended with motion. Perturbation and disorder follow the daemoniacal phasmata; but spectacles attend the archons, conformable to each of the particulars which we have already mentioned; the material archons, indeed, being borne along tumultuously; but those of a leading characteristic, presenting themselves to the view, firmly established in themselves. The phasmata of heroes are subject to motion and mutation; but those of souls resemble, indeed, the heroic, but at the same time are less than these. In addition also to these peculiarities, divine beauty, indeed, shines with an immense splendour as it were, fixes the spectators in astonishment, imparts a divine joy, presents itself to the view with ineffable symmetry, and is exempt from all other species of pulchritude. But the blessed spectacles of archangels have indeed themselves the greatest beauty, yet are not so ineffable and admirable as those of the Gods. Those of angels divide, in a partible manner, the beauty which they receive from archangels. But the daemoniacal and heroical self-visive spirits, have both of them beauty in definite forms, yet the former is adorned in reasons which define the essence, and the latter exhibits fortitude. The phasmata of archons may be divided in a twofold respect. For some of them exhibit a beauty which is spontaneous, and of a ruling characteristic; but others, an elegance of form which is fictitious and renovated. And the phasmata of souls are, indeed, adorned in definite reasons, but these reasons are more divided than those in heroes, are partibly circumscribed, and are vanquished by one form. If, however, it be requisite to define all of them in common, I say that each participates of beauty according to its arrangement, the peculiar nature which it possesses, and its allotment.

[1] The *cosmocrators*, or governors of the world, are the *planets*. See the fourth book of my translation of Proclus on the Timaeus of Plato.
[2] Morphe pertains to the colour, figure, and magnitude of superficies.

Chap. IV.

PROCEEDING, therefore, to other peculiarities of them, we say, that with the Gods, indeed, there is acuteness and rapidity in the energies, which shine forth with greater celerity than those of intellect itself, though in themselves they are immoveable and stable. With archangels, the celerities are, in a certain respect, mingled with efficacious energies. Those of angels partake of a certain motion, and do not, similarly with archangels, possess a power which is effective by speaking. The operations of demons appear to be more rapid than they are in reality. In the motions of the heroic phasmata, a certain magnificence presents itself to the view; but in accomplishing what they wish to effect, their energies are not so rapid as those of daemons. In the phasmata of archons, the first energies appear to be most excellent and authoritative; but the second have a more abundant representation, yet in actions fall short of the end. And the phasmata of souls are seen to be more moveable, yet are more imbecile, than those of heroes.

In addition to these things also, the magnitude of the epiphanies [or manifestations] in the Gods, indeed, is so great as sometimes to conceal all heaven, the sun and the moon; and the earth itself, as the Gods descend, is no longer able to stand still. When archangels appear, certain parts of the world are moved, and a divided forerunning light precedes them. But they exhibit a magnitude of light commensurate to the magnitude of their domination. The angelic light is less than the archangelic, and more divided, but in daemons it is still more divided, and the magnitude of the manifestation is not always equal in them. The manifestation of heroes is still less than that of daemons, but exhibits more of an elevated condition. Again, the manifestation of such archons as preside over mundane forms, presents itself to the view as above measure great; but such of them as are distributed about matter, exhibit in their manifestations an abundance of pride and arrogance. Those of souls are not all of them seen to be equal, but appear to be less than those of heroes. And, in short, the magnitude of the manifestation is appropriately present in each of these, according to the magnitude of their powers, and the amplitude of the empire through which they extend themselves, and in which they exercise their authority.

After these things, therefore, we shall define the reasons of the self-apparent statues [or images]. Hence, in the forms of the Gods which are seen by the eves, the most clear spectacles of truth itself are perceived, which are also accurately splendid, and shine forth with an evolved light. The images of archangels present themselves to the view true and perfect; but those of angels preserve, indeed, the same form, but fail in plenitude of indication. The images of daemons are obscure; and those of heroes are seen to be still inferior to these. With respect, also, to archons, the images of such as are mundane, are clear; but of such as are material, obscure. Both, however, are seen to be of an authoritative nature. And the images of souls appear to be of a shadowy form.

In a similar manner, likewise, we must determine concerning the light of these powers. For the images of the Gods, indeed, are replete with a fulgid light. Those of archangels are full of supernatural light. Those of angels are luminous; but demons present themselves to the view with a turbid fire. The light of heroes is mingled with many things. And, with respect to archons, the light of those that have the government of the world is more pure; but of those that preside over matter, exhibits itself mingled from things of a dissimilar and contrary nature. And the light of souls manifests itself to be partibly filled with many of the mixtures which exist in generation.

Conformably, also, to what has been said, the fire of the Gods, indeed, shines forth with an indivisible and ineffable light, and fills all the profundities of the world, in an empyrean, [1] but not in a mundane, manner. But the fire of archangels is impartible indeed, but is seen to possess about itself an abundant multitude, either preceding or following after itself. The fire of angels is divided, except that it exhibits itself in the most perfect ideas. That of demons is still more shortly circumscribed by a distribution into parts, is effable, and does not astonish the sight of those that have seen more excellent natures. The fire of heroes has, after a certain manner, the same things as that of daemons, but at the same time falls short of the most accurate similitude to it. Moreover, with respect to archons, the fire of those that are of a more elevated order, is more pellucid; but of those that are material, is more dark. And the fire of souls is seen to be much divided and multiform, and is comingled from many of the natures that are in the world. Again, the fire of the Gods appears to be entirely stable. That of archangels is tranquil; but that of angels is stably moved. The fire of daemons is unstable; but that of heroes is, for the most part, rapidly moved. The fire of those archons that are of the first rank is tranquil; but of those that are of the last order is tumultuous. And the fire of souls is transmuted in a multitude of motions.

[1] For πυριως in this place, I read εμπψριως. For the empyrean world, according to the Chaldeans, is above the material worlds, and emits a supermundane fire or light.

Chap. V.

MOREOVER, that which purifies souls is perfect in the Gods; but in archangels it is anagogic. Angels alone dissolve the bond of generation. Daemons draw souls down into nature; but heroes lead them to a providential attention to sensible works. Archons either deliver to them the government of mundane concerns, or the inspection of material natures. And souls, when they become apparent, tend in a certain respect to generation.

Farther still, consider this, also, that you should attribute everything which is pure and stable in the visible image to the more excellent genera. Hence, you should ascribe to the Gods that which in the image is transcendently splendid, and which is firmly established in itself. That which is splendid, but is established as in another thing, you should give to archangels; but that which remains in another to angels. To all these, therefore, you should oppose, that which is rashly borne along, is unestablished, and filled with foreign natures, the whole of which is adapted to inferior orders.

These, also, may now be divided according to the difference of commixture. For mundane vapours are mingled with daemons, and are unstably borne along, contrary to the motion of the world. Genesiurgic compositions of pneumatic substances are mingled with heroes, about which substances, also, they are moved. The archons of the world remain invariably the same, exhibiting the mundane nature which they possess. But the archons of matter are full of material substances. And souls are filled with an abundance of stains and foreign spirits, together with which, when they become visible, each of these genera presents itself to the view.

The following, also, will be no small indications to you [of the difference of these powers]. With the Gods matter is immediately consumed. With archangels it is consumed in a short time. With angels there is a solution of, and elevation from, matter. By daemons matter is elegantly adorned. With heroes there is a coadaptation to it, in appropriate measures, and a skilful providential attention to it. And with respect to archons, those that are the governors of the world are present with matter in a transcendent manner, and in this way unfold themselves into light. But those that are material, exhibit themselves as entirely replete with matter. With respect to souls, also, those that are pure, present themselves to the view out of matter, but those of a contrary description are seen surrounded with it.

Chap. VI.

MOREOVER, the gifts arising from the manifestations are not all of them equal, nor have the same fruits. But the presence [1] of the Gods, indeed, imparts to us health of body, virtue of soul, purity of intellect, and in one word elevates every thing in us to its proper principle. And that, indeed, in us which is cold and destructive it annihilates; that which is hot it increases, and renders more powerful and predominant; and causes all things to accord with soul and intellect. It also emits a light, accompanied with intelligible harmony, and exhibits that which is not body as body to the eyes of the soul, through those of the body. The presence of archangels imparts likewise the same things, except that it does not impart them always, nor in all things, nor does it bestow goods which are sufficient, perfect, and incapable of being taken away; nor is their appearance accompanied with a light equal to that of the Gods. The presence of angels imparts divisibly still more partible goods, and the energy through which it becomes visible falls very short of comprehending in itself a perfect light. That of daemons renders the body, indeed, heavy, afflicts with diseases, draws down the soul to nature, does not depart from bodies, and the sense allied to bodies, and detains about this terrestrial place those who are hastening to divine fire, and does not liberate from the bonds of Fate. The presence of heroes is in other respects similar to that of daemons, but is attended with this peculiarity, that it excites to certain generous and great undertakings. The appearance which is visible by itself, of the mundane archons, imparts mundane goods, and every thing pertaining to human life; but that of the material archons extends material benefits, and such works as are terrestrial. Moreover, the vision of souls that are undefiled, and established in the order of angels, is anagogic, and the saviour of the soul, is accompanied with sacred hope, and imparts those goods which sacred hope vindicates to itself. But the vision of other souls draws down to generation, corrupts the fruits of [sacred] hope, and fills the spectators with passions which fix them to body.

[1] For περιουσια here, it is necessary to read παρουσια

Chap. VII.

MOREOVER, in the manifestations there is an indication of the order which the powers that are seen possess. For the Gods are surrounded by either Gods or angels; but archangels have angels either preceding or coarranged with them, or following them behind, or are accompanied by a certain other multitude of angels, who attend on them as guards. Angels exhibit, together with themselves, the peculiar works of the order to which they belong. Good daemons permit us to survey, in conjunction with themselves, their own works, and the benefits which they impart; but avenging daemons exhibit the species of punishments [which they inflict]; and such other daemons as are depraved are surrounded by certain noxious, blood-devouring, and fierce wild beasts. [1] Archons [of the first rank] exhibit, together with themselves, certain portions of the world; but other archons attract to themselves the inordination and confusion of matter. With respect to soul, if it ranks as a whole, and does not belong to any particular species, it presents to the view a formless fire, extended through the whole world, which is indicative of the total, one, indivisible, and formless soul of the universe; but a purified soul exhibits a fiery form, and a pure and unmingled fire. Then, also, the most inward light of it is seen, and an undefiled and stable form, and it most willingly and joyfully follows its elevating leader, and unfolds, by its works, its own appropriate order. But the soul which verges downward draws along with it the signs of bonds and punishments, is heavy with material spirits, is detained by the anomalous tumults of matter, and exhibits before itself, genesiurgic presiding daemons. And, in short, all these genera exhibit their proper orders; *viz.* the aerial genera exhibit aerial fire; the terrestrial a terrestrial and blacker fire; and the celestial a more splendid fire. But in these three boundaries all the genera are distributed according to a triple order of beginning, middle, and end. And the Gods, indeed, exhibit the supreme and most pure causes of this triple order. But the genera of angels depend on those of archangels. The genera of daemons appear to be subservient to those of angels; and in a similar manner to these, the genera of heroes are ministrant. They are not, however, subservient to angels in the same way as daemons. Again, the genera of archons, whether they preside over the world or over matter, exhibit the order which is adapted to them. But all the genera of souls present themselves to the view as the last of more excellent natures. Hence, also, they exhibit places in conjunction with themselves; souls of the first rank primary, but those of the second rank secondary, places, and the rest conformably to their arrangement, in each of these three genera.

[1] These are terrestrial daemons, to whom the Chaldean oracle alludes, which says, "The wild beasts of the earth shall inhabit thy vessel," i.e. as Psellus explains it, the composite temperature of the soul.

Chap. VIII.

MOREOVER, with respect to the tenuity and subtilty of light, the Gods extend a light so subtle that corporeal eyes cannot sustain it, but are affected in the same manner as fishes, when they are drawn upward from turbid and thick water into attenuated and diaphanous air. For men who survey divine fire are not able to breathe, through the subtilty of it, but become languid as soon as they perceive it, and are deprived of the use of their connascent spirit. Archangels, also, emit a light which is intolerable to respiration, yet their splendour is not equally pure with that of the Gods, nor similarly overpowering. The presence of angels renders the temperature of the air tolerable, so that theurgists are capable of being united to it. But when daemons are present, the whole air is not at all affected; nor does the air, which surrounds them, become more attenuated; nor does a light precede them, in which, being previously received and preoccupied by the air, they unfold the form of themselves; nor are they surrounded by a certain splendour, which diffuses its light everywhere. When heroes appear, certain parts of the earth are moved, and sounds are heard around them; but, in short, the air does not become more attenuated, nor incommensurate to theurgists, so as to render them unable to receive it. But when archons are present, an assemblage of many luminous appearances runs round them, difficult to be borne, whether these appearances are mundane or terrestrial. They have not, however, a supermundane tenuity, nor even that of the supreme elements. And to the psychical appearances the air is more allied, and, being suspended from them, receives in itself their circumscription.

Chap. IX.

IN the last place, the dispositions of the of those that invoke the Gods to appear receive, when they become visible, a liberation from the passions, a transcendent perfection, and an energy entirely more excellent, and participate of divine love and an immense joy. But when archangels appear, these dispositions receive a pure condition of being, intellectual contemplation, and an immutable power. When angels appear, they participate of intellectual wisdom and truth, pure virtue, stable knowledge, and a commensurate order. But when daemons are seen, they receive the appetite of generation and a desire of nature, together with a wish to accomplish the works of Fate, and a power effective of things of this kind. If heroes are seen, they derive from the vision other such like manners and many impulses, which contribute to the communion of souls. But when soul these dispositions come into contact with archons, mundane or material, motions are excited in conjunction with the soul. And, together with the vision of souls, the spectators derive genesiurgic tendencies and connascent providential inspections, for the sake of paying attention to bodies, and such other peculiarities as are allied to these.

In addition to these things, also, the manifestation of the Gods imparts truth and power, rectitude of works, and gifts of the greatest goods; but the manifestation of other powers is appropriately accompanied by such things as are commensurate to their several orders. Thus the manifestation of arch-angels imparts truth, not simply about all things, but definitely of certain things; and this not always, but sometimes; nor indefinitely to all, or every where, but with limitation, in a certain place, or to a certain individual. In like manner it does not impart a power effective of all things, nor always without distinction, nor every where; but a power which is effective sometimes, and in a certain place. But the manifestation of angels, in a still greater degree than that of archangels, divides, in imparting good, the circumscriptions which are always defined by them in more contracted boundaries. Again, the manifestation of daemons does not impart the goods of the soul, but either those of the body, or goods pertaining to the body. And they impart these when the order of the world permits them. After the same manner, likewise, the manifestation of heroes imparts second and third goods, and regards as its scope the whole terrestrial and mundane polity of souls. With respect to archons, the manifestation of some of these imparts mundane benefits, and all the goods of life; but that of others of an inferior rank imparts not a few of the prerogatives of material natures. And souls, when they appear, procure for those that behold them things which contribute to the benefit of human life. Thus, therefore, we have appropriately defined the gifts of these powers, conformably to the proper order of each; and the particulars in the manifes-tations about which you inquired, have received a fit reply. And thus much for these questions.

Chap. X.

WHAT you introduce, however, for the purpose of obtaining a knowledge of these things, whether it be your own opinion, or whether you have heard it from others, is neither true nor rightly asserted. For you say, *"that to speak boastingly, and to exhibit an adumbrative phantasm, are common to Gods and daemons, and to all the more excellent genera of be-ings."* But the thing is not as you apprehend it to be. For a God, an angel, and a good daemon, instruct men in what their proper essence consists; and never use an addition in their language which transcends their power, or their ap-propriate good. For truth is coexistent with the Gods, in the same manner as light with the sun. And, at the same time, we say, that divinity is not in want of any beauty or virtue which it is possible to add to him through language. Moreover, angels and daemons always receive truth from the Gods, so that they never assert any thing contrary to this, each of them being essentially perfect, nor can they add any thing to it for the sake of commendation.

When, therefore, does the deception mentioned by you " *of speakingly boastingly* " take place. For when a certain error happens in the theurgic art, and not such *autopc,* or self visible, images are seen as ought to occur, but others, instead of these, then inferior powers assume the form of the more venerable orders, and pretend to be those whose forms they assume; and hence arrogant words are uttered by them, and such as exceed the authority which they possess. For, as it appears to me, if any fraud germinates from the first principle, much falsehood is derived from the perversion, which it is necessary the priest should learn from the whole order in the phasmata, and by the proper observation of which they are able to confute and reject the fictitious [1] pretext of these inferior powers, as by no means pertaining to true and good spirits. Nor is it proper to introduce errors in the true judgment of things; for neither in other sciences or arts do we judge of their works from the aberrations which may happen to take place in them. You should not, therefore, here characterize things which are scarcely performed with rectitude through ten thousand labours, from the errors which may, through ignorance, befall them; but rather assert something else of them. For if the works which take place from the appearance of these powers are such as you say, *viz.* if they are arrogant and false, yet the operations about fire of true spirits are genuine and true. For, as in all other things, such as are principal primarily begin from themselves, and impart to themselves that which they give to others; as, for instance, in essence, in life, and in motion; thus also the natures which supply all beings with truth, primarily proclaim the truth of themselves, and precedaneously unfold the essence of themselves to the spectators. Hence, likewise, they exhibit to theurgists a fire which is of itself visible. For it is not the province of heat to refrigerate, nor of light to darken or conceal any thing; nor with any other nature which essentially performs a certain thing, is a power present of at the same time effecting the contrary. But things which do not possess a [true] nature, and which are contrary to things that exist essentially; these are able to receive contraries, and are adapted to fall into evil.

We must say the same thing, therefore, concerning phantasms. For if these are not true, but other things are so which have a real existence, thus also in the appearances of spirits, they seem to be such as things which are true beings; at the same time they participate of falsehood and deception, in the same manner as the forms which present themselves to the view in mirrors; and thus vainly attract the mind about things which never take place in any of the more excellent genera. These phantasms, likewise, will consist in deceptive perversions. For that which is an imitation of [real] being, and is an obscure assimilation, and becomes the cause of deception, pertains to no one of the true and clearly existing genera. But the Gods, indeed, and those powers that follow the Gods, reveal true images of themselves, but by no means extend phantasms of themselves, such as exist in water, or in mirrors. For on what account should they exhibit these? Shall we say, as bringing with them an indication of their own essence and power? This, however, is by no means the case. For these phantasms become the cause of deception to those that believe in them, and withdraw the spectators from the true knowledge of the Gods. Shall we say, then, that it is because they afford a certain utility to those that behold them? But what advantage can be derived from falsehood? If, therefore, this is not the case, may it not be natural to divinity to extend a phantasm from itself? But how can that which is firmly established in itself, and which is the cause of essence and truth, produce in a foreign seat a certain deceitful imitation of itself? By no means, therefore, does divinity either transform himself into phantasms, nor extend these from himself to other things, but emits, by illumination, true representations of himself, in the true manners of souls. Conformably to this, also, the attendants of the Gods are emulous of the self-visible truth of the Gods. But that which you now say, *"that it is common to Gods and daemons, and the rest of the more excellent genera, to produce fictitious images, and to speak boastingly of themselves,"* confounds all the genera of superior beings in each other, and leaves no difference whatever between them. For thus all things will be common to them, and nothing singularly excellent will be given to transcendent natures. It will, therefore, be more just to ask, in opposition to you, in what will the genus of the Gods be superior to that of daemons? These genera, however, have nothing in common, nor is the communion between them phantastic, nor is it fit from such natures as are last, and from the errors which take place in them, to estimate first essences, and the true impressions of forms which are in them. For by thus thinking concerning these essences, we shall think justly, and in a way pleasing to the Gods.

[1] For πεπλανημενην here, it seems requisite to read πεπλασμενην. Gale also, in his version, in this place has fictum.

Chap. XI.

IN what follows, in which you think that ignorance and deception about these things are impiety and impurity, and in which you exhort us to the true developement of these particulars, is not, indeed, attended with any ambiguity, but is acknowledged by all men. For who will not grant that the science which apprehends real being, is most adapted to a divine cause, but that ignorance which is hurried along to nonbeing, since it is most remote from a divine cause, falls off from truly existing forms? Since, however, what is said by you is not sufficient, I will add what is wanting; and because what you assert is rather philosophical and logical, than conformable to the efficacious art of priests, on this account I think it is necessary to say something more theurgical about these particulars.

For, let *"ignorance and deception be error and impiety,"* yet it does not follow that, on this account, things which are offered to the Gods, and divine works, are false. For a conception of the mind does not conjoin theurgists with the Gods; since, if this were the case, what would hinder those who phi-losophize theoretically, from having a theurgic union with the Gods? Now, however, in reality, this is not the case. For the perfect efficacy of ineffable works, which are divinely performed in a way surpassing all intelligence, and the power of inexplicable symbols, which are known only to the Gods, impart theurgic union. Hence, we do not perform these things through intellectual perception; since, if this were the case, the intellectual energy of them would be imparted by us; neither of which is true. For when we do not energize in-tellectually, the *synthemata [1]* themselves perform by themselves their proper work, and the ineffable power of the Gods itself knows, by itself, its own images. It does not, however, know them, as if excited by our intelli-gence; for neither is it natural that things which comprehend should be ex-cited by those that are comprehended, nor perfect by imperfect natures, nor wholes by parts. Hence, neither are divine causes precedaneously called into energy by our intellections; but it is requisite to consider these, and all the best dispositions of the soul, and also the purity pertaining to us, as certain concauses; the things which properly excite the divine will being divine syn-themata themselves. And thus, things pertaining to the Gods, are moved by themselves, and do not receive from any inferior nature a certain principle in themselves of their own proper energy.

I have, however, been thus prolix, in order that you may not think all the authority of the energy in theurgic operations is in our power, and that you may not suppose the true work of them consists in our conceptions, or the falsehood of them in our deception. For though we may know the peculiari-ties which are consequent to each genus, yet we may not obtain the truth which is in their works. Nevertheless, efficacious union [with divine natures] is not effected without knowledge; yet knowledge does not possess a same-ness with this union. So that neither is divine purity obtained through right knowledge, as neither is purity of body procured through health; but divine purity is more undefiled than knowledge, and is more transcendently united. Hence neither this, nor any thing of the like kind which is in us, and is human, cooperates any thing to the end of divine actions.

Accept, therefore, this, which is said indeed incidentally, but is a sufficient reply to the whole of your conception concerning the theurgic art. Those as-sertions, also, of yours pertain to the same thing, in which you say, *"that the science of the Gods is sacred and useful, and call the ignorance of things hon-ourable and beautiful darkness, but the knowledge of them light; and also add, that the ignorance of these things fills men with all evils, through ineruidtion and audacity, but the knowledge of them is the cause of all good."* For all these assertions tend to the same thing with the preceding, and obtain together with them an appropriate discussion. It is necessary, therefore to omit them, and to pass on to the inquiries concerning divination, and concisely dissolve them.

[1] i.e. The inexplicable theurgic signs or symbols.

60

Section III.

Chap. I.

IN the first place, therefore, you ask me to explain to you distinctly, *"what that is which is effected in the foreknowledge of future events?"* Immediately, however, that which you endeavour to learn is impossible. For, according to the meaning of your question, you think that foreknowledge is something which is generated, or subsists in becoming to be, and pertains to things which have a natural subsistence. It is not, however, one of the things which have their existence in becoming to be, nor is it effected after the manner of physical mutation, nor is it invented and devised as something useful for the purposes of life, nor in short, is it a human work, but is divine and supernatural, and is supernally sent to us from the heavens. It is also unbegotten and eternal, and spontaneously has a precedaneous subsistence.

The greatest remedy, therefore, for all such doubts is this, to know the principle of divination, that it neither originates from bodies, nor from the passions about bodies, nor from a certain nature, and the powers about nature, nor from any human apparatus, or the habits pertaining to it. But neither does it originate from a certain art, externally acquired, about a certain part of such things as are subservient to life. For the whole authority of it pertains to the Gods, and is imparted by them; it is also effected by divine works, or signs; and it possesses divine spectacles, and scientific theorems. All other things, however, are subjected as instruments to the gift of foreknowledge transmitted from the Gods; *viz.* such things as pertain to our soul and body, and such as are in the nature of the universe, or are inexistent in particular natures. But some things are previously subjacent, as in the order of matter, such as places, or certain other things of the like kind.

If some one, however, dismissing primordial causes, should refer divination to secondary offices, such as the motions of bodies, or the mutations of passions, or certain other motions, or the energies of human life, or animal or physical reasons, and should think that in so doing he asserts something manifest; or if, considering the symmetries of these with reference to each other, as causes, he should apprehend that he can assign something accurate concerning divination, he wholly deviates from the truth. But the one right boundary, and the one principle of all these particulars, is by no means to produce without a cause the foreknowledge of futurity, from things which have no prescience in themselves, but to survey from the Gods who contain in themselves the terminations of all the knowledge of beings, divination distributed about the whole world, and about all the natures that are separately contained in it. For such a cause as this is primordial, and is especially most common, containing in itself primarily those things which it gives to its participants, and particularly imparting truth, of which divination is in want; and antecedently comprehending the essence and cause of future events, from which foreknowledge necessarily and incessantly proceeds. Let such a principle as this, therefore, be the origin in common of all divination, from which it is possible to discover scientifically all the species of it; which we shall now unfold, conformably to the questions proposed by you.

Chap. II.

CONCERNING the divination, therefore, which takes place in sleep, you say as follows: *"We frequently obtain through dreams, when we are asleep, a knowledge of future events, not being in an ecstasy, through which we are much agitated, for the body is quiet, but we do not apprehend what we see in the same clear manner as when we are awake."* It is usual, however, for what you here say, to happen in human dreams, and in dreams which are excited by the soul, or by some of our conceptions, or by reason, or by imaginations, or certain diurnal cares. And these, indeed, are sometimes true and sometimes false; and in some things they apprehend reality, but in many deviate from it. But the dreams which are denominated *theopemptoi*, or *sent from God*, do not subsist after the manner which you mention; but they take place either when sleep is leaving us, and we are beginning to awake, and then we hear a certain voice, which concisely tells us what is to be done; or voices are heard by us, between sleeping and waking, or when we are perfectly awake. And sometimes, indeed, an invisible and incorporeal spirit surrounds the recumbents, so as not to be perceived by the sight, but by a certain other cosensation and intelligence. The entrance of this spirit, also, is accompanied with a noise, and he diffuses himself on all sides without any contact, and effects admirable works conducive to the liberation of the passions of the soul and body. But sometimes a bright and tranquil light shines forth, by which the sight of the eyes is detained, and which occasions them to become closed, though they were before open. The other senses, however, are in a vigilant state, and in a certain respect have a cosensation of the light unfolded by the Gods; and the recumbents hear what the Gods say, and know, by a consecutive perception, what is then done by them. This, however, is beheld in a still more perfect manner, when the sight perceives, when intellect, being corroborated, follows what is performed, and this is accompanied with the motion of the spectators. Such, therefore, and so many being the differences of these dreams, no one of them is similar to human dreams. But wakefulness, [1] a detention of the eyes, a similar oppression of the head, a condition between sleeping and waking, an instantaneous excitation, or perfect vigilance, are all of them divine indications, and are adapted to the reception of the Gods. They are also sent by the Gods, and a part of divine appearances antecedes according to things of this kind.

Take away, therefore, from divine dreams, among which also divination is contained, *"the being asleep,"* and also the assertion, *"that we do not apprehend what we see in sleep, in the same clear manner as when we are awake."* For the Gods are no less clearly present with us in these dreams than when we are awake. And, if it be requisite to speak the truth, the presence of the Gods, in the former case, is necessarily clearer and more accurate, and produces a more perfect perception than in the latter. Some, therefore, not knowing these indications of prophetic dreams, and conceiving that they have something in common with human dreams, rarely and casually obtain a foreknowledge of futurity, and in consequence of this, reasonably doubt how dreams contain any truth. And this, also, appears to me to disturb you, in consequence of your not knowing the true indications of dreams. It is necessary, however, that, admitting these to be the elements of the true knowledge of dreams, you should attend to the whole of the discussion concerning divination in sleep.

[1] For υπνοσ here, it is necessary to read αυπνοσ . For Iamblichus has before shown that divine dreams are not produced in sleep, but either when sleep leaves us, or between sleeping and waking, or when we are perfectly awake. The necessity of this emendation is also evident from what Iamblichus shortly after adds, *viz. that we must take away from divine dreams the being asleep*; i.e. the being in a profound sleep.

Chap. III.

THE wise, [1] therefore, speak as follows: The soul having a twofold life, one being in conjunction with body, but the other being separate from all body; when we are awake we employ, for the most part, the life which is common with the body, except when we separate ourselves entirely from it by pure intellectual and dianoetic energies. But when we are asleep, we are perfectly liberated, as it were, from certain surrounding bonds, and use a life separated from generation. Hence, this form of life, whether it be intellectual or divine, and whether these two are the same thing, or whether each is peculiarly of itself one thing, is then excited in us, and energizes in a way conformable to its nature. Since, therefore, intellect surveys real beings, but the soul contains in itself the reasons of all generated natures, it very properly follows that, according to a cause which comprehends future events, it should have a foreknowledge of them, as arranged in their precedaneous reasons. And it possesses a divination still more perfect than this, when it conjoins the portions of life and intellectual energy to the wholes from which it was separated. For then it is filled from wholes with all scientific knowledge, so as for the most part to attain by its conceptions to the apprehension of every thing which is effected in the world. Indeed, when it is united to the Gods, by a liberated energy of this kind, it then receives the most true plenitudes of intellections, from which it emits the true divination of divine dreams, and derives the most genuine principles of knowledge. But if the soul connects its intellectual and divine part with more excellent natures, then its phantasms will be more pure, whether they are phantasms of the Gods, or of beings essentially incorporeal, or, in short, of things contributing to the truth of intelligibles. If, also, it elevates the reasons of generated natures, contained in it to the Gods, the causes of them, it receives power from them, and a knowledge which apprehends what has been, and what will be; it likewise surveys the whole of time, and the deeds which are accomplished in time, and is allotted the order of providentially attending to and correcting them in an appropriate manner. And bodies, indeed, that are diseased it heals; but properly disposes such things as subsist among men erroneously and disorderly. It likewise frequently delivers the discoveries of arts, the distributions of justice, and the establishment of legal institutions. Thus in the temple of Aesculapius, diseases are healed through divine dreams; and, through the order of nocturnal appearances, the medical art is obtained from sacred dreams. Thus, too, the whole army of Alexander was preserved, which would otherwise have been entirely destroyed in the night, in consequence of Bacchus appearing in sleep, and pointing out a solution of the most grievous calamities. The city Aphutis, likewise, when besieged by King Lysander, was saved through a dream sent to him by Jupiter Ammon. For afterwards, he most rapidly withdrew his army from thence, and immediately raised the siege.

What occasion, however, is there to be prolix in mentioning every particular of things which happen daily, and which exhibit an energy superior to all language? What, therefore, has been said concerning divine divination in sleep is sufficient to show what it is, how it is effected, and what advantage it affords to mankind.

[1] In the original there is nothing more than λεγουσι δε ταδε in this place; but the sense requires that we should read λεγουσι δε οι σοφοι ταδε. And this emendation is confirmed by the versions of Scutellius and Gale.

Chap. IV.

AFTERWARDS, also, you say, *"that many, through enthusiasm and divine inspiration, predict future events, and that they are then in so wakeful a state, as even to energize according to sense, aid yet they are not conscious of the state they are in, or at least, not so much as they were before."* I wish, therefore, here to point out to you the signs by which those who are rightly possessed by the Gods may be known. For they either subject the whole of their life, as a vehicle or instrument to the inspiring Gods; or they exchange the human for the divine life; or they energize with their own proper life about divinity. But they neither energize according to sense, nor are in such a vigilant state as those who have their senses excited from sleep (for neither do they apprehend future events); nor are they moved as those are who energize according to impulse. Nor, again, are they conscious of the state they are in, neither as they were before, nor in any other way; nor, in short, do they convert to themselves their own intelligence, or exert any knowledge which is peculiarly their own.

The greatest indication, however, of the truth of this is the following. Many, through divine inspiration, are not burned when fire is introduced to them, the inspiring influence preventing the fire from touching them. Many, also, though burned, do not apprehend that they are so, because they do not then live an animal life. And some, indeed, though transfixed with spits, do not perceive it; but others that are struck on the shoulders with axes, and others that have their arms cut with knives, are by no means conscious of what is done to them. Their energies, likewise, are not at all human. For inaccessible places become accessible to those that are divinely inspired; they are thrown into fire, and pass through fire, and over rivers, like the priest in Castabalis, without being injured. But from these things it is demonstrated, that those who energize enthusiastically are not conscious of the state they are in, and that they neither live a human nor an animal life, according to sense or impulse, but that they exchange this for a certain more divine life, by which they are inspired and perfectly possessed.

Chap. V.

THERE are, therefore, many species of divine possession, and divine inspiration is multifariously excited; whence, also, the signs of it are many and different. For either the Gods are different, by whom we are inspired, and thus produce a different inspiration; or the mode of enthusiasms being various, produces a different afflatus. For either divinity possesses us, or we give up ourselves wholly to divinity, or we have a common energy with him. And sometimes, indeed, we participate of the last power of divinity, sometimes of his middle, and sometimes of his first power. Sometimes, also, there is a participation only, at other times communion likewise, and sometimes a union of these divine inspirations. Again, either the soul alone enjoys the inspiration, or the soul receives it in conjunction with the body, or it is also participated by the common animal.

From these things, therefore, the signs of those that are inspired are multiform. For the inspiration is indicated by the motions of the [whole] body, and of certain parts of it, by the perfect rest of the body, by harmonious orders and dances, and by elegant sounds, or the contraries of these. Either the body, likewise, is seen to be elevated, or increased in bulk, or to be borne along sublimely in the air, or the contraries of these, are seen to take place about it. An equability, also, of voice, according to magnitude, or a great variety of voice after [1] intervals of silence, may be observed. And again, sometimes the sounds have a musical intension and remission, and sometimes they are strained and relaxed after a different manner.

[1] For κατα τα μεταξυ διαλαμβαναμενα κ. λ, I read μενα κ. λ.

Chap. VI.

THAT, however, which is the greatest thing is this, that he who [appears to] draw down a certain divinity, sees a spirit descending and entering into some one, recognizes its magnitude and quality, and is also mystically persuaded and governed by it. But a species of fire is seen by the recipient, prior to the spirit being received, which sometimes becomes manifest to all the spectators, either when the divinity is descending, or when he is departing. And from this spectacle the greatest truth and power of the God, and especially the order he possesses, as likewise about what particulars he is adapted to speak the truth, what the power is which he imparts, and what he is able to effect, become known to the scientific. Those, however, who, without these blessed spectacles, draw down spirits invisibly, are without vision, as if they were in the dark, and know nothing of what they do, except some small signs which become visible through the body of him who is divinely inspired, and certain other things which are manifestly seen, but they are ignorant of all the most important particulars of divine inspiration, which are concealed from them in the invisible. But to return from this digression: if the presence of the fire of the Gods, and a certain ineffable species of light, externally accede to him who is possessed, and if they wholly fill him, have dominion over and circularly comprehend him on all sides, so that he is not able to exert any one proper energy, what sense, or animadversion, or appropriate projection of intellect, can there be in him who receives a divine fire? What human motion, likewise, can then intervene, or what human reception of passion or ecstasy, or of aberration of the phantasy, or of any thing else of the like kind, such as is apprehended by the multitude, can take place? Let such, therefore, be the divine indications of true inspiration from the Gods, which he who attends to will not wander from a right knowledge concerning it.

Chap. VII.

IT is not, however, sufficient to learn these things alone, nor will he who only knows these become perfect in divine science. But it is requisite also to know what enthusiasm is, and how it is produced. It is falsely, therefore, supposed to be a motion of dianoia, in conjunction with daemoniacal inspiration. For human dianoia is not moved, if it is thus enthusiastically affected; nor is the inspiration produced by daemons, but by the Gods. Neither is enthusiasm simply an ecstasy; for it is a re-elevation and transition to a more excellent condition of being. But delirium and ecstasy evince a perversion to that which is worse. Hence, he who is an advocate for the latter, speaks, indeed, of things which happen to those that energize enthusiastically, yet does not teach that which is precedaneous. But this consists in being wholly possessed by divinity, which is afterwards followed by mental alienation. No one, therefore, can justly apprehend that enthusiasm is something pertaining to the soul, or to some one of its powers, or to intellect or energies, or to corporeal imbecility, or that it cannot subsist without the debility of the body. For neither is the work of divine inspiration human, nor does the whole of it depend on human powers and energies; but these, indeed, have the relation of a subject, and divinity uses them as instruments. He accomplishes, however, the whole work of divination through himself, and being separated in an unmingled manner from other things, neither the soul nor the body being at all moved, he energizes by himself. Hence, when divinations are rightly effected in the way which I have mentioned, then they subsist without falsehood. But when the soul has been previously disturbed, or is moved in the interim, or the body intervenes, and confounds the divine harmony, then divinations become turbulent and false, and the enthusiasm is no longer true nor genuine.

Chap. VIII.

IF, therefore, true divination was a solution of the divine part of the soul from the other parts of it, or if it was a separation of intellect, or a certain extension of it; or if it was a vehemence and extension of energy or passion, or an acuteness and motion of dianoia, or a fervour of intellect; then, since all such like particulars are excited by our soul, enthusiasm might be reasonably supposed to be the offspring of the soul. If, however, the body, on account of certain temperaments, whether they are such as are melancholic, or any other, or, to speak more particularly, on account of heat, or cold, or moisture, or a certain specific quality of these, or the mixture or temperature of these in a certain proportion, or the pneumatic part of the soul, or the more and the less of these; if any one of these is established as the cause of enthusiastic alienation, in this case, the alienation will be a corporeal passion, and will be excited by physical motions. But if its excitation originates from both the soul and the body, so far as these coalesce with each other, a motion of this kind will be common to the animal [produced by the union of the two]. The enthusiastic energy, however, is not the work either of the body or the soul, or of both conjoined. For these do not contain in themselves a certain cause of divine alienation, nor are things of a more excellent nature adapted to be generated by such as are less excellent.

But it is necessary to investigate the causes of divine mania. And these are the illuminations proceeding from the Gods, the spirits imparted by them, and the all perfect domination of divinity, which comprehends indeed every thing in us, but exterminates entirely our own proper consciousness and motion. This divine possession, also, emits words which are not understood by those that utter them; for they pronounce them, as it is said, with an insane mouth, and are wholly subservient, and entirely yield themselves to the energy of the predominating God. The whole of enthusiasm is a thing of this kind, and is effected by these causes, though this must not be considered as asserted with consummate accuracy.

Chap. IX.

WHAT you afterwards say is as follows: *"That some of those who suffer a mental alienation,, energize enthusiastically on hearing cymbals or drums, or a certain modulated sound, such as those who are Corybantically inspired, those who are possessed by Sabazius, and those who are inspired by the mother of the Gods."* It is necessary, therefore, to discuss the causes of these things, and to show how they are definitely produced.

That music, therefore, is of a motive nature, and is adapted to excite the affections, and that the melody of pipes produces or heals the disordered passions of the soul, changes the temperaments or dispositions of the body, and by some melodies causes a Bacchic fury, but by others occasions this fury to cease; [1] and, likewise, how the differences of these accord with the several dispositions of the soul, and that an unstable and variable melody is adapted to ecstasies, such as are the melodies of Olympus, [2] and others of the like kind; all these appear to me to be adduced in a way foreign to enthusiasm. For they are physical and human, and the work of our art; but nothing whatever of a divine nature in them presents itself to the view.

We must rather, therefore, say, that sounds and melodies are appropriately consecrated to the Gods. There is, also, an alliance in these sounds and melodies to the proper orders and powers of the several Gods, to the motions in the universe itself, and to the harmonious sounds which proceed from the motions. Conformably, therefore, to such like adaptations of melodies to the Gods, the Gods themselves become present. For there is not any thing which intercepts; *so that whatever has but a casual similitude to, directly participates of, them.* A perfect possession, likewise, immediately takes place, and a plenitude of a more excellent essence and power. Not that the body and the soul are in each other, and sympathize, and are copassive with the melodies; but because the inspiration of the Gods is not separated from divine harmony, but is originally adapted and allied to it, on this account it is participated by it in appropriate measures. Hence also, it is excited and restrained according to the several orders of the Gods. But this inspiration must by no means be called an ablation, purgation, or medicine. For it is not primarily implanted in us from a certain disease, or excess, or redundance; but the whole principle and participation of it are supernally derived from the Gods.

Neither is it proper to say that the soul primarily consists of harmony and rhythm. For thus enthusiasm would be adapted to the soul alone. It is better, therefore, to deny this, and to assert that the soul, before she gave herself to body, was an auditor of divine harmony; and that hence, when she proceeded into body, and heard melodies of such a kind as especially preserve the divine vestigie of harmony, she embraced these, from them recollected divine harmony, and tends and is allied to it, and as much as possible participates of it. Hence the cause of divine divination may, after this manner, be assigned in common.

[1] "Among the deeds of Pythagoras," says Iamblichus, in his Life of that father of philosophy, (chap. xxv.) "it is said, that once through the spondaic [i.e. Doric] song of a piper he extinguished the rage of a Tauromenian lad, who had been feasting by night, and intended to burn the vestibule of his mistress, in consequence of seeing her coming from the house of his rival. For the lad was inflamed and excited [to this rash attempt] by a Phrygian song; which, however, Pythagoras most rapidly suppressed. But Pythagoras, as he was astronomizing, happened to meet with the Phrygian piper at an unseasonable time of night, and persuaded him to change his Phrygian for a spondaic song; through which the fury of the lad being immediately repressed, he returned home in an orderly manner, though a little before this he could not be in the least restrained, nor would, in short, bear any admonition; and even stupidly insulted Pythagoras when he met him. When a certain youth, also, rushed with a drawn sword on Anchilus, the host of Empedocles, because, being a judge, he had publicly condemned his father to death, and would have slain him as a homicide, Empedocles changed the intention of the youth, by singing to his lyre that verse of Homer,

> Nepenthe, without gall, o'er every ill
> Oblivion spreads. ODYSS. lib. 4.

And thus snatched his host Anchilus from death, and the youth from the crime of homicide. It is also related, that the youth from that time became the most celebrated of the disciples of Pythagoras. Farther still, the whole Pythagoric school produced, by certain appropriate songs, what they called *exartysis*, or adaptation; *synarmoga*, or elegance of manners; and *epaphe*, or contact, usefully conducting the dispositions of the soul to passions contrary to those which it before possessed. For when they went to bed, they purified the reasoning power from the perturbations and noises to which it had been exposed during the day, by certain odes and peculiar songs, and by this means procured for themselves tranquil sleep, and few and good dreams. But when they rose from bed, they again liberated themselves from the torpor and heaviness of sleep, by songs of another kind. Sometimes, also, by musical sounds alone, unaccompanied with words, they healed the passions of the soul and certain diseases, enchanting, as they say, in reality. And it is probable that from hence this name *epode*, i.e. enchantment, came to be generally used. After this manner, therefore, Pythagoras, through music, produced the most beneficial correction of human manners and lives."

Proclus also, in his MS. Commentary on the First Alcibiades of Plato, observes, "that of musical instruments some are repressive, and others motive; some are adapted to rest, and others to motion. The repressive, therefore, are most useful for education, leading our manners into order, repressing the turbulency of youth, and bringing its agitated nature to quietness and temperance. But the motive instruments are adapted to enthusiastic energy; and hence, in the mysteries and mystic sacrifices, the pipe is useful; for the motive power of it is employed for the purpose of exciting the reasoning power to a divine nature. For here it is requisite that the irrational part should be laid asleep, and the rational excited. Hence those that instruct youth use repressive instruments, but initiators such as are motive. For that which is disciplined is the irrational part; but it is reason which is initiated, and which energizes enthusiastically."

See, likewise, on this subject, Ptolem. Harmonic. lib. iii. cap. 7 and 8, who observes among other things, "that our souls directly sympathize with the energies of melody, recognizing, as it were, their alliance to them-and that at one time the soul is changed to a quiet and repressed condition, but at another to fury and enthusiasm. Ταις ενεργειασις της μελῳδιας συμπασχειν ημων αντικρυς τας ψυχας, την συγγενειαν ωσπερ επιγινωσκουσας -------------et, ποτε μεν εις ησυχιαν και κατασολην τρεπεσθαι, ποτε δεεις οῖσρον και ενθψσιασμον. And, in the last place, see Plato in his Io, and Aristotle in his Politics.

[2] Proclus in Polit. p. 365, says, "that the melodies of Olympus were the causes of ecstasy." Τα του Ολυμπου μελη ἐκσατικα.

Chap. X.

LET us, however, discuss what pertains to divination more particularly; not asserting this, that nature leads each thing to its like; for the enthusiastic energy is not the work of nature; nor again asserting that the temperature of the air, and of that which surrounds us, produces also a different temperature in the body of those that energize enthusiastically; since inspiration, which is the work of the Gods, is not changed by corporeal powers or temperaments. Nor must we say, that the much celebrated inspiration of divinity is adapted to passions and generated natures. For the gift of the proper energy of the Gods to men is impassive and superior to all generation. But since the power of the Corybantes is, in a certain respect, of a guardian and efficacious nature, [1] and that of Sabazius appropriately pertains to Bacchic inspiration, the purifications of souls, [2] and the solutions of ancient divine anger, [3] on this account the inspirations of them entirely differ from each other.

With respect, however, to the mother of the Gods, you, indeed, seem to think that those who are possessed by the Goddess are males; for, conformably to this, you denominate them Metrizantes. But the thing is not truly so. For those who are precedaneously inspired by the mother of the Gods are women; but the males that are thus inspired are very few in number, and such as are more effeminate. This enthusiasm, however, has a vivific and replenishing power, [4] on which account, also, it in a remarkable degree differs from all other mania. Proceeding, therefore, in this way, in what remains of the present discussion, and fitly distinguishing the inspirations of the Nymphs, or of Pan, and the other differences of them, according to the powers of the Gods, we shall separate them conformably to their appropriate peculiarities; and we shall also be able to explain through what cause they leap and dwell in mountains, why some of them appear to be bound, and why they are worshiped through sacrifices. All these, likewise, we shall ascribe to divine causes, as containing in themselves all the authority of these particulars; but we shall not say that either a certain collected redundancy of body or soul requires to be purified, or that the periods of the seasons are the causes of such like passions, or that the reception of the similar, and the ablation of the dissimilar, bring with them a certain remedy for an excess of this kind. For all such like particulars are corporeal-formed, and are entirely separated from a divine and intellectual life. But each thing energizes conformably to its nature; so that the spirits which are excited by the Gods, and which produce in men Bacchic inspiration, expel every other human and physical motion; and it is not proper to assimilate their energies to those which are usually exerted after our manner; but it is fit to refer them to perfectly different and primordial divine causes. One species, therefore, of divine inspiration is of this kind, and is after this manner produced.

[1] The Nature of the Corybantes, and the order to which they belong, is unfolded as follows by Proclus, in Plat. Theo lib. vi. cap. 13. "To what has been said we shall add the theory pertaining to the unpolluted [*] Gods among the ruling divinities [i.e. among the divinities that subsist immediately after the intellectual Gods]. For Plato also gives us an opportunity of mentioning these, since it is necessary that the rulers and leaders of wholes should subsist analogous to the intellectual kings, though they make their progression in conjunction with division, and a separation into parts. For as they imitate the paternal generative and convertive powers of the intellectual kings, thus also it is necessary that they should receive the immutable monads in themselves, according to the ruling peculiarity, and establish over their own progressions secondary causes of a guardian characteristic. And the mystic tradition, indeed, of Orpheus makes mention of these more clearly. But Plato being persuaded by the mysteries, and by what is performed in them, indicates concerning these unpolluted Gods. And in the Laws, indeed, he reminds us of the inflation of the pipe by the Corybantes, which represses every inordinate and tumultuous motion. But in the Euthydemus, he makes mention of the collocation on a throne, which is performed in the Corybantic mysteries; just as in other dialogues he mentions the Curetic order, speaking of the armed sports of the Curetes. For the Curetes are said to surround and to dance round the Ilemiurgus of wholes, when he was unfolded into light from Rhea. In the intellectual Gods, therefore, the first Curetic order is allotted its hypostasis. But the order of the Corybantes, which precedes Core [i.e. Proserpine], and guards her on all sides, as the theology says, is analogous to the Curetes in the intellectual order. If, however, you are willing to speak conformably to Platonic custom, because these divinities preside over purity, and preserve the Curetic order undefiled, and also preserve immutability in their generations, and stability in their progressions [**] into

the worlds, on this account they were called Corybantes. For το κορον, *to koron*, is every where significant of purity, as Socrates says in the Cratylus; since, also, you may say that our mistress Core was no otherwise denominated than from purity and an unpolluted life. But, in consequence of her alliance to this order, she produces twofold guardian triads, one in conjunction with her father, but the other herself by and from herself, imitating in this respect the whole vivific Goddess [Rhea] who constitutes the first Curetes."

[*] These Gods are called *unpolluted*, because they are the causes of *purity*. For every God begins his own energy from himself, and is that primarily which his effects are secondarily.

[**] For περιοδοις here, it is necessary to read προοδοις.

[2] Servius, in commenting on the "Mystica vannus Iacchi" of Virgil, observes, that the sacred rites of Bacchus pertained to the purification of souls, "Liberi patris sacra ad purgationem animarum pertinebant." And elsewhere he says, "Animae aere ventilantur, quod erat in sacris Liberi purgationis genus." Euripides also, in Bacchis, exclaims,

Ω μακαρ οσις ευδαιμων τελετας θεων

Ειδως, βιοταν εγισευει,

Και θιασευεται ψυχαν,

Εν ορεσι Βακχευων

Οσιοισι καθαρμοις.

i.e. " O blessed and happy he, who knowing the mysteries of the Gods, sanctifies his life, and purifies his soul, celebrating orgies in the mountains, with holy purifications."

[3] "In the greatest diseases and labours (says Plato in the Phxdrus) to which certain persons are sometimes subject *through the ancient indignation of the Gods, in consequence of former guilt*, mania when it takes place, predicting what they stand in need of, discovers a liberation from such evils by dying to prayer and the worship of the Gods. Hence, obtaining by this means purifications and the advantages of initiation, it renders him who possesses it free from disasters both for the present and future time, by discovering to him who is properly insane, and possessed by divinity, a solution of the present evils." And the Platonic Hermias beautifully unfolds the meaning of this ancient indignation of the Gods, through former guilt, as follows: " Offences which have been committed for a great length of a time, are more difficult to be washed away, and a liberation from them can alone be effected by the telestic art; but those that have been committed for a shorter time are more easily cured. Thus, also, we see in the medical art, that maladies which have existed but for a little time, if they are paid attention to at their commencement, are easily remedied, but that when they are of long standing, they are more difficultly healed. For the evil in this case becomes as it were natural and confirmed by habit, and resembles an indurated ulcer. A similar thing to this, therefore, takes place in guilty conduct. Hence, if he who has committed an injury, immediately repents, and acknowledges his guilt to him whom he has injured, he dissolves the injury, and renders himself no longer obnoxious to justice. But when some one dissolves an injury committed by his father, by restoring, for instance, land which he had unjustly taken, he then makes himself to be unobnoxious to justice, and lightens and benefits the soul of his father. These things, however, the telestic art more swiftly remedies. Moreover, if it should happen that the whole race of some one successively use land which had originally been plundered, in this case, the injury in the first place becomes immanifest, and on this ac-

count is more difficult to be cured; and, in the next place, time causes the evil to become as it were natural. Hence the Gods frequently predict to men that they should go to such or such places, and that an apology should be made to this man, who was never known to them, and that he should be appeased, in order that thus they may obtain a remedy and be liberated from their difficulties, and that the punishments inflicted on them by the Furies may cease. The Gods, however, predict, not for the purpose of taking away punishment, but in order that justice may be done, and that we may be amended. The telestic art, therefore, renders him better who possesses the mania which it imparts, and through him saves also many others. Thus, for instance, it is related of one who was cutting down an oak, and though he was called on by a Nymph not to cut it down, yet persisted in felling it, that he was punished for so doing by the avenging Furies, that he was in want of necessary food, and that if at any time he met with it, it was immediately taken from him, till one who possessed the telestic art told him to raise an altar and sacrifice to this Nymph, for thus he would be liberated from his calamities. Another person, likewise, who had slain his mother, was freed from the punishment inflicted on him by the Furies by migrating to another country, conformably to the mandate of divinity, and there fixing his abode."
[4] This is because Rhea, the mother of the Gods, is a vivific Goddess, being filled indeed (says Proclus, in Plat. Theol. lib. v, c. xi.) from the father prior to her P. e. from Saturn with intelligible and prolific power, but filling the Demiurgus [Jupiter], who derives his existence from her, with vivific abundance.

Chap. XI.

ANOTHER species of divine divination which is much celebrated, most manifest and manifold, is that of oracles, about which you say as follows: "There are some who drink water, as the priest of Clarius, in Colophon; [1] but others are seated at the mouth [of a cavern], as those who prophesy at Delphi; and others imbibe the vapour from water, as the prophetesses in Brandchidae." [2] You have, therefore, made mention of these three oracles by name, not that there are only these, for there are many more which you have omitted, but as these are more celebrated than the rest, and, at the same time, because through these you may be sufficiently instructed in the mode of divination sent to men from the Gods, hence, as it appears to me, you were satisfied with these. We, therefore, likewise shall discuss these three, omitting to speak about the many other oracles that exist.
It is acknowledged then by all men, that the oracle in Colophon gives its answers through the medium of water. For there is a fountain in a subterranean dwelling from which the prophetess drinks; and on certain established nights, after many sacred rites have been previously performed, and she has drank of the fountain, she delivers oracles, but is not visible to those that are present. That this water, therefore, is prophetic, is from hence manifest. But how it becomes so, this, according to the proverb, is not for every man to know. For it appears as if a certain prophetic spirit pervaded through the water. This is not, however, in reality the case. For a divine nature does not

pervade through its participants in this manner, according to interval and division, but comprehends as it were externally, and illuminates the fountain, [3] and fills it from itself with a prophetic power. For the inspiration which the water affords is not the whole of that which proceeds from a divine power, but the water itself only prepares us, and purifies our luciform spirit, [4] so that we may be able to receive the divinity; while, in the mean time, there is a presence of divinity prior to this, and illuminating from on high. And this, indeed, is not absent from any one, who through aptitude is capable of being united to it. But this divine illumination is immediately present, and uses the prophetess as an instrument; she neither being any longer mistress of herself, nor capable of attending to what she says, nor perceiving where she is. Hence, after prediction, she is scarcely able to recover herself. And before she drinks the water, she abstains from food for a whole day and night; and retiring to certain sacred places, inaccessible to the multitude, begins to receive in them the enthusiastic energy. Through her departure, therefore, and separation from human concerns, she renders herself pure, and by this means adapted to the reception of divinity: and from hence she possesses the inspiration of the God, shining into the pure seat of her soul, becomes full of an unrestrained afflatus, and receives the divine presence in a perfect manner, and without any impediment.

But the prophetess in Delphi, whether she gives oracles to mankind through an attenuated and fiery spirit, bursting from the mouth of the cavern, or whether being seated in the adytum on a brazen tripod, or on a stool with four feet. she becomes sacred to the God; whichsoever of these is the case, she entirely gives herself up to a divine spirit, and is illuminated with a ray of divine fire. And when, indeed, fire ascending from the mouth of the cavern circularly invests her in collected abundance, she becomes filled from it with a divine splendour. But when she places herself on the seat of the God, she becomes coadapted to his stable prophetic power: and from both these preparatory operations she becomes wholly possessed by the God. And then, indeed, he is present with and illuminates her in a separate manner, and is different from the fire, the spirit, the proper seat, and, in short, from all the visible apparatus of the place, whether physical or sacred.

The prophetic woman too in Brandchidae, whether she holds in her hand a wand, [5] which was at first received from some God, and becomes filled with a divine splendour, or whether seated on an axis, she predicts future events, or dips her feet or the border of her garment in the water, or receives the God by imbibing the vapour of the water; by all these she becomes adapted to partake externally [6] of the God.

But the multitude of sacrifices, the sacred law of the whole sanctimony, and such other things as are performed in a divine manner, prior to the prophetic inspiration, *viz.* the baths of the prophetess, her fasting for three whole days, her retiring into the adyta, and there receiving a divine light, and rejoicing for a considerable time-all these evince that the God is entreated by prayer to approach, that he becomes externally present, and that the prophetess, before she comes to her accustomed place, is inspired in a wonderful manner; and that, in the spirit which rises from the fountain, another more ancient God, who is separate from the place, shines forth to the view, and who is also the cause of the place, of the country, and of the whole divination.

[1] See, concerning this oracle, Scholiastes Apollonii ad i. librum, et Tecitus ii. Annal.
[2] This oracle is mentioned by Herodotus, 1. i., by Strabo, 1. xiv, and by Ammian. Marcell. lib. xxix.
[3] See Plutarch in his treatise De Defectu Oraculorum.
[4] See Plutarch in the above mentioned treatise. Concerning this luciform spirit, or vehicle, which is immortal, and which is called by Olympiodorus αυγοειδες χιτων, a *luciform vestment*, see my Translation of the fifth book of Proclus on the Timaeus.
[5] It was usual for those who prophesied to carry a wand. Tiresias had a sceptre, and Abaris an arrow. The Scholiast on Nicander says, that the Egyptian and Scythian magi, and also many of those in Europe, prophesied with wands. And Eustathius on the Odyssey, p. 1657, observes, "that there is a certain magic in divine wands," esse in ραβδοις θειοις τινα μαγειαν.
[6] That is, to partake of an illumination, which has no σχεσισ, or habitude, to any thing material.

Chap. XII.

IT appears, therefore, that the divination of oracles accords with all the hypotheses which we have before adduced concerning prediction. For if a power of this kind was inseparable from the nature of places, and of the bodies which are the subjects of it, or proceeded [1] according to a motion defined by number, it would not be able to foreknow, with invariable sameness, things which exist every where and always. But being separate and liberated from places and things which are measured by the numbers of time, and also from those which are detained in place, it is equally present with all things wherever they may be, and subsists simultaneously with all the natures that are produced according to time. It likewise comprehends in one the truth of all things, through its separate and transcendent essence.

Hence, if this is rightly asserted by us, the prophetic power of the Gods is not partibly comprehended by any place, or partible human body, nor by the soul, which is detained in one certain species of divisible natures; but being separate and indivisible, it is wholly every where present with the natures which are capable of receiving it. It likewise externally illuminates and fills all things, pervades through all the elements, comprehends earth and air, fire and water, and leaves nothing destitute of itself, neither animals nor any of the productions of nature, but imparts from itself a certain portion of foreknowledge, to some things in a greater, and to others in a less, degree. Moreover, existing itself prior to all things, by its own separate nature, it becomes sufficient to fill all things, so far as each is able to partake of it.

Chap. XIII.

LET us, therefore, now direct our attention to another species of divination, which is not public, but of a private nature, concerning which you say, *"that some become enthusiastic by standing on characters, as those that are, filled from the intromission of spirits."* This species, therefore, through those who badly use it, cannot easily be comprehended in one definition. But it is obvious and superficial, and known to many, and employs a falsehood and deception which are not to be endured; nor is it at all attended with the presence of a certain divinity, but it produces a certain motion of the soul, which is adverse to the Gods, and attracts from them an obscure and adumbrative representation, which, through the evanescent nature of its power, is usually disturbed by daemoniacal depraved spirits. That, however, which is truly a representation of the Gods, is in other respects genuine and pure, immutable and true, and is inaccessible to, and unimpeded by, spirits of a contrary nature. For, as darkness is not adapted to sustain the splendour of the glittering light of the sun, but suddenly becomes totally invisible, entirely recedes, and immediately vanishes; thus, also, when the power of the Gods, which fills all things with good, abundantly shines forth, no place is left for the tumult of evil spirits, nor can it present itself to the view; but, as if it was nothing, it departs into nonentity, not being able to be at all moved, when more excellent natures are present, or to disturb [1] such natures in their illuminations.

Since, therefore, these differ so greatly, I shall not use any other indications, in order to distinguish them, than those which are adduced by you. For when you say, *"some standing on characters,"* you seem to signify nothing else than the cause of all the evils pertaining to these things. For there are some who, neglecting the whole business of the telesiurgic theory, both concerning the invoking [priest] and the inspector (εποπτης), and also despising the order of religion, and the most holy endurance of labours for a long time, and rejecting the sacred laws and ordinances, and other religious ceremonies, think that the standing on characters is alone sufficient, and that by doing this for one hour, they can cause a certain spirit to enter; though how is it possible that any thing beautiful or perfect can be effected by these? Or how, by ephemeral works, can a contact be produced with the eternal and true essence of the Gods in sacred deeds? Through these things, therefore, it appears that such like rash men entirely err, and that they do not deserve to be ranked among diviners.

[1] Proclus, in his MS. Commentary on the First Alcibiades of Plato, observes, " that in the mysteries some one of the more imperfect daemons assumes the appearance of one that is more perfect, and draws down to himself souls that are not yet purified, and separates them from the Gods. Hence, in the most holy of the mysteries [i.e. in

the Eleusinian mysteries], prior to the manifest presence of the God [who is invoked], certain terrene daemons present themselves to the view, disturbing those that are initiated, divulsing them from undefiled good, and exciting them to matter. On this account the Gods [in the Chaldean oracles] order us not to behold them, till we are guarded by the powers imparted by the mysteries. For they say,

Ου γαρ χρη κεινους σε βλεπειν πριν σωμα τελεσθεις.

i.e. It is not proper you should behold them till your body is purified by initiation. And they add the reason,

Οτι τας ψυχας τελγοντες αει τελετων απαγουσι,

i.e. For these daemons alluring souls, always draw them away from the mysteries.

Conformably to this, also, Proclus in Plat. Theol. p. 7, says, ωσπερ εν ταις των τελετων αγιωταταις φασι τους μυσας, τεν πρωτην πολυειδεσι, και πολυμορφοις των θεων προβεβλημενοις γενεσιν απανταν, εισιοντας δε, ακλινεις, και ταισ τελεταις πεφραγμενους, αυτην την θειαν ελλεμψιν ακραιφνως εγκολπιζεσθαι, και γψμνιτας (ως αν εκεινοι φαιεν) του θειου μεταλαμβανειν, τον αυτον οιμαι τροπον και εν τη θεωρια των ολων. i.e. " As in the most holy of the mysteries, they say, that the mystics at first meet with the multiform and many shaped genera [i.e. with evil daemons], which are hurled forth before the Gods, but on entering the interior parts of the temple, unmoved, and guarded by the mystic rites, they genuinely receive in their bosom divine illumination, and divested of their garments, as they would say, participate of a divine nature; the same mode, as it appears to me, takes place in the speculation of wholes."

That mitred sophist, Warburton, as I have elsewhere called him, from not understanding the former part of this latter extract from Proclus, ridiculously translates the words, πολυειδεσι, και πολυμορφοις των θεων προβεβλημενοις γενεσιν, "multiform shapes and species, that prefigure the first generation of the Gods." See his Divine Legation of Moses, book ii. p. 152, 8vo. a work replete with distorted conceptions and inaccurate translations. And yet, as great a sophist as Warburton was, and notwithstanding the work I have just mentioned abounds with false opinions, and such as are of the most pernicious kind, yet he is compelled by truth to acknowledge, in book ii. p. 172, "that the wisest and best men in the Pagan world are unanimous in this, that the mysteries were instituted pure, and proposed the noblest end by the worthiest means," But this by the way.

Chap. XIV.

CONCERNING another kind of divination, also, you say as follows: *"Others who are conscious what they are doing in other respects, are divinely inspired according to the phantastic part, some indeed receiving darkness for a cooperator, others certain potions, but others in cantations and compositions. And some energize according to the imagination through water,* [1] *others in a wall, others in the open air, and others in the light of the sun, or some other celestial body."* The whole, however, of this kind of divination of which you now speak, since it is multiform, may be comprehended in one power, which may be called the eduction of light. [2] But this illuminates with divine light the etherial and luciform vehicle [3] with which the soul is surrounded, from which divine visions occupy our phantastic power, these visions being excited by the will of the Gods. For the whole life of the soul and all the powers that are in it, being in subjection to the Gods, are moved in such a way as the Gods, the leaders of the soul, please.

And this takes place in a twofold manner, either from the Gods being present with the soul, or imparting to the soul from themselves a certain forerunning light; but, according to each of these modes, the divine presence and the illumination have a separate subsistence. The attentive power, therefore, and dianoia [4] of the soul, are conscious of what is effected, since the divine light does not come into contact with these; but the phantastic part is divinely inspired, because it is not excited to the modes of imaginations by itself, but by the Gods, the phantasy being then entirely changed from human custom.

Since, however, a contrary is receptive of a contrary, according to a mutation and departure from itself, and that which is allied to another thing, and familiar [5] with it through similitude, is capable of receiving it, hence the illuminators receive darkness as a cooperator, and employ in illuminating the light of the sun, or of the moon, or, in short, of the air.

Sometimes, likewise, they use collocations of such things as are adapted to the Gods that are about to descend, or they employ incantations or compositions, and these appropriately prepared for the reception, presence, and manifestation of the Gods. And again, sometimes they introduce light through water, because this being diaphanous, is aptly disposed to the reception of light. But at other times, they cause light to shine forth on a wall, having previously prepared the wall for the reception of light in the best manner by the sacred descriptions of characters; and, at the same time, they fix the light in a certain solid place, so that it may not be widely diffused.

Many other modes, also, of introducing light might be mentioned; but all of them may be referred to one mode, that of irradiation, where ever it may be effected, and through whatever instruments the Gods may illuminate. Since, therefore, this illumination accedes externally, and has every thing which it possesses subservient to the will and intelligence alone of the Gods, and as the greatest thing pertaining to it, possesses a sacred irradiating light, either supernally derived from ether, or from the air, or the moon, or the sun, or from some other celestial sphere,-this being the case, it is evident from all these particulars, that such a mode of divination as this is unrestrained, primordial, and worthy of the Gods.

[1] This divination according to the imagination through water, may be illustrated by the following extract from Damascius (apud Photium) Γυνη ιερα θεομοιρον εχουσα φυσιν παραλογοτατην. υδωρ γαρ εγχεασα ακραιφνες ποτηριω τινι των υαλινων, εωρα κατα του υδατος εισω του ποτηριου τα φασματα των εσομενων πραγματων, και προυλεγεν απο της οψεως αυτα απερ εμελλεν εσεσθαι παντως. η δε πειρα του πραγματος ουκ ελαθεν ημας. i.e. "There was a sacred woman who possessed in a wonderful manner a divinely gifted nature. For pouring pure water into a certain glass cup, she saw in the water that was within the cup the luminous appearances of

78

future events, and from the view of these she entirely predicted what would happen. But of this experiment we also are not ignorant."

[2] "The Platonists," says Psellus (ad Nazianzenum) " assert that light is spread under divine substances, and is rapidly seized, without any difficulty, by some who possess such an excellent nature as that which fell to the lot of Socrates and Plotinus. But others, at certain periods, experience a mental alienation about the light of the moon."

[3] Concerning this vehicle, in which the phantastic power resides, see vol. ii. of my translation of Proclus on the Timaeus of Plato, p. 407; the Introduction to my translation of Aristotle on the Soul; and the long extract from Synesius on Dreams, in vol. ii, of my Proclus on Euclid.

[4] i.e. The discursive energy of reason.

[5] Proclus in Plat. Polit. having observed that Socrates in the Phaedrus, when he speaks in a divinely inspired manner, and poetically adopts such names as are employed by the poets, and says that it is not possible for one who speaks with an insane [i.e. with an inspired] mouth to abstain from them, adds " that an alliance to the damoniacal genus, preparing the soul for the reception of divine light, excites the phantasy to symbolic narration." Η προς δαιμονιον γενος οικειοτης, η προευτρεπιζουσα την του θειου φωτος παρουσιαν, ανακινει της φαντασιαν εις της συμβολικην απαγγελιαν. p. 396.

Chap. XV.

LET US, therefore, pass on to the mode of divination which is effected through human art, and which possesses much of conjecture and opinion. But concerning this you say as follows: *"Some also establish the art of the investigation of futurity through the viscera, through birds, and through the stars."* And there are, indeed, many other arts of this kind, but the above are sufficient to exhibit the whole artificial species of divination. Universally, therefore, this art employs certain divine signs, which derive their completion from the Gods, according to various modes. But from divine portents, according to an alliance of things to the signs which are exhibited, art in a certain respect decides, and from certain probabilities conjecturally predicts. The Gods, therefore, produce the signs, either through nature, which is subservient both generally and particularly to the generation of effects; or through genesiurgic daemons, who presiding over the elements of the universe, partial bodies, and every thing contained in the world, conduct with facility the phaenomena, conformably to the will of the Gods. But these signs symbolically premanifest the decrees of divinity and of futurity, as Heraclitus says, *"neither speaking nor concealing, but signifying;"* [1] because they express the mode of fabrication through premanifestation. As, therefore, the Gods generate all things through forms, [2] in a similar manner they signify all things through signs, impressed as it were by a seal (δια συνθηματων). Perhaps, likewise, they render by this mean our intelligence more acute. And thus much has been said by us in common concerning the whole of this kind of human art.

[1] These words of Heraclitus are also quoted by Plutarch in his treatise De Defectu Oraculorum.
[2] For εικονων here, I read ειδων.

Chap. XVI.

DESCENDING, however, to particulars, the soul of animals, the dmmon who presides over them, the air, the motion of the air, and the circulation of the heavens, variously change the viscera, [1] conformably to the will of the Gods. But an indication that they are so changed is this, that they are frequently found without a heart, [2] or deprived of the most principal parts, without which it is not at all possible for animals to be supplied with life. With respect to birds, likewise, the impulse of their proper soul moves them, and also the daemon who presides over animals; and, together with these, the revolution of the air, and the power of the heavens which descends into the air, accord with the will of the Gods, and consentaneously lead the birds to what the Gods ordained from the first. Of this the greatest indication is, that birds frequently precipitate themselves to the earth, and destroy themselves, which it is not natural for any thing to do; but this is something supernatural, so that it is some other thing which produces these effects through birds.

Moreover, the lations of the stars approximate to the eternal circulations of the heavens, not only locally, but also in powers, and the irradiations of light. But these are moved conformably to the mandates of the celestial Gods. For the most pure, agile, and supreme part of the air, is adapted to be enkindled [i.e. is most inflammable], so that when the Gods assent, it is immediately set on fire. And if some one thinks that certain effluxions of the celestial bodies are imparted to the air, his opinion will not be discordant with what is frequently effected by the divine art. The union, also, and sympathy of the universe, and the simultaneous motion of the most remote parts, as if they were near, and belonged to one animal, cause these signs to be sent from the Gods to men in the most luminous manner, primarily, indeed, through the heavens, but afterwards through the air.

From all that has been said, therefore, this becomes manifest, that the Gods, employing many instruments as media, send indications to men; and that they also use the ministrant aid of daemons and souls, and the whole of nature, and of every thing in the world which is willingly obedient to them, they being the primordial leaders of all these, and transmitting the motion which descends from them wherever they please. Hence, they being separate from all things, and liberated from all habitude and coarrangement with things in generation, lead all that generation and nature contains, according to their own proper will. This explanation, therefore, of divination accords with the doctrine of the fabricative energy and providence of the Gods. For it does not draw down the intellect of more excellent natures to sublunary concerns and to us, but this intellect being established in itself, converts to itself signs and the whole of divination, and discovers that these proceed from it.

[1] Herodian, lib. viii. observes, that the Italians very much believed in the indications of future events through the viscera: and Strabo, lib. xvii. asserts the same thing. [2] The auspices were said to be pestiferous when there was no heart in the entrails, or when the head was wanting in the liver. This was the case with the animals that were sacrificed by Caesar on the day in which he was slain. The same thin- also happened to Caius Marius, when he was sacrificing at Utica. But when Pertinax was sacrificing, both the heart and the liver of the victim were wanting, whence his death was predicted, which happened shortly after. In the sacrifices, likewise, which Afarcellus performed prior to the unfortunate battle with the Carthabiniaus, the liver was found to be without a head, as Plutarch and Livy, Pliny and Valcrius Maximus relate.

Chap. XVII.

IN the next place you inquire *"concerning the mode of divination, what it is, and what the quality is by which it is distinguished,"* which we have already explained, both generally and particularly. But you, in the first place, represent diviners as asserting, *"that all of them obtain a foreknowledge of future events through Gods or daemons, and that it is not possible for any others to know that which is future, than those who are the lords of futurity."* Afterwards you doubt, *"whether divinity is so far subservient to men, as not to be averse to sonic becoming diviners from meal."* You do not, however, properly apprehend the abundance of the power of the Gods, their transcendent goodness, and the cause which comprehends all things, when you denominate their providential care and defence of us subserviency. And, besides this, you are ignorant of the mode of divine energy, that it is not drawn down and converted to us, but that it has a separate precedency, and gives itself, indeed, to its participants, yet neither departs from itself, nor becomes diminished, nor is ministrant to those that receive it; but, on the contrary, uses all things as subservient to itself. The present doubt also appears to me to be erroneous in another respect, for supposing the works of the Gods to be like those of men, it inquires how they are effected. For because we are converted to our works, and sometimes adhere to the passions of the things which we providentially attend to, on this account you badly conjecture that the power of the Gods is subservient to the natures which are governed by them. But this power is never drawn down to its participants either in the production of the worlds, or in the providential inspection of the realms of generation, or in predicting concerning it. For it imparts to all things good, and renders all things similar to itself. It likewise benefits the subjects of its government most abundantly, and without envy, and by how much the more it abides in itself, by so much the more it is filled with its own proper perfection. And it does not itself, indeed, become any thing belonging to its participants, but it causes the things which receive it to partake of its peculiarities, and preserves them in an all-perfect manner. It also abides at the same time perfectly in itself, and comprehends them at once in itself, but is neither vanquished nor comprehended by any one of them. In vain, therefore, are men disturbed by a suspicion of this kind. For divinity is not divided together with the above mentioned modes of divination, but produces all of them impartibly. Nor does he effect different things at a different time, in a distributed manner, but produces all of them according to one energy, collectively and at once. Nor is he detained about signs, being comprehended in, or divided about, them; but contains them in himself, and in one order, and comprehends them in unity, and produces them from himself, according to one invariable will.

If, also, the power of the Gods proceeds in premanifestation as far as to things inanimate, such as pebble stones, rods, [1] pieces of wood, stones, corn, or wheat, this very thing is most admirable in the presignification of divine prophesy; because it imparts soul to things inanimate, motion to things immoveable, and makes all things to be clear and known, to partake of reason, and to be defined by the measures of intellection, though possessing no portion of reason from themselves. Another divine miracle also divinity appears to me to exhibit through signs in these things. For, as he sometimes makes some stupid man to speak wisely, through which it becomes manifest to every one, that this is not a certain human but a divine work; thus, also, he reveals through things which are deprived of knowledge, conceptions which precede all knowledge. And, at the same time, he declares to men that the signs which are exhibited are worthy of belief, and that they are superior to nature, from which he is exempt. Thus he makes things to be known which are naturally unknown, and things which are without knowledge gnostic. Through them, also, he inserts in us wisdom, and through every thing which is in the world excites our intellect to the truth of real beings, of things which are in generation, and of future events. From these things, therefore, I think it is manifest, that the mode of divination is perfectly contrary to what you suspected it to be. For it is of a ruling and primordial nature, of an unrestrained power, and transcendent nature, comprehending in itself all things, but not being comprehended by any thing, nor enclosed by its participants. For it ascends into, and rules over, all things simultaneously, and without circumscription, and collectively signifies future events. Hence, from what has been said, you may easily dissolve these vulgar doubts, which disturb most men, and may in a becoming manner elevate yourself to the intellectual, divine, and irreprehensible presignification of the Gods from all things. Through this, therefore, we have evinced, that divinity is not drawn down to the signs employed by divination.

[1] Gale observes that this appears to have been a very ancient mode of divination, and does not differ from that which is comprehended under the term wood. Hence the Scholiast, in Nicandri Theriaca, says, "that the 'Magi and Seythians predicted from

the wood of the tamarisk. For in many places they predict from rods. And that Dinon, in the first book of his third Syntaxis, observes, "that the Median diviners predict from rods." The Scholiast likewise adds the testimony of Metrodorus, who says, "that the tamarisk is a most ancient plant, and that the Egyptians, in the solemnity of Jupiter, were crowned with the tamarisk, and also the Magi among the Medes." He adds, "that Apollo also ordained that prophets should predict from this plant, and that in Lesbos he wears a tamarisk crown, has often been seen thus adorned, and that in consequence of this he was called by the Lesbians μυρικαιον, *Muricaion*, [from μυρικη, the tamarisk]." What the Scholiast here says, is confirmed by Herodotus, in lib. iv. and elsewhere. To this, also, what every where occurs about prediction from the laurel pertains. For if the leaves of the laurel when committed to the fire made a noise, it was considered as a good omen, but if they made none, a bad one.

Chap. XVIII.

ANOTHER contest, however, awaits us, not less than that in which we have been before engaged, and which you immediately announce, concerning the causes of divination, *"whether a God, an angel, or a daemon, or some other power, is present in manifestations, or divinations, or certain other sacred energies."* But our reply to your question is simply this, that it is not possible for any thing to be performed in a manner adapted to sacred concerns in divine works, without the presence of some one of the more excellent natures, as inspecting and giving completion to the sacred energy. And where the felicitous operations are perfect, sufficient to themselves, and unindigent, of these the Gods are the leaders. but where they are media, and in a small degree fall short of the extremes, they have angels as the powers that perfect and unfold them into light. And it is the province of daemons to effect those operations which rank as the last. But the right performance of actions which are effected in a divine manner, is entirely to be ascribed to some one of the more excellent natures. For since it is not possible to speak rightly about the Gods without the Gods, much less can any one perform works which are of an equal dignity with divinity, and obtain the foreknowledge of every thing without [the inspiring influence of] the Gods. For the human race is imbecile, and of small estimation, sees but a little, and possesses a connascent nothingness; and the only remedy of its inherent error, perturbation, and unstable mutation, is its participation, as much as possible, of a certain portion of divine light. But he who excludes this, does the same thing as those who attempt to produce soul from things inanimate, or to generate intellect from things unintelligent. For without the cooperation of a cause, he constitutes divine works from things which are not divine.

Let it be granted, therefore, that a God, a daemon, or an angel, gives completion to more excellent works, yet we must not on this account admit what you adduce as a thing acknowledged, *"that they affect these things, in consequence of being drawn through us by the necessities with which invocation is attended."* For divinity is superior to necessity, and this is likewise the case with all the choir of more excellent natures that is suspended from him. Nor is he alone exempt from the necessity which is introduced by men, but also from that which comprehends in itself the world; because it is not the province of an immaterial nature, and which does not receive any adventitious order, to be subservient to any necessity introduced from any thing else. And in the next place, invocation, and the things performed by a scientific operator, accede and are conjoined to more excellent natures through similitude and alliance, and do not accomplish their energies through violence. Hence, the effects which are seen to take place in diviners, do not happen as you think, from the scientific theurgist being passively affected; nor is divination thus effected through necessity, passion preoccupying the predictor; for these things are foreign from, and incongruous to, the essence of more excellent natures.

Chap. XIX.

BUT neither does the cause [of the energies] of more excellent natures subsist as a certain middle instrument, [1] nor does he who invokes operate through him who prophesies; for to assert these things is impious. And it is much more true to say, that God is all things, is able to effect all things, and that he fills all things with himself, and is alone worthy of sedulous attention, [2] esteem, the energy of reason, and felicitous honour; that which is human being vile, of no account, and ludicrous, when compared with that which is divine. Hence I laugh, when I hear it said, that divinity is spontaneously present with certain persons or things, either through the period of generation, or through other causes. For thus that which is unbegotten will no longer be more excellent, if it is led by the period of generation; nor will it be primarily the cause of all things, if it is coarranged with certain things, according to other causes. These assertions, therefore, are unworthy of the conceptions which we should frame of' the Gods, and foreign from the works which are effected in theurgy. [3] But an investigation of this kind suffers the same things the multitude suffer, about the fabrication of the universe and providence. For not being able to learn what the mode is in which these are effected, and refusing to ascribe human cares and reasonings to the Gods, they wholly abolish the providential and fabricative energy of divinity. As, therefore, we are accustomed to answer these, that the divine mode of production and providential inspection is very different from that which is human, and which it is not proper wholly to reject through ignorance, as if it had not from the first any subsistence; thus, also, it may be justly contended against you, that all prediction, and the performance of divine works, are the works of the Gods, as they are not effected through other and these human causes, but through such as are alone known to the Gods

[1] Gale, in his translation, has totally mistaken the meaning of the original in this place, and it is not unusual with him to do so. For the original is αλλ' ουδε ως οργανον τι μεσον εσι το των κρειττονων αιτιον, και δρα δια του θεσπιζοντος ο καλων. This he thus translates: "Sed neque dicendum est fatidicum animum esse instrumentum intermedium divinorum, sacerdotem vero invocantem esse tanquam efficientem causam." In consequence, also, of this mistake, he erroneously conceives that Iamblichus dissents from himself.

[2] God is all things causally, and is able to effect all things. He likewise does produce all things, yet not by himself alone, but in conjunction with those divine powers which continually germinate, as it were, from him, as from a perennial root. Not that he is in want of these powers to the efficacy of his productive energy, but the universe requires their cooperation, in order to the distinct subsistence of its various parts and different forms. For as the essence of the first cause, if it be lawful so to speak, is full of deity, his immediate energy must be deific, and his first progeny must be Gods. But as he is ineffable and superessential, all things proceed from him ineffably and superessentially. For progression, are conformable to the characteristics of the natures from which they proceed. Hence the cooperation, energy of his first progeny is necessary to the evolution of things into effable, essential, and distinct subsistence. *The supreme God, therefore*, is, as Iamblichus justly observes, *alone worthy of sedulous attention, esteem, the energy of reason, and felicitous honour;* but this is not to the exclusion of paying appropriate attention and honour to other powers that are subordinate to him, who largely participate of his divinity, and are more or less allied to him. For in reverencing and paying attention to these appropriately, we also attend to and reverence him. For that which we sedulously attend to, honour, and esteem in them, is that alone which is of a deified nature, and is therefore a portion, as it were, of the ineffable principle of all things.

Gale, from not understanding this, exclaims, "if these things are true, (viz. that God is alone worthy of sedulous attention, &c.) as they are, indeed, most true, to what purpose, O Iamblichus, is that mighty study and labour about demons and other spirits?" But the answer to this, by regarding what has been above said, is easy. For mighty study and labour about these intermediate powers is necessary, in order to our union with their invisible cause. For as we are but the dregs of the rational nature, and the first principle of things is something so transcendent as to be even beyond essence, it is impossible that we should be united to him without media; *viz.* without the Gods, and their perpetual attendants, who are on this account *the true saviours of souls.* For in a union with the, supreme deity our true salvation consists.

[3] For these conceptions and these works teach us, that in reality we, through sacred operations, approach to divinity, but that divinity does not draw near to us. Hence Proclus in Alcibiad. εν ταις κλησεσι, και εν ταις αυτοψιαις προσιεναι πως μηιν φαινεται το θειον, ημων επανατεινομενων επ' αυτο. i.e. "In invocations of the Gods, and when they are clearly seen, divinity, in a certain respect, appears to approach to us, though it is we that are extended to him."

Chap. XX.

OMITTING, therefore, these things, we may reasonably adduce a second cause, assigned by you, of the above mentioned particulars: *viz. "that the soul says and imagines these things, and that they are the passions of it, excited from small incentives.*" Neither, however, does nature possess these passions, nor does reason admit them. For every thing which is generated is generated from a certain cause, and that which is of a kindred nature derives its completion from a kindred nature. But a divine work is neither casual, for a thing of this kind is without a cause, and is not entirely arranged, nor is it produced by a human cause. For this is a thing foreign and subordinate; but that which is more perfect cannot be produced from the imperfect. All works, therefore, which have a similitude to divinity germinate from a divine cause. For the human soul is contained by one form, and is on all sides darkened by body, which he who denominates the river of Negligence, or the water of Oblivion, or ignorance and delirium, [1] or a bond through passions, [2] or the privation of life, or some other evil, will not by such appellations sufficiently express its turpitude. How, therefore, is it possible that the soul, which is detained by so many evils, can ever become sufficient to an energy of this kind? It is, indeed, by no means reasonable to suppose that she can. For if at any time we appear to be capable of effecting this, it is alone through participating of, and being illuminated by, the Gods, that we enjoy the divine energy. Hence the soul does not participate of divine works, so far as she possesses her own proper virtue and wisdom; though if works of this kind pertained to the soul, every soul would perform them, or that soul alone which possessed its proper perfection. Now, however, neither of these is sufficiently prepared for this purpose; but even the perfect soul is imperfect as with reference to divine energy. The theurgic energy, therefore, is a different thing, and the felicitous accomplishment of divine works is imparted by the Gods alone. For if this were not the case, the worship of the Gods would not, in short, be requisite, but divine goods might be present with us from ourselves, without the exercise of religion. If, therefore, these opinions are insane and stupid, it is proper to abandon an hypothesis of this kind, as not affording a cause which deserves to be mentioned of the accomplishment of divine works.

[1] Gale, in his note on these words, after having observed that Porphyry says, that ignorance, darkness, and folly attend the soul in its lapse into body; and that, according to Servius, the soul, when it begins to descend into body, drinks of folly and oblivion, quotes also Irenaeus (lib. ii. c. 59), who makes the following stupid remark: "Souls entering into this life [it is said] drink of oblivion, before they enter into bodies, from the daemon who is above this ingress. But whence do you know this, O Plato, since your soul also is now in body? For if you remember the daemon, the cup, and the entrance, it is likewise requisite that you should know the rest." To this it is easy to reply, that a soul purified and enlightened by philosophy, like that of Plato, is able to recognise many things pertaining to its preexistent state, even while in the present body, in consequence of partially emerging from corporeal darkness and oblivion; but that it is not capable of knowing every thing *distinctly,* till it is perfectly liberated from the delirium of the body. And Gale, no less sillily, adds, "respondebunt Platonici haec omnia cognovisse Platonem ex narratione, quae circumferebatur de Ere Armenio, qui Lethes aquam non biberat. i.e. "The Platonists will answer that Plato knew all these thin;s from the narration of the Armenian Erus [in the Republic] who did not drink of the water of Lethe." For Plato did not obtain this knowledge

from any historical narration, but from possessing in a transcendent degree the cathartic and theoretic virtues, and from energizing enthusiastically (or according to a divinely inspired energy) through the latter of these virtues.

[2] Agreeably to this, Porphyry says in his Αφορμαι προς τα νοετα, or Auxiliaries to Intelligibles, ψυχη καταδειται προς σωμα, τη επισροφη τη προς τα παθη τα απ' αυτου. ------ And ψσυχη εδησεν εαυτην εν τω σωματι. i.e. "The soul is bound to the body, by a conversion to the passions arising from her union with it." And, "the soul binds herself in the body." Philolaus also says, that the ancient theologists and prophets asserted, ως δια τινας τιμωριας α ψυχα τω σωματι συνεζευκται, και καθαπερ εν σαματι τουτω τεθαπται, "that the soul is conjoined to the body, on account of certain punishments, and that it is buried in it as in a sepulchre."

Chap. XXI.

Is, therefore, what you add in the third place more true; *viz. "that there is a certain mixed origin, of hypostasis, consisting of our soul and divine inspiration externally derived?"* Consider this then more accurately, lest we should be deceived by it, being impeded by its plausibility. For wherever one thing is effected from two, this one thing is wholly of a similar species, nature, and essence. Thus the elements which concur in the same thing, produce one certain thing from many, and many souls coalesce in one total soul. That, however, which is perfectly exempt, can never become one with that which departs from itself; [1] so that neither will there be one certain form of hypostasis with the soul and divine inspiration. For if divinity is unmingled, the soul will not be mingled with it; and if he is immutable, he will not be changed through a concretion into that which is common, from the simplicity of his subsistence. Some, therefore, prior to us, were of opinion that certain small sparks excite in us divine forms. It is impossible, however, that these sparks, whether they are physical, or in some other way corporeal-formed, should be transferred from things of a casual nature to things which are divine. But in what is now asserted by you, the soul is said to be a concause of the divine comixture; and it is evident, this being admitted, that the soul becomes of an equal dignity with the Gods, that it gives a certain part to them and receives a part from them, and that it also affords a measure to natures more excellent than itself, and is itself bounded by them. That likewise follows which is asserted by some, and is most dire, that the Gods precedaneously subsisting in the order of elements, are inherent in their effects, and there will be a certain thing produced in time, and from a mixture according to time, which will contain the Gods in itself. What, likewise, is this comingled form of subsistence? For if it is both [soul and divine inspiration externally derived], it will not be One thing consisting of two, but a certain composite, and a coacervation from two things. But if it is as something different from both, eternal natures will be mutable, and divine natures will in no respect differ from physical substances in generation. [2] And as it is absurd to admit that an eternal nature is produced through generation, it is still more absurd

87

to suppose that any thing which consists of eternal natures can be dissolved. Neither, therefore, is this opinion concerning divination by any means reasonable; and besides this, it is also paradoxical, whether it is considered as one supposition or as two.

[1] This assertion, that the nature which is perfectly exempt can never become one with that which departs from itself, is opposed by Gale, who says that man is composed of soul and body, and yet the latter is far inferior to, and less excellent than, the former. But in adducing this instance, he clearly shows that he does not understand what Iamblichus says. For the human soul being a medium between a certain impartible and partible essence, so far as it partakes of the partible essence, has a certain alliance with body, and is not perfectly exempt from it. Bid this is not the case with divine inspiration and our soul: for the former in a perfectly exempt manner transcends the latter. Let it, therefore, be granted him that, as Psellus says, "hypostatic union conducts different essences or natures to one hypostasis," yet such a union can never take place between two things, one of which has no habitude, proximity, or alliance to the other. Gale was led into this mistake by not properly attending to the words *perfectly exempt*, το παντελως εξηρημενον, which are here employed by Iamblichus. But such mistakes are usual with Gale, from his inaccurate and rambling manner of thinking. He likewise forgot, at the time he was writing notes on Iamblichus, that he was the master of a grammar school, and not a philosopher.

From what has been said, the absurdity, also, of their opinion is immediately obvious, who fancy that the divine essence can be mingled and united with the mortal nature. For if such a union were possible, it Would benefit and exalt the latter, but injure and degrade the former. Just as in the union of tile rational soul with the body (as Proclus beautifully observes in Tim. p, 339), "the former, by verging to a material life, kindles indeed a light n the body, but becomes herself situated in darkness; and by giving life to file body, destroys both herself and her own intellect [in as great a degree as these are capable of receiving destruction]. For thus the mortal nature participates of intellect, but the intellectual part of death, and the whole, as Plato observes in the Laws, becomes a prodigy composed of the mortal and the immortal, of the intellectual and that which is deprived of intellect. For this physical law which binds the soul to the body is the death of the immortal life, but vivifies the mortal body."

[2] Here again Gale, from not understanding, opposes Iamblichus. For he says, "sed neξ hoc sequitur. S. Maximus, ubi hypostaticam unionem declarat; haec inquit, cernuntur in corpore et anima. Una ex utroque confit hypostasis composita. Servat autem in se naturam perfectam utriusque sc. corporis et animae, και την τουτων διαφοραν ασυμφυρτον και τα ιδιωματα ασυμφυρτα και ασυγχυτα, i.e. "But neither does this follow. S. Maximus, where he unfolds hypostatic union, says these things are perceived in the soul and body. One composite hypostasis is produced from both. But this hypostasis preserves in itself the perfect nature of each, and likewise the difference of these unmingled, and the peculiarities unmingled and unconfused." This hypostatic union, however, as we have before observed, cannot take place between divine inspiration and the soul, because the former is *perfectly exempt* from the latter.

Gale adds, "Quaero autem quid velit Iamblichus per αμφοιν? Opinor, ψυχην et την αξωθεν θειαν επιπνοιαν. Non facile evincetεπιπνοιαν esse αιδιον τι, utpote quae sit transiens dei actio." i.e. "I ask what Iamblichus means by *both*. I think *the soul and divine inspiration externally* derived. But he will not easily prove that inspiration is something eternal, because it is a transient energy of God." Gale is right in his conjecture, that Iamblichus by the word both in this place, means the soul and divine inspiration externally derived; for it can admit of no other meaning; but when he adds, that inspiration cannot be something eternal, because it is a transient energy of divinity, he shows himself to be as bad a theologist as he is a philosopher. For God being an eternal, or rather a supereternal nature, his energies have nothing to do with time and its transitive progressions, but are stably simultaneous; so that transition does not exist in his inspiring influence, but in the recipients of it, these being of a temporal and mutable nature. Hence it is just as absurd to call any energy of divinity transient, as it would be to say that the light of the sun is transient, because it shines through diaphanous, but not through opaque, substances.

Chap. XXII.

You say, therefore, "*that the soul generates the power which has an imaginative perception of futurity, through motions of this kind, or that the things which are adduced from matter constitute daemons through the powers that are. inherent in them, and especially things adduced from the matter which is taken from animals.*" It appears to me, however, that what is now asserted by you exhibits a dire illegality with reference to the whole of theology and the theurgic energy. For one absurdity in it, and which is the first that presents itself to the view, is this, that it makes daemons to be generable and corruptible. And another, which is more dire than this, is that things which are prior will be produced from things which are posterior to themselves. For daemons exist prior to soul, and to the powers which are distributed about bodies. In addition to these things, also, how can the energies of a partible soul which is detained in body, become essence, and be by themselves separate out of soul? Or how can the powers which are divided about, be separated from bodies, though they have their very being in bodies? And Who is it that liberating them from a corporeal condition of subsistence, again collects the corporeal dissolution, and causes it to coalesce in one thing? For thus a thing of this kind will be a demon, who will have an existence prior to his being constituted. This assertion, likewise, is attended with certain common doubts. For how can divination be produced from things which have no divining power? And how can soul be generated from things which are without soul? And, in short, how can things which are more perfect be the progeny of such as are more imperfect? The mode, likewise, of production appears to me to be impossible. For it is impossible that essence should be produced through the motions of the soul, and through the powers which are in bodies. For from things which are without essence, it is impossible that essence should be generated.

Whence, also, does the imagination, receiving from a certain thing a divining power, become prophetic of futurity? For we do not see that any one of the things which are sown through generation possess any thing more than what is imparted to it by its first generating cause. But, in the present instance, the imagination will receive a certain more excellent addition from that which has no existence. Unless some one should say, that daemons preside over the matter which is derived from animals, and that when this matter is adduced, the presiding daemon is sympathetically moved towards it. According to this opinion, therefore, daemons are not generated from the powers in bodies; but preceding and having an existence prior to bodies, they are moved in conformity to them. Let it, however, be admitted, that daemons are thus sympathetic, yet I do not see after what manner there will be something true respecting futurity. For the foreknowledge and premanifestation of futurity is not the province of a copassive and material power, which is detained in a certain place and body; but, on the contrary, this pertains to a power which is liberated from all these. Such, therefore, are the corrections of this opinion.

Chap. XXIII.

THE animadversions which are after this adduced, at first, indeed, doubt about the mode of divination, but as they proceed, endeavour entirely to subvert it. We shall, therefore, discuss both these. And, in the first place, we shall begin to dissolve the former of these doubts. *"For in sleep, when we are not employed about any thing, have sometimes obtain a knowledge of the future."* Not that the cause of divination is derived both from us and externally: for in things the principle of which definitely subsists in us, and that which is consequent is externally derived, if these two have a coarrangement and connexion with each other, in this case the works of the two are definitely effected, and the things which are suspended from them follow their precedaneous causes. But when the cause is independent of us, and preexists by itself, the end is not defined on account of us, but the whole depends on things external to us. Now, therefore, since the truth which is in dreams does not entirely concur with our works, but frequently shines forth from itself, it shows that divination is externally derived from the Gods, that it possesses an independent power, and that it benevolently unfolds futurity when it pleases, and in such a way as it pleases. These things, therefore, should have an answer of this kind.

Chap. XXIV.

IN what follows, while you endeavour to unfold divination, you entirely subvert it. For if a passion of the soul is admitted to be the cause of it, what wise man will attribute to an unstable and stupid thing orderly and stable foreknowledge? Or how is it possible that the soul, which is in a sane and stable condition according to its better powers, *viz.* those that are intellectual and dianoetic, should be ignorant of futurity; but that the soul which suffers according to disorderly and tumultuous motions, should have a knowledge of what is future? For what has passion in itself adapted to the theory of beings? And is it not rather an impediment to the more true intellection of things? Farther still, therefore, if the things contained in the world were constituted through passions, in this case passions, through their similitude, would have a certain alliance to them. But if they are produced through reasons and through forms, there will be another foreknowledge of them, which is liberated from all passion. Again, passion alone perceives that which is present, and which now has a subsistence; but foreknowledge apprehends things which do not yet exist. Hence, to foreknow is different from being passively affected.

Let us, however, consider your arguments in support of this opinion. That *"the senses are occupied,"* therefore tends to the contrary to what you say; for it is an indication that no human phantasm is then excited. But *"the fumigations which are introduced,"* have an alliance to divinity, but not to the soul of the spectator. And *"the invocations"* do not excite the inspiration of the reasoning power, or corporeal passions in the recipient; for they are perfectly unknown and arcane, and are alone known to the God whom they invoke. But that *"not all men, but those that are more simple and young are more adapted to divination,"* manifests that such as these are more prepared for the reception of the externally acceding and inspiring spirit. From these indications, however, you do not truly conjecture that enthusiasm is a passion. For it follows from these signs, that the influx of it, in the same manner as the inspiration, is externally derived. In this way, therefore, these things subsist.

Chap. XXV.

THAT which follows in the next place, descends from a divine alienation of mind to an ecstasy of the reasoning power which leads it to a worse condition, and absurdly says, *"that the cause of divination is the mania which happens in diseases."* For, as we may conjecture, it assimilates enthusiasm to the redundancy of the black bile, to the aberrations of intoxication, and to the fury which happens from mad (logs. It is necessary, therefore, from the beginning, to divide ecstasy into two species, one of which leads to a worse condition of being, and fills us with stupidity and folly; but the other imparts goods which are more honourable than human temperance. One species also debates to a disorderly, confused, and material motion; but the other gives itself to the cause which rules over the orderly distribution of things in the world. And the one, indeed, as being deprived of knowledge, wanders from wisdom; but the other conjoins with natures that transcend all our wisdom. The one, likewise, is unstable, but the other is immutable. The one is preternatural, but the other is above nature. The one draws down the soul, but the other elevates it. And the one entirely separates us from a divine allotment, but the other connects us with it.

Why, therefore, does your assertion so much wander from the proposed hypothesis, as to decline from things primary and good to the last evils of insanity? For in what is enthusiasm similar to melancholy, or intoxication, or any other delirium excited by the body? Or what prediction can ever be produced from diseases of the body? Is not a derivation of this kind a perfect corruption, but divine inspiration the perfection and salvation of the soul? And does not depraved enthusiasm take place through imbecility, but the enthusiasm which is more excellent through a plenitude of power? In short, the latter being quiescent, according to its own proper life and intelligence, gives itself to be used by another [power which is superior to itself]; but the former, energizing according to its proper energies, renders these most depraved and turbulent. This, therefore, is a difference the most manifest of all others, because all the works of divine natures differ [in a transcendent degree] from the works of other beings. For as the more excellent genera are exempt from all others, thus also their energies do not resemble those of any other nature. Hence, when you speak of divine mania, immediately remove from it all human perversions. And if you ascribe a sacred *"sobriety and vigilance"* to divine natures, you must not consider human sobriety and vigilance as similar to it. But by no means compare the diseases of the body, such as suffusions, and the imaginations excited by diseases, with divine imaginations. For what have the two in common with each other? Nor again, must you compare *"an ambiguous state,"* such as that which takes place between a sober condition of mind and ecstasy, with sacred visions of the Gods, which are defined by one energy. But neither must you compare the most manifest surveys of the Gods with the imaginations artificially procured by enchantment. For the latter have neither the energy, nor the essence, nor the truth of the things that are seen, but extend mere phantasms, as far as to appearances only.

All such doubts as these, however, which are adduced foreign to the purpose, and tend from contraries to contraries, we do not consider as pertinent to the present hypothesis. Hence, as we have shown the unappropriateness of them, we do not think it requisite to discuss them any further, because they are contentiously introduced, and not with philosophical investigation.

Chap. XXVI.

THERE are many other contentious innovations also, which may be the subject of wonder. But some one may justly be astonished at the contrariety of opinions produced by admitting either that the truth of divination is with enchanters, the whole of which subsists in mere appearances alone, but has no real existence; or that it is with those who are incited by passion or disease, since every thing which they have the boldness to utter is fraudulently asserted. For what principle of truth, or what auxiliary of intelligence, either smaller or greater, can there be in those who are thus insane? It is necessary, however, not to receive truth of such a kind as that which may be fortuitous; for this, it is said, may happen to those that are rashly borne along. Nor must such truth be admitted as that which subsists between agents and patients, when they are concordantly homologous with each other; for truth of this kind is present with the senses and imaginations of animals. Hence this truth has nothing peculiar, or divine, or superior to common nature. But the truth of divination is established in energy with invariable sameness, has the whole knowledge of beings present with it, and is connascent with the essence of things. It likewise employs stable reasons, and perfectly, aptly, and definitely knows all things. This truth, therefore, is adapted to divination. Hence, it is very far from being a certain natural prescience, such as the preperception which is inherent in some animals of earthquakes and rain. For this arises from sympathy, when certain animals are moved in conjunction with certain parts and powers of the universe; or when, through the acuteness of a certain sense, they antecedently perceive things which happen in the air, before they accede to places about the earth.

If, therefore, these assertions are true, though we derive from nature impressions by which we obtain a knowledge of things, or come into contact with futurity, it is not proper to consider an impression of this kind as prophetic foreknowledge; but it is, indeed, similar to this knowledge, yet falls short of it in stability and truth, is conversant with that which frequently, but not always, happens, and apprehends the truth in certain, but not in all things. Hence, if there is a discipline which foresees the future in the arts, as, for instance, in the piloting or medical art, this does not all pertain to divine foreknowledge. For it conjectures the future by certain signs, and these such as are not always credible, nor such as have that of which they are the signs, connected with them with invariable sameness. But with divine providence, a stable knowledge of the future precedes; [and this is attended with] an immutable faith suspended from causes; an indissoluble comprehension of all things in all; and a perpetually abiding and invariable knowledge of all things as present and definite.

Chap. XXVII.

MOREOVER, neither is it sufficient to assert, *"that nature, art, and the sympathy of things in the universe, as if they were the parts of one animal, contain premanifestations of certain things with reference to each other; nor that bodies are so prepared, that there is a presignification of some by others."* For these things, which are very clearly seen, exhibit a certain divulsed vestige of divine prediction, in a greater or less degree; since it is not possible for any thing to be perfectly destitute of divine divination. But as in all things the image of good exhibits a similitude of divinity; thus, likewise, in all things a certain obscure or more manifest image of divine prediction shines forth to the view. Nevertheless, no one of these is such as the divine species of divination; nor must the one, divine, and unmingled form of it be characterized from the many phantasms which proceed from it into generation. Nor, if there are certain other false and deceitful resemblances, which are still more remote from reality, is it fit to adduce these in forming a judgment of it. But the divine form or species of divination is to be apprehended according to one intelligible and immutable truth; and the mutation which subsists differently at different times is to be rejected as unstable and unadapted to the Gods. If, therefore, that which is truly divination is a thing of this kind, i.e. is a divine work, who would not blush to ascribe it to nature, which produces its effects without reason and intellect, as if nature elaborated in us a certain prophetic apparatus, and inserted this aptitude in some things in a greater but in others in a less degree? For in those things in which men receive auxiliaries from nature in the attainment of their proper perfection, in these, also, certain aptitudes of nature precede; but in things in which no human work is proposed [to be effected], in these neither does the end pertain to us. And when a certain good, which is more ancient than our nature, has a prior arrangement, it is not possible in this case that a certain natural excellence should become the prepared subject of it. For in those things of which there are perfections, in these imperfect preparations are ingenerated; but both these are the habits of men [and not of Gods]. Hence, of those things which are not present with us, so far as we are men, there will not be a preparative from nature. There is not, therefore, a natural seed in us of divine prediction. If some one, however, should in a more general way assert, that there is a certain human divination, of this there will be a certain physical preparation. But with respect to that which may be truly denominated divination, and which pertains to the Gods, it is not proper to think that this is ingrafted by nature. For both other things, and also the indefinite, according to the more and the less, are the attendants on this. Hence it is separated from divine divination, which abides in stable boundaries. On this account, also, it is requisite strenuously to contend against him who asserts that divination originates from us. You likewise adduce clear indications of this from the works performed in predicting what is future. For you say, *"that those who invoke [the divinities for the purposes of divination] have about them stones and herbs, bind certain sacred bonds, which they also dissolve, open places that are shut, and change the deliberate intentions of the recipients, so as to render them worthy, though they were before depraved."* All these particulars, therefore, signify that the inspiration accedes externally. It is requisite, however, not only to preassume this, but also to define what the inspiration of divine origin is, which produces divine divination. For if this is not done, we shall not previously know what its peculiarity is, in consequence of not attributing

94

to it its proper character, and adapting this to it as a certain seal. And this, indeed, has been accurately done by us a little before.

Chap. XXVIII.

You adduce, however, as a thing by no means to be despised, *"the artificers of efficacious images."* But I should wonder if these were admitted by any one of the theurgists who survey the true forms of the Gods. For why should any one exchange truly existing beings for images, and descend from the first to the last of things? Or do we not know that all things effected by an adumbration of this kind, have an obscure subsistence, are the phantasms only of that which is true, and appear to be good, but in no respect are so? Other things, also, of this kind that accede, are borne along in a flowing condition of being; but obtain nothing genuine, or perfect, or manifest. But this is evident from the mode of their production for not divinity, but man is the maker of them. Nor are they produced from uniform and intelligible essences, but from matter, which is assumed for this purpose. What good, therefore, can germinate from matter, and from the material and corporeal-formed powers which are in bodies? Or is not that which derives its subsistence from human art, more imbecile than men themselves, who impart existence to it? By what kind of art, likewise, is this image fashioned? For it is said, indeed, to be fashioned by demiurgic art; but this is effective of true essences, and not of certain images. Hence the image-producing art is distant by a great interval from the seminal production of realities. Besides, neither does it preserve a certain analogy with divine fabrication. For divinity does not fabricate all things, either through the celestial physical motions, or through a partial matter, or through powers thus divided; but he produces the worlds by conceptions, will, and immaterial forms, and through an eternal and supermundane soul. The maker of images, however, is said to elaborate them through the revolving stars. But the thing does not in reality subsist so as it appears to do. For since there are certain infinite powers in the celestial Gods, the last genus of all the powers in them is physical. But again, of this power one portion being inherent in spermatic reasons [or productive powers], and prior to these reasons being established in immoveable natures, essentially precedes generation. But another portion being inherent in sensible and visible motions and powers, and in celestial effluxions and qualities, has dominion over the whole visible order of things. This last power, therefore, in all these rules over the circumterrestrial manifest generation in places about the earth. Many other arts, however, as for instance, the medical [1] and gymnastic, use this power, which has dominion over visible generation, and the qualities of the effluxions sent from the heavens employ it, and likewise all such arts as in their operations communicate with nature. And moreover, the image-making; art attracts a certain very obscure genesiurgic portion from the celestial effluxions.

Such, therefore, as the truth is, such also it is requisite to unfold it to others. It must be said, then, that the maker of images neither uses the celestial circulations, nor the powers which are inherent in them, nor those powers which are naturally established about them; nor, in short, is it possible to come into contact with them. But he artificially, and not theurgically, applies himself to the last effluxions which openly proceed from the nature of them, about the last part of the universe. For these effluxions, I think, being mingled with a partial matter, are capable of being changed and transformed differently at different times. They likewise receive the transposition, from some things to others, of the powers which are in partial natures. The variety, however, of such like energies, and the composition of a multitude of material powers, are not only entirely separated from divine fabrication, but also from natural production. For nature produces her proper works collectively, and at once, and accomplishes all things by simple and incomposite energies. Hence it remains that a commixture of this kind, about the last and manifest celestial effluxion, and about the things which are moved by a celestial nature, is artificial.

[1] Hippocrates was of opinion that physicians ought to be skilled in astronomy. And Galen derides those physicians who deny that astronomy is necessary to their art. See his treatise entitled Si quis sit Medicus eundem esse philosophum. And in lib. viii. cap. 20, of his treatise De Ingenio Sanitatis, he calls physicians that are ignorant of astronomy homicides. But by astronomy here, both Hippocrates and Galen intended to signify what is now called astrology. Roger Bacon also, in his Epistle to Pope Clement, says, "Opera quae fiunt hic inferius, variantur secundum diversitatem coelestium constellationum, ut opera medicinae et alkimiae." i.e. "The works which are performed in these inferior realms are varied according to the diversity of the celestial constellations, as, for instance, the works of medicine and alchemy." If, however, as Galen says, and doubtless with great truth, physicians that are ignorant of this are homicides, how numerous must the medical homicides be of the present age!

Chap. XXIX.

WHY, therefore, does the maker of images, who effects these things, desert himself, though he is better than these images, and consists of things of a more excellent nature, and confide in inanimate idols, which are inspired with the representation alone of life, contain a renovated harmony, and which is externally multiform, and are in reality diurnal? Shall we say that something genuine and true is inherent in them? Nothing, however, which is fashioned by human art is genuine and pure. But you will say, that simplicity and uniformity of energy predominate in the whole of their composition. This is very far from being the case. For the idol, according to its visible composition, is mingled from all-various and contrary qualities. Shall we say then, that a certain pure and perfect power is manifest in them? By no means. For a thing of this kind possesses an adventitious multitude of efflux-ions, collected from many places, and which shows itself to be imbecile and evanescent. But if these particulars, which we have enumerated, are not found to take place in images, is stability present with them, as it is said to be [by the patrons of these images]? By no means, likewise, is this the case. For these idols are extinguished with much greater rapidity than the images which are seen in mirrors. For they are immediately formed by the accession of fumigations from exhaling vapours; but when the fumigation is mingled with, and diffused through, the whole air, then the idol is likewise immedi-ately dissolved, and is not naturally adapted to remain for the smallest por-tion of time. Why, therefore, should the man who is a lover of truth, pay at-tention to these useless delusions? I, indeed, do not think them to be of any value. For if the makers of these images know that the fictions about which they are busily employed, are nothing more than the formations of passive matter, the evil arising from an attention to them will be simple. But in addi-tion to this, these idol-makers are similar to the images in which they con-fide. And if they pay attention to these idols as if they were Gods, the absurdi-ty will be so great, as neither to be effable by words, nor to be endured in deeds. For a certain divine splendour never illuminates a soul of this kind, because it is not adapted to be imparted to things which are entirely repug-nant to it; neither have those things which are detained by dark phantasms a place for its reception. This delusive formation, therefore, of phantasms, will be conversant with shadows, which are very remote from the truth.

Chap. XXX.

You say, however, "*that the makers of images observe the motion of the celestial bodies, and can tell from the concurrence of what star, with a certain star or stars, predictions will be true or false; and also whether the things that are performed will be inanities, or significant and efficacious.*" But neither will these phantasms, on this account, possess any thing divine. For the last of the things which are in generation are moved in conjunction with the celestial courses, and are copassive with the effluxions which descend from the heav-enly bodies. Moreover, if any one considers these things accurately, he will find that they demonstrate the contrary to what is here asserted. For how is it possible that things which are in every respect mutable, and this with facil-ity, and which are all-variously turned by external motions, so as to become inefficacious, or prophetic, or significant, or effective, or at different times different, should contain in themselves, by participation, any portion, how-ever small, of divine power? What then, are the powers which are inherent in matter the elements of daemons? By no means: for no partial sensible bodies generate daemons; but much more are these generated and guarded by daemons. Neither is any man able to fashion, as by a machine, certain forms of daemons; but, on the contrary, he is rather fashioned and fabricated by them, so far as he participates of a sensible body. But neither is a certain daemoniacal multitude generated from the elements of sensibles; since, on the contrary, this multitude is simple, and energizes uniformly about composite natures. Hence, neither will it have sensibles more ancient, or more stable than itself; but being itself more excellent than sensibles, both in dignity and power, it imparts to them the permanency which they are able to receive. Unless indeed, you denominate idols daemons, not rightly employing an appellation of this kind. For the nature of daemons is one thing, and that of idols another. The order of each, likewise, is very different. Moreover, the leader of idols is different from the great leader of daemons. And this, also, you admit. For you say, " that no God or daemon is drawn down by idols." What, therefore, will be the worth of a sacred deed, or of the foreknowledge of what is future, if it is entirely destitute of divinity and a daemon? So that it is requisite to know what the nature is of this wonder-working art, but by no means to use or confide in it.

Chap. XXXI.

AGAIN, therefore, still worse than this is the explanation of sacred operations, which assigns as the cause of divination, *"a certain genus of daemons, which, is naturally fraudulent, omniform, and various, and which assumes the appearance of Gods and daemons, and the souls of the deceased."* I shall, therefore, relate to you, in answer to this, what I once heard from the prophets of the Chaldeans.

Such Gods as are truly divinities, are alone the givers of good; alone associate with good men, and with those that are purified by the sacerdotal art, and from these amputate all vice, and every passion. When these, also, impart their light, that which is evil, and at the same time daemoniacal, vanishes from before more excellent natures, in the same manner as darkness when light is present; nor is it able to disturb theurgists in the smallest degree, who receive from this light every virtue, obtain worthy manners, become orderly and elegant in their actions, are liberated from passions, and purified from every disorderly motion, and from atheistical and unholy conduct. But those who are themselves flagitious, and who leap, as it were, to things of a divine nature in an illegal and disorderly manner, these, through the imbecility of their proper energy, or through indigence of inherent power, are not able to associate with the Gods. Because, likewise, they are excluded, through certain defilements, from an association with pure spirits, they become connected with evil spirits, are filled from them with the worst kind of inspiration, are rendered depraved and unholy, become replete with intemperate pleasures, and every kind of vice, are emulous of manners foreign to the Gods, and, in short, become similar to the depraved daemons, with whom they are connascent. These, therefore, being full of passions and

98

vice, attract to themselves, through alliance, depraved spirits, and are excited by them to every kind of iniquity. They are also increased in wickedness by each other, like a circle conjoining the beginning to the end, and similarly making an equal compensation. Hence deeds which are the nefarious offences of impiety, which are introduced into sacred works in a disorderly manner, and which are also confusedly performed by those who betake themselves to such works, and at one time, as it seems, cause one divinity to be present instead of another, and again, introduce depraved daemons instead of Gods, whom they call equal to the Gods (αντιθεους) - such deeds as these you should never adduce in a discourse concerning sacerdotal divination. For good is more contrary to evil than to that which is not good. As, therefore, the sacrilegious are in the most eminent degree hostile to the religious cultivation of the Gods; thus, also, those who are conversant with daemons who are fraudulent, and the causes of intemperance, are undoubtedly hostile to theurgists. For from these every depraved spirit departs, and when they are present, is entirely subverted. Every vice, too, and every passion, are by these perfectly amputated: for a pure participation of good is present with the pure, and they are supernally filled with truth from a divine fire. These, therefore, suffer no impediment from evil spirits, nor are these spirits any obstacles to the goods of their souls. Nor are theurgists disturbed by pride, or flattery, or the enjoyment of exhalations, or any violence; but all these, as if struck by lightning, yield and recede, without touching the theurgist, or being able to approach to them. Hence this genus of divination is undefiled and sacerdotal, and is truly divine. This, also, does not, as you say it does, require me, or any other as an arbiter, in order that I may prefer it to a multitude of other things; but it is itself exempt from all thins, is supernatural and has an eternal preexistence, neither receiving a certain opposition, nor a certain transcendency, which has a prearrangement in many things, because it is of itself liberated, and uniformly precedes all things. And to this it is requisite that you, and every one who is a genuine lover of the Gods, should give himself wholly; since by this mean irreprehensible truth will be obtained in divinations, and perfect virtue in souls; and through both these, an ascent will be afforded to theurgists to intelligible fire, which ought to be preestablished as the end of all foreknowledge, and of every theurgic operation. Hence you in vain adduce the opinion of those who think that divination is effected by an evil daemon, since these do not deserve to be mentioned in speculations concerning the Gods. At the same time, likewise, they are ignorant of the means of distinguishing truth from falsehood, because they are from the beginning nourished in darkness, and are wholly incapable of knowing the principles from which these are produced. Here, therefore, we shall terminate our discussion concerning the mode of divination.

Section IV.

Chap. I.

LET us then, in the next place, consider the opposing arguments, what they are, and what reason they possess. And if we should discuss some things a little more abundantly, in consequence of speaking freely and at leisure, it is requisite that you should promptly attend to, and endure what, we say. For it is necessary that great labour should be bestowed on the greatest disciplines, and that they should be accurately explored for a long time, if you intend to know them perfectly. Do you, therefore, conformably to the present hypothesis, propose the arguments which occasion the doubt, and I will answer you. Say then, *"it very much perplexes me to understand how superior beings, when invoked, are commanded by those that invoke them, (is if they were their inferiors."* But I will unfold to you the whole division, which is worthy of regard, concerning the powers that are invoked; from which you will be able clearly to define what is possible and what is impossible, in the subjects of your investigation. For the Gods, indeed, and the natures that are more excellent than we, through the wish of what is beautiful, and from an unenvying and exuberant fullness of good, benevolently impart to those that are worthy, such things as are fit for them, commiserating the labours of sacerdotal men, but being delighted with those that they have begotten, nourished, and instructed. But the middle genera are the inspective guardians of judgment. These inform us what ought to be done, and from what it is fit to abstain. They also give assistance to just works, but impede such as are unjust; and as many endeavour to take away unjustly the property of others, or basely to injure or destroy some one, they cause these to suffer the same things as they have done to others. But there is, likewise, another most irrational genus of daemons, [1] which is without judgment, and is allotted only one power, through an arrangement by which each of these daemons presides over one work alone. As therefore, it is the province of a sword to cut, and to do nothing else than this, thus also of the spirits which are distributed in the universe, according to the partible necessity of nature, one kind divides, but another collects, things which are generated. This, however, is known from the phaenomena. For the Charonean [2] spiracles, as they are called, emit from themselves a certain spirit, which is able to corrupt promiscuously every thing that falls into them. Thus, therefore, of certain invisible spirits, each is allotted a different power, and is alone adapted to do that which it is ordained to perform. He, therefore, who turns from their natural course things which contribute to the universe in an orderly manner, and illegitimately performs a certain thing, in this case receives the injury arising from that which he uses badly. This, however, pertains to another mode of discussion.

[1] According to Proclus, in Alcibiad. Prior. there are three orders of daemons, the first of which are more *intellectual*, the second are of a more *rational nature*, and the third, of which Iamblichus is now speaking, are *various, more irrational, and more material.*

[2] Charonea is a country of Asia Minor, bordering on the river Meander; and in it there are spiracles which exhale a foul odour. According to Pliny, there are places of this kind in Italy, in the country of Puteoli, now Puzzulo. In Amsanetus, also, a place in the middle of Italy, in the country of the Samnites, there were sulphureous waters, the steams of which were so pestilential, that they killed all who came near them. Hence Cicero, in lib. i. De Divin. " Quid enim? Non videmus, quam sint varia terrarum genera? Ex quibus et mortifera quaedam pars est, ut et Amsancti in Hirpinis, et in Asia Plutonia."

Chap. II.

BUT we sometimes see that take place which is now proposed to be considered. For it happens that spirits are commanded [to do this or that] who do not use a reason of their own, and have not the principle of judgment. Nor does this occur irrationally. For our dianoia naturally possessing the power of reasoning about and judging of things as they are, and comprehending in itself many powers of life, is accustomed to command the most irrational spirits, and such as derive their perfection from one energy alone. Hence, it invokes these as more excellent natures, because it endeavours to attract to particulars from the whole world, in which we are contained, things which contribute to wholes. [1] And it commands them as inferior natures, because frequently certain parts of things in the world [such as our reasoning power] are more pure and perfect than things which extend themselves to the whole world. Thus, for instance, if one thing is intellectual [as is the case with our dianoia], but another is wholly inanimate or physical, then that which proceeds to a less extent has a more principal power than that which is more extended, though the former falls far short of the latter in magnitude and multitude of domination. For these things, also, another reason may be assigned, and which is as follows: in all theurgical operations the priest sustains a twofold character; one, indeed, as man, and which preserves the order possessed by our nature in the universe; but the other, which is corroborated by divine signs, and through these is conjoined to more excellent natures, and is elevated to their order by an elegant circumduction, this is deservedly capable of being surrounded with the external form of the Gods. Conformably, therefore, to a difference of this kind, the priest very properly invokes, as more excellent natures, the powers derived from the universe, so far as he who invokes is a man; and again, he commands these powers, because through arcane symbols, he, in a certain respect, is invested with the sacred form of the Gods.

[1] And these irrational spirits, so far as they contribute to wholes, are more excellent than we are, though through being irrational they are inferior to us.

Chap. III.

DISSOLVING, however, the doubts in a way still more true, we think it requisite, in invoking superior natures, to take away the evocations which appear to be directed to them as to men, and also the mandates in the performance of works, which are given with great earnestness. For if the communion of concordant friendship, and a certain indissoluble connexion of union, are the bonds of sacerdotal operations, in order that these operations may be truly divine, and may transcend every common action known to men, no human work will be adapted to them; nor will the invocations of the priest resemble the manner in which we draw to ourselves things that are distant; nor are his mandates directed as to things separated from him, in the way in which we transfer one thing from others. But the energy of divine fire shines forth voluntarily, and in common, and being self-invoked and self-energetic, energizes through all things with invariable sameness, both through the natures which impart, and those that are able to receive, its light. This mode of solution, therefore, is far superior, which does not suppose that divine works are effected through contrariety, or discrepancy, in the way in which generated natures are usually produced; but asserts that every such work is rightly accomplished through sameness, union, and consent. Hence, if we separate from each other that which invokes and that which is invoked, that which commands and that which is commanded, that which is more and that which is less excellent, we shall, in a certain respect, transfer the contrariety of generations to the unbegotten goods of the Gods. But if we despise all such things, as it is just we should, as of an earth-born nature, and ascribe that which is common and simple, as being more honourable, to the powers who transcend the variety which is in the realms of generation, the first hypothesis of these questions will be immediately subverted, so that no reasonable doubt concerning them will be left.

Chap. IV.

WHAT then shall we say concerning the next inquiry to this, *viz.* "*why the powers who are invoked think it requisite that he who worships then should be just, but they when called upon to act unjustly do not refuse so to act?*" To this I reply, that I am dubious with respect to what you call acting justly, and am of opinion that what appears to us to be an accurate definition of justice does not also appear to be so to the Gods. For we, looking to that which is most brief, direct our attention to things present, and to this momentary life, and the manner in which it subsists. But the powers that are superior to us know the whole life of the soul, and all its former lives; and, in consequence of this, if they inflict a certain punishment from the prayer of those that invoke them, they do not inflict it without justice, but looking to the offences committed by souls in former lives; [1] which men not perceiving think that they unjustly fall into the calamities which they suffer.

[1] See the justice of providence in this respect most admirably defended by Plotinus, in the first of his treatises on providence, which treatise forms one of the five books of Plotinus translated by me, in 8vo. 1794.

Chap. V.

THE multitude, also, are accustomed to doubt in common the very same thing concerning providence, *viz.* why certain persons are afflicted unde-servedly, as they have not done any thing unjustly prior to their being thus afflicted. For neither here is it possible to understand [perfectly] what the soul is, and its whole life, how many offences it has committed in former lives, and whether it now suffers from its former guilt. In this life, also, many unjust actions are concealed from human knowledge, but are known to the Gods, since neither is the same scope of justice proposed to them as to men. For men, indeed, define justice to be the soul's performance of its own prop-er business, [1] and the distribution of desert, conformably to the established laws, and the prevailing polity. But the Gods, looking to the whole orderly arrangement of the world, and to the subserviency of souls to the Gods, form a judgment of what is just. Hence the judgment of just actions with the Gods is different from what it is with us. Nor is it wonderful, if we are unable, in most things, to arrive at the supreme and most perfect judgment of more excellent natures. What also hinders, but that to each thing by itself, and in conjunction with the whole alliance of souls, justice may in a very transcend-ent manner be decreed by the Gods? For if a communion of the same nature in souls, both when they are in and when they are out of bodies, produces a certain identical connexion and common order with the life of the world, it is likewise necessary that a fulfilment of justice should be required by wholes, and especially when the magnitude of the unjust deeds antecedently commit-ted by one soul transcends the infliction of one punishment due to the of-fences. But if any one should add other definitions, through which he can show that what is just subsists with the Gods in a way different from that in which it is known by us, from these also our design will be facilitated. For me, however, the before mentioned canons are alone sufficient for the purpose of manifesting the universal genus, and which comprehends every thing per-taining to the medicinal punishments inflicted by divine justice.

[1] In the original, την ιδιαν ψυχης αυτοπραγιαν, which Gale very inadequately translates *proprium animae officum.*

Chap. VI.

IN order, therefore, that from an abundance of arguments we may contend against the objection which is now adduced, we will grant, if you please, the contrary to what we have asserted, *viz.* that certain unjust things are performed in this business of invocations. That the Gods, however, are not to be accused as the causes of these is immediately manifest. For those that are good are the causes of good; and the Gods possess good essentially. They do nothing, therefore, that is unjust. Hence other causes of guilty deeds must be investigated. And if we are not able to discover these causes, it is not proper to throw away the true conception respecting the Gods, nor on account of the doubts whether these unjust deeds are performed, and how they are effected, to depart from notions concerning the Gods which are truly clear. For it is much better to acknowledge the insufficiency of our power to explain how unjust actions are perpetrated, than to admit any thing impossible and false respecting the Gods; since all the Greeks and Barbarians truly opine the contrary to be the case with divine natures. After this manner, therefore, the truth respecting these particulars subsists.

Chap. VII.

MOREOVER, it is necessary to add the causes whence evils [1] sometimes arise, and to show how many and of what kind they are. For the form of them is not simple; but, being various, is the leader of the generation of various evils. For if what we a little before said, concerning images and evil daemons, who assume the appearance of Gods and good daemons, is true, an abundant evil-producing tribe, about which a contrariety of this kind usually happens, will from hence appear to flow. *For an evil daemon requires that his worshipper should be just, because he assumes the appearance of one belonging to the divine genus; but he is subservient to what is unjust, because he is depraved.* The same thing, likewise, that is said of good and evil may be asserted of the true and the false. As, therefore, in divinations we attribute true predictions to the Gods alone, but when we detect any falsehood in predictions we refer this to another genus of cause, *viz.* that of daemons; thus, also, in things just and unjust, the beautiful and the just are to be alone ascribed to Gods and good daemons; but such daemons as are naturally depraved, perpetrate what is unjust and base. And that, indeed, which consents and accords with itself, and always subsists with invariable sameness, pertains to more excellent natures; but that which is hostile to itself, which is discordant, and never the same, is the peculiarity in the most eminent degree of daemoniacal dissension, about which it is not at all wonderful that things of an opposing nature should subsist; but perhaps the very contrary, that this should not be the case, would be more wonderful.

Chap. VIII.

W<small>E</small> may, however, beginning from another hypothesis, demonstrate the same thing. We must admit that the corporeal parts of the universe are neither sluggish nor destitute of power, but as much as they excel our concerns in perfection, beauty, and magnitude, by so much also is the power which is present with them greater. Each, likewise, by itself is capable of effecting different things, and produces certain different energies. They are also capable of effecting things much more numerous on each other. And besides this, a certain multiform production extends to parts from wholes; partly from sympathy, through similitude of powers, and partly from the aptitude of the agent to the patient. If, therefore, certain evils and destructions happen to parts, they are salutary and good as with reference to wholes and the harmony of the universe, but to parts they introduce a necessary corruption, either from not being able to bear the energies of wholes, or from a certain other commixture and temperament of their own imbecility, or, in the third place, from the privation of symmetry in the parts to each other.

Chap. IX.

A<small>FTER</small> the body of the universe, also, many things are generated by the nature of it. For the concord of similars, and the contrariety of dissimilars, effect not a few things. Farther still, the assemblage of many things into the one animal of the universe, and the powers in the world, whatever the number and quality of them may be, effect, in short, one thing in wholes and another in parts, on account of the divided imbecility of parts. Thus, for instance, the friendship, love, and contention which subsist in energy in the universe, become passions in the partial natures by which they are participated. Those things, likewise, that are preestablished in forms and pure reasons in the nature of wholes, participate of a certain material indigence, and privation of *morphe*, in things which subsist according to a part. And things which are conjoined to each other in wholes are separated in parts. Hence partible natures, which participate of wholes in conjunction with matter, degenerate from them in all things, and also from what is beautiful and perfect. But some parts are corrupted, in order that wholes may be preserved in a condition conformable to nature. Sometimes, likewise, parts are compressed and weighed down, though at the same time wholes remain impassive to a molestation of this kind.

Chap. X.

WE shall collect, therefore, what happens from these conclusions. For if certain invocators employ the physical or corporeal powers* of the universe, an involuntary gift of energy [from these powers], and which is without vice, takes place. He, likewise, who uses this gift [sometimes] perverts it to things of a contrary nature, and to base purposes. And the gift, indeed, is moved contrarily together with the passions, and sympathetically through similitude; but he who uses the thing which is imparted, deliberately draws it, contrary to justice, to what is evil and base. And the gift, indeed, causes things which are most remote to cooperate through the one harmony of the world. But if some one understanding this to be the case should iniquitously endeavour to draw certain portions of the universe to other parts, these parts are not the cause of the evil that ensues; but the audacity of men, and the transgression of the order in the world, pervert things that are beautiful and legal. Hence neither do the Gods effect what appears to be base, but this is accomplished by the natures and bodies that proceed from them; nor do these very natures and bodies impart improbity from themselves, as it is thought they do; but they send their proper effluxions to places about the earth, for the salvation of wholes, and those who receive them transmute them by their commixture and perversion, and transfer what is given to a purpose different from that for which it was imparted. From all these particulars, therefore, it is demonstrated that a divine nature is not the cause of evils and unjust deeds.

[1] Sec cap. 40, 41, 12, of Ennead iv. lib. iv. of Plotinus, from which the doctrine of this chapter is derived.

Chap. XI.

MOREOVER, you inquire, and at the same time doubt, *"how it comes to pass that the Gods do not hear him who invokes them, if he is impure from venereal connexions; but, at the same time, they do not refuse to lead any one to illegal venery."* You have, indeed, a clear solution of these things from what has been before said; if they are done contrary to [human] laws, but are effected according to another order and cause more excellent than laws. Or if it happens that things of this kind are conformable to the mundane harmony and friendship, yet produce a conflict in parts through a certain sympathy. Or if the communication of good, which is beautifully imparted, is perverted by those that receive it to the contrary.

Chap. XII.

IT is necessary, however, to discuss these things particularly, and to show how they subsist, and what reason they possess. It is requisite, therefore, to understand that the universe is one animal; and that the parts in it are, indeed, separated by places, but through the possession of one nature hasten to each other. [1] The whole collective power, however, and the cause of mixture, spontaneously draws the parts to a mingling with each other. But it is also possible for this spontaneous attraction to be excited and extended by art more than is fit. The cause itself, therefore, of this mixture extending from itself to the whole world, is good, and the source of plenitude; has the power of harmonically procuring communion, consent, and symmetry; and inserts, by union, the indissoluble principle of love, which principle retains and preserves both things that are in existence, and such as are becoming to be. But in the parts, through their separation from each other and from wholes, and because, from their own proper nature, they are imperfect, indigent, and imbecile, their mutual connection is accompanied with passion; by which, in most of them, desire and a connascent appetite are inherent. Art [2] therefore, perceiving this innate desire thus implanted by nature, and distributed about it (art itself also being multiformly distributed about nature), variously attracts and derives it as through a channel. Hence it transfers that which in itself is orderly and arranged into the privation of order, and fills that which is beautiful and commensurate with deformity. But the venerable end in each particular thing, which is connascent with union, it transfers to another indecorous plenitude, which is an assemblage of different things according to a common passion. It likewise imparts a matter from itself, which is unadapted to the whole generation of what is beautiful, either because it does not entirely receive it, or because it transfers it to other things. It also mingles many different physical powers, which it manages as it pleases for the purposes of generation. Hence we have universally shown, that the apparatus of a venereal connexion of this kind proceeds from a certain human art, and not from a certain daemoniacal or divine necessity.

[1] Agreeably to this, Plotinus, also, in Ennead iv. lib. iv. cap. 3Q, παν τουτο το εν, και ως ζωον εν· ζωον τε οντος, και εις εν τελουντος, ουδεν ουτω πορρω τοπου ως μη εγγυς ειναι τη του ενος ζωον προς το συμπαθειν φυσει. i.e. "This universe is one, and is as one animal. But being an animal and completely effecting one thing, nothing in it is so distant in place as not to be near to the nature of the one animal, on account of its sympathy with the whole of itself."
[2] This art is no other than magic, of which the following account, from a very rare Greek manuscript of Psellus, On Demons according to the Dogmas of the Greeks, will, I doubt not, be acceptable to the reader, as it illustrates what is here said by Iamblichus, and shows that magic is not an empty name, but possesses a real power, though at present this art seems to be totally lost. Ficinus published some extracts from this manuscript in Latin; but Gale does not appear to have had it in his posses-

n. Η γοητεια δε εστι τεχνη τις περι τους ενυλους και χθονιους δαιμονας φαντασιοσκοπουσα τοις εποπταις τα τουτων ειδωλα, και τους μεν ωσπερ εξ αδου αναγουσα, τους δε υψοθεν καταγουσα, και τουτους κακωτικους, και ειδωλα αττα υφιστησι φαντασματα τοις θεωποις των τουτων, και τοις μεν ρευματα τινα εκειθεν κυμαινοντα επαφιησι· τοις δε δεσμων ανεσεις και πρυφας, και χαριτας επαγγελλεται. επαγεται δε τας τοιαυτας δυναμεις, και ασμασι και επασμασιν. η δε μαγεια πουδυναμον το χρεμα τοις Ελλησιν εδοξε. μεριδα γουν ειναι ταυτην φασιν εσχατην της ιεατικης επιστημης. ανιχνευουσα γαρ των υπο την σεληνην παντων την τε ουσαν και φυσιν, καιδυναμιν και ποιοτηρα. λεγω δε στοιχειων και των τουτων μεριδων, ζωων, παντοδαπων φυτων, και των εντευθεν καρπων, λιθων, βοτανων, και απλως ειπειν, παντος πραγματος, υποστασιν τε και δυναμιν. εντευθεν αρα τα εαυτης επγαζεται. αγαλματα τε υφιστησιν υγειας περιποιητικα, και σχηματα ποιειται παντοδαπα· και νοσοποια δεμιουργηματα ετερα. και αετοι μεν, και δρακοντες, βιωσιμοι αυτοις προς υγειαν υποθεσις· αιλουροι δε και κυνες, και κορακες αγρυπνητικα συμβολα. κηρος δε και πηλος εις τας των μοριων συμπασεις παραλαμβανονται. φανταζει δε πολλακις, και πυρος ουρανιου ενδοσεις, και διαμειδιωσι επι τουτων αγαλματα· πυρί δε αυτοματω λαμπαδες αναπτονται. i.e. "Goeteia, or witchcraft, is a certain art respecting material and terrestrial daemons, whose images it causes to become visible to the spectators of this art. And some of these daemons it leads up, as it were from Hades, but others it draws down from on high; and these, too, such as are of an evil species. This art, therefore, causes certain phantastic images to appear before the spectators. And before the eyes of some, in- deed, it pours exuberant streams; but to others it promises freedom from bonds, del- icacies, and favours. They draw down, too, powers of this kind by songs and incanta- tions. But magic, according to the Greeks, is a thing of a very powerful nature. For they say that this forms the last part of the sacerdotal science. Magic, indeed, investi- gates the nature, power, and quality of every thing sublunary; of the elements, and their parts, of animals, all various plants and their fruits, of stones, and herbs: and in short, it explores the essence and power of every thing. From hence, therefore, it produces its effects. And it forms statues which procure health, makes all various figures, and things which become the instruments of disease. It asserts, too, that ea- gles and dragons contribute to health; but that cats, dogs, and crows are symbols of vigilance, to which, therefore, they contribute. But for the fashioning of certain parts wax and clay are used. Often, too, celestial fire is made to appear through magic; and then statues laugh, and lamps are spontaneously enkindled."

This curious passage throws light on the following extract from the first book of the Metaphorsis of Apuleius: "Magico susurranime, amnes agiles reverti, mare pigrum colligari, ventos inanimes expirare, solem inhiberi, lunam despumari, stellas evelli, diem tolli, noctem teneri." i.e. "By magical incantation rapid rivers may be made to run back to their fountains, the sea be congealed, winds become destitute of spirit, the sun be held back in his course, the moon be forced to scatter her foam, the stars be torn from their orbits, the day be taken away, and the night be detained." For it may be inferred from Psellus, that witches formerly were able to cause the appear- ance of all this to take place. It must also be observed, that this MS. of Psellus On De- mons forms no part of his treatise On the Energy of Daemons, published by Gaulmi- nus; for it never was published.

Chap. XIII.

CONSIDER, therefore, also another genus of causes; how a stone or a herb frequently possess from themselves a nature corruptive, or again collective of generated natures. For this is not only the case with these, but this physical power is also in greater natures and greater things, which those who are not able to infer by a reasoning process, will perhaps transfer the works and energies of nature to more excellent beings [i.e. to Gods, angels, and daemons]. Now, therefore, it is acknowledged that the tribe of evil daemons has a very extended power in generation, in human affairs, and in such things as subsist about the earth. Hence, why is it wonderful that a tribe of this kind should effect such works as these? For every man is not able to distinguish a good from an evil daemon, or by what peculiarities the one is separated from the other. Hence those, who are not able to perceive the difference between the two, absurdly reason concerning the cause of them, and refer this cause to genera superior to nature and the daemoniacal order. If, also, certain powers of a partial soul are assumed in order to effect these things, whether such a soul is detained in body, or has left the testaceous and terrestrial body, but wanders about the places of generation in a turbid and humid spirit; this, indeed, will be a true opinion, but separates the cause of these things at the greatest distance from more excellent natures. By no means, therefore, is that which is divine, or any good daemon, subservient to the illegal desires of men in venereal concerns. For of these things there are many other causes.

Section V.

Chap. I.

THE doubt mentioned by you in the next place, is, as I may say, an inquiry which is made in common both by the learned and the unlearned, I mean concerning sacrifices, *"what utility or power they possess in the universe, and with the Gods, and on what account they are performed, appropriately indeed to the powers who are honoured by them, but usefully to those by whom the gifts are offered."* In the same place, also, another objection occurs, viz. *"that the interpreters of prophecies and oracles ought to abstain from animals, lest the Gods should be polluted by the vapours arising from them. For this is contrary to the assertion, that the Gods (tile especially allured by the vapours of animals."*

Chap. II.

THE hostile opposition, therefore, in the things that are now proposed, may be easily dissolved by demonstrating the dignity of wholes with respect to parts, and by recalling to your recollection the exempt transcendency of the Gods above men. But what I mean is this, that the soul, which ranks as a whole, presides over all the mundane body, [1] and that the celestial Gods ascend, as into a vehicle, into a celestial body, neither receiving any injury from thence, nor any impediment in their intellections. But to a partial soul, the communion with body is noxious in both these respects. If, therefore, some one perceiving this, should nevertheless introduce such a doubt as the following, that if the body is a bond to our soul, it will also be a bond to the soul of the universe, and that if a partial soul is converted to the body on account of generation, in a similar manner the power of the Gods is converted to generation; in answer to this every one may reply, that he who thus doubts does not know how much superior beings transcend men, and wholes parts. Since, therefore, the objections pertain to things different from each other, they do not produce any ambiguity.

[1] Hence Iamblichus (apud Stob. Eclog. Phys. p. 114), says, Ουχ η εστι πασων ψυχων κοινωνια προς τα σωματα, αλλ' η μεν ολη ωσπερ Πλωτινω δοκει, προσιον εαυτη το σωμα εχει εν εαυτη, αλλ' ουκ αυτη προσεισι τω σωματι, ουδε περιεχεται υπ' αυτου. αι δε μερισται προσερχονται τοις σωμασι, και των σωματων γιγνονται. i.e. "There is not the same communion of all souls with bodies; but the soul which ranks as a whole (as it also appeared to Plotinus), approaching to itself, contains body in itself, but does not itself approach to body, nor is comprehended by it. Partible souls, however, accede to bodies, and give themselves up to them."
    Conformably to this Porphyry also, in his Αφορμαι προς τα νοητα, No. 30, says, "No *whole* and perfect essence is converted to its own progeny; but all perfect natures are led back to the causes by which they were generated, even as far as to the mundane body. For this body, being perfect, is elevated to the mundane soul which is intellectual, and through this is circularly moved. But the soul of this body is elevated to intellect, and intellect to that which is first. All things, therefore, extend themselves to this, beginning from that which is last, according to the peculiar ability of each. But the reduction to that which is first is either proximate or remote. Hence these are not only said to aspire after divinity, but also to enjoy him as far as they are able. But in partial natures, and which are able to verge to many things, a conversion to their progeny belongs. Hence in these guilt, in these disgraceful perfidy, is found. Matter, therefore, defiles these, because they decline to it, at the same time that they possess the power of converting themselves to a divine nature."

Chap. III.

HERE, therefore, the same reasoning is likewise sufficient. For with us the enjoyment of bodies which once were united to soul, impresses in us heaviness and defilement, ingenerates in us voluptuousness, and produces many other diseases in the soul. But with the Gods, and with mundane and total causes, this is by no means the case. For the exhalation which ascends after a divine manner from animals that are sacrificed, as it is comprehended by, and does not comprehend, the Gods, and as it is also connected with the universe, but does not conjoin wholes and the Gods to itself, is in consequence of this coadapted to superior beings and to total causes, but does not restrain them and coadapt them to itself.

Chap. IV.

NOR is that which so greatly disturbs you, and for which you so strenuously contend, attended with any difficulty, I mean abstinence from animals, [1] if it is rightly understood. For those who worship the Gods do not abstain from animals, lest the Gods should be defiled by the vapours arising from them. For what exhalation from bodies can approach those who, before any thing material can come into contact with their power, intangibly amputate matter? Nor is it the power of the Gods only that abolishes all bodies, and causes them to vanish, without any approximation to them; but a celestial body, also, is unmingled with all the material elements; [2] nor does it receive into itself any thing extraneous, nor impart any portion of itself to things of a foreign nature. How, therefore, can any terrestrial vapour, which is not elevated five stadia from the earth before it again flows down to the earth, either nourish a circulating and immaterial body, or, in short, produce in it a certain defilement, or any other passion? For it is acknowledged that an ethereal body is void of all contrariety, is liberated from all mutation, is entirely pure from the possibility of being transmuted into any thing else, and is perfectly free from a tendency to, and from the middle, because it is either without any tendency, or is convolved in a circle. Hence, it is not possible that bodies, which consist of different powers and motions, which are all-variously changed, and are moved either upwards or downwards, should have any communion of nature or power with celestial bodies, or that any exhalation of the former should be mingled with the latter. As the former, therefore, are entirely separated from the latter, they will not effect any thing in them. For celestial bodies being unbegotten, are not capable of receiving any mutation from generated natures. How, therefore, can the Gods be defiled by such like vapours, who suddenly, as I may say, at one stroke, amputate the vapours ascending from all matter and material bodies?

This, therefore, it is not fit to suspect of the Gods [viz. that they can be defiled by vapours]; but it is much more requisite to think that things of this kind are foreign to us and to our nature. For things which are divided, and also material and kindred natures, are able to have a certain communion with each other in acting and suffering; but things which are essentially different, and such as are entirely transcendent, and which employ other natures and powers, these cannot act on or receive any thing from each other. The defilement, therefore, produced by material natures, falls on things which are detained by a material body; and from these it is necessary those should be purified who are capable of being defiled by matter. But how can those beings be defiled by material essences who neither have a divisible nature nor possess the power of receiving in themselves the passions of matter? How, likewise, can divinity, who has nothing in common with us, in consequence of antecedently existing superior to human imbecility, be polluted by my passions, or by those of any other man?

Neither of these, therefore, at all pertains to the Gods; neither our being filled with material bodies; (for there is nothing, in short, of this kind with them, nor are they defiled by our stains, since they are entirely pure and incorruptible), nor if there are certain material vapours of bodies which are emitted about the earth; for these vapours are most remote from the essence and power of the Gods. Hence the whole hypothesis of contrariety is subverted if no part of it pertains to the Gods. For how, in short, can that which is not possess in itself a certain contest [with any thing]? You in vain, therefore, suspect things of this kind to be absurd, and you adduce doubts unworthy of the Gods, since they cannot be reasonably applied even to good men. For no man who possesses intellect, and is free from passion, would ever permit himself to be allured by the exhalation of vapours, and much less would any one of the beings more excellent than man stiffer himself to be thus allured. These things, however, will be discussed shortly after. But now, since this contrariety is, through many solutions, subverted, we shall here finish what we have to say about the first doubt.

[1] Iamblichus here alludes to the excellent treatise of Porphyry, περι της των εμψυχων αποχησ, On Abstinence from animal Food, from which work the English reader will find several admirable extracts in one of the Introductory Dissertations prefixed to my translation of Proclus on Euclid.
[2] A celestial body, as is beautifully shown by Proclus in Tim. lib. iii, contains the summits of all the elements, but is characterized by vivific unburning fire; so that, in short, it is vitalized extension.

Chap. V.

YOUR next inquiry is of greater consequence, and is concerning things of a greater nature. How, therefore, shall I be able, briefly and sufficiently, to give you an answer to a question which is extremely difficult, and requires a long explanation? Nevertheless I will answer it, and without failing in alacrity. I will also endeavour to follow what you have concisely indicated and tacitly signified. But I will unfold to you my dogma concerning sacrifices [which is as follows]. It is by no means requisite that sacrifices should be offered for the sake of honour alone, in the same manner as we honour benefactors; nor for the sake of returning thanks for the goods imparted to us by the Gods; nor yet for the sake of first fruits, or as a remuneration by certain gifts of more venerable goods bestowed on us by the Gods. For these things are also common to men, and are assumed from the common polity of mankind, but by no means preserve the transcendency of the Gods and the order of them as exempt causes.

Chap. VI.

BUT the greatest thing in sacrifices, *viz.* their efficacious power, and why especially they are so very beneficial that without them we are neither liberated from pestilence, nor famine, nor sterility of fruits, nor obtain seasonable showers of rain, nor things of much greater consequence than these, I mean such as contribute to the purification of the soul, or an emancipation from generation; these are not at all indicated by such modes of sacrifices as you adduce. Hence no one can justly approve of them, because they assign a cause of the works performed in sacrifices unadapted to their dignity. And if some one should approve of them it will be only in a secondary way, and as suspended from primary, more ancient, and venerable causes.

Chap. VII.

THE discussion therefore requires should show what it is through which sacrifices are effective of things, and are suspended from the Gods, the precedaneous causes of that we effects. If then we say that the communion of similar powers, or the dissension of contraries, or a certain aptitude of the agent to the patient in the universe, as in one animal, every where possessing one and the same life, coexcites adapted similars, pervading with invariable sameness according to one sympathy, and existing most near in things most remote: if we should say this, we should thus assert something of what is true, and which necessarily accompanies sacrifices, yet we should not demonstrate the true mode of their subsistence. For the essence of the Gods is not placed in nature and in physical necessities, so as to he coexcited by physical passions, or by the powers which extend through all nature; but independently of these, it is defined by itself, having nothing in common with them, neither according to essence, nor according to power, nor any thing else.

Chap. VIII.

THE same absurdities likewise happen from assigning, as the causes of what is effected by sacrifices, either certain numbers that are with us, such, for instance, as assuming the number sixty in the crocodile, [1] as adapted to the sun; or physical reasons, as the powers and energies of animals, for instance, of the dog, [2] the cynocephalus, [3] and the weasel, [4] these being common to the moon; or material forms, such as are seen in sacred animals; [5] according to the colours, and all the forms of the body; or any thing else pertaining to the bodies of animals, or of other things which are offered; or a certain member, as the heart of a cock; [6] or other things of the like kind which are surveyed about nature, if they are considered as the causes of the efficacy in sacrifices. For from these things the Gods are not demonstrated to be supernatural causes; nor, as such, to be excited by sacrifices. But they are considered as physical causes detained by matter, and as physically involved in bodies, and coexcited and becoming quiescent together with them, these things also existing about nature. If, therefore, any thing of this kind takes place in sacrifices, it follows as a concause, and as having the relation of that without which a thing is not effected; and thus it is suspended from precedaneous causes.

[1] The number sixty is no less manifest in the crocodile than in the sun. For according to Aristotle (in Hist. Anim. lib. v.) the crocodile brings forth sixty eggs of a white colour and sits on them for sixty days.
[2] "Isis," says Gale, "is the moon. And a dog attended Isis when she was diligently seeking her husband Osiris. But the moon perpetually seeks the sun, and therefore that sagacious animal, the dog, accords with Isis. In the solemnities, also, of Isis, dogs preceded the procession." After this manner others besides Gale, who have not penetrated the depths of the philosophy and theology of Plato, would doubtless explain what is fabulously said of Isis. In reality, however, Isis is not the moon, but one of the divinities that revolve in the lunar sphere as an attendant on the moon, and who, in modern language, is one of the satellites of that planet. For, as I have shown from Proclus, in the Introduction to my translation of the Timaeus of Plato, every planetary sphere is an ολοτησ, *or a part of the universe having a total subsistence, i.e. ranking as a whole*, and is surrounded with a number of satellites analogous to the choir of the fixed stars. Of these satellites, likewise, the leaders of which are the planets, the first in order are Gods; after these, daemons revolve in lucid orbicular bodies; and these are followed by partial souls, such as ours. See Proclus in Tim. p. 275 and p. 279. This theory, as I have elsewhere observed, is the grand key to the theology and mythology of the ancients, as it shows at one view why the same God is so often celebrated with the names of other Gods; which induced Macrobius to think that all the Gods were nothing more than different powers of the sun. The English reader will find an abundant confirmation of what is here said in the fourth book of my translation of the above mentioned admirable work of Proclus.
[3] "The Egyptians," says Horapollo, lib. i. "wishing to signify the moon, paint a cynocephalus, because this animal is variously affected by the course of the moon."
[4] In the original μυγαλη. "This word," says Gale, "is written variously, viz. as μυγάλη, μυγαλὴ and μυγαλῆ. It is also variously translated, for it is either ratfus, or rnzzs araneus." Plutarch, in the fourth book of his Symposiacs, Quest. 5, says, "that the Egyptians were of opinion that darkness was prior to light, and that the latter was produced from mice in the fifth generation, at the time of the new moon. And

further still, they assert that the liver of the weasel diminishes in the wane of the moon."

[5] With the Egyptians many animals were sacred; for the worship of which the following admirable apology is made by Plutarch in his treatise of Isis and Osiris:

"It now remains that we should speak of the utility of these animals to man, and of their symbolical meaning; some of them partaking of one of these only, but many of them of both. It is evident, therefore, that the Egyptians worshiped the ox, the sheep, and the ichneumon, on account of their use and benefit, as the Lemnians did larks, for discovering the eggs of caterpillars and breaking them; and the Thessalians storks, because, as their land produced abundance of serpents, the storks destroyed all of them as soon as they appeared. Hence, also, they enacted a law, that whoever killed a stork should be banished. But the Egyptians honoured the asp, the weasel, and the beetle, in consequence of observing in them certain dark resemblances of the power of the Gods, like that of the sun in drops of water. For at present, many believe and assert that the weasel engenders by the ear, and brings forth by the mouth, being thus an image of the generation of reason [or the productive principle of things]. But the genus of beetles has no female; and all the males emit their sperm into a sphericle piece of earth, which they roll about, thrusting it backwards with their hind feet, while they themselves move forward; just as the sun appears to revolve in a direction contrary to that of the heavens, in consequence of moving from west to east. They also assimilated the asp to a star, as being exempt from old age, and performing its motions, unassisted by organs, with agility and ease. Nor was the crocodile honoured by them without a probable cause; but is said to have been considered by them as a resemblance of divinity, as being the only animal that is without a tongue. For the divine reason is unindigent of voice, and proceeding through a silent path, and accompanied with [*] justice, conducts mortal affairs according to it. They also say it is the only animal living in water that has the sight of its eyes covered with a thin and transparent film, which descends from his forehead, so that he sees without being seen, which is likewise the case with the first God. But in whatever place the female crocodile may lay her eggs, this may with certainty be concluded to be the boundary of the increase of the Nile. For not being able to lay their eggs in the water, and fearing to lay them far from it, they have such an accurate presensation of futurity, that though they enjoy the benefit of the river in its access, during the time of their laying and hatching, yet they preserve their eggs dry and untouched by the water. They also lay Sixty eggs, are the same number of days in hatching them, and those that are the longest lived among them live just so many years, which number is the first of the measures employed by those who are conversant with the heavenly bodies.

"Moreover, of those animals that were honoured for both reasons, we have before spoken of the dog. But the ibis, killing indeed all deadly reptiles, was the first that taught men the use of medical evacuation, in consequence of observing that she is after this manner washed and purified by herself. Those priests, also, that are most attentive to the laws of sacred rites, when they consecrate water for lustration, fetch it from that place where the ibis had been drinking; for she will neither drink nor come near unwholesome or infected water; but with the distance of her feet from each other and her bill she makes an equilateral triangle. Farther still, the variety and mixture of her black wings about the white represents the moon when she is gibbous.

"We ought not, however, to wonder if the Egyptians love such slender similitudes, since the Greeks also, both in their pictures and statues, employ many such like resemblances of the Gods. Thus in Crete there was a statue of Jupiter without ears. For it is fit that he who is the ruler and lord of all things should hear no one. [**] Phidias also placed a dragon by the statue of Minerva, and a snail by that of Venus at Elis, to show that virgins require a guard, and that keeping at home and silence become married women. But the trident of Neptune is a symbol of the third region of the world, which the sea possesses, having an arrangement after the heavens and the air. Hence, also, they thus denominated Amphitrite and the Tritons. The Pythagoreans, likewise, adorned numbers and figures with the appellations of the Gods. For they called the equilateral triangle, Minerva Coryphagenes, or begotten from the summit, and Tritogeneia because it is divided by three perpendiculars drawn from the three angles. But they called *the one* Apollo, being persuaded to this by the obvious meaning of the word Apollo [which signifies a privation of multitude] and by the simplicity of the monad [†]. The duad they denominated strife and audacity, and the triad justice. For since injuring and being injured are two extremes subsisting according to excess and defect, justice, through equality, has a situation in the middle. But what is called the tetractys, being the number 36, was, as is reported, their greatest oath, and was denominated the world. For this number is formed from the composition of the four first even and the four first odd numbers, collected into one sum. [††] If, therefore, the most approved of the philosophers did not think it proper to neglect or despise any occult signification of a divine nature when they perceived it even in things which are inanimate and incorporeal, it appears to me that they, in a still greater degree, venerated those peculiarities depending on manners which they saw in such natures as had sense, and were endued with soul, with passion, and ethical habits. We must embrace, therefore, not those who honour these things, but those who reverence divinity through these, as through most clear mirrors, and which are produced by nature, in a becoming manner, conceiving them to be the instruments or the art of the God by whom all things are perpetually adorned. But we ought to think that no inanimate being can be more excellent than one that is animated, nor an insensible than a sensitive being, not even though someone should collect together all the gold and emeralds in the universe. For the divinity is not ingenerated either in colours, or figures, or smoothness; but such things as neither ever did, nor are naturally adapted to participate of life, have an allotment more ignoble than that of dead bodies. But the nature which lives and sees, and has the principle of motion from itself, and a knowledge of things appropriate and foreign to its being, has certainly derived an efflux and portion of that wisdom which, as Heraclitus says, considers how both itself and the universe is governed. Hence the divinity is not worse represented in these animals than in the workmanships of copper and stone, which in a similar manner suffer corruption and decay, but are naturally deprived of all sense and consciousness. This then I consider as the best defence that can be given of the adoration of animals by the Egyptians."

[*] Instead of και δικησ, I read και μετα δικησ.

[**] i.e. Should be perfectly impartial.

[†] Instead of διπλοτατοις μοναδος, as in the original, which is nonsense, it is necessary to read, as in the above translation, απλοτητι της μοναδος.

[††] For 2+4+6+8=20; and 1+3+5+7=16; and 20+16=36.

[6] The cock was sacred to Apollo, and therefore its heart was believed to be the instrument of divination in sacrifices. The chemic Olympiodorus says, "that the cock obscurely signifies the essence of the sun and moon." See, in tile additional notes, what is said by Proclus concerning the cock, in his treatise On Magic.

Chap. IX.

IT is better, therefore, to assign as the cause of the efficacy of sacrifices friendship and familiarity, and a habitude which binds fabricators to the things fabricated, and generators to the things generated. Hence when, this common principle preceding, we take a certain animal, or any thing which germinates in the earth, and which genuinely and purely preserves the will of its maker; then, through a thing of this kind, we appropriately move the demiurgic cause, which presides over it in an undefiled manner. But these causes being many, and some, as the daemoniacal causes, having a proximate arrangement; but others, as divine causes, being arranged above these; and farther still, one most ancient and venerable cause being the leader of these; all the causes are moved in conjunction by a perfect sacrifice. Each thing, likewise, is in a kindred manner adapted to the sacrifice, according to the order which it is allotted. But if any sacrifice is imperfect, it proceeds to a certain extent, but is not capable of proceeding any further. Hence many are of opinion that sacrifices are to be offered to good daemons, many to the last powers of the Gods, and many to the mundane or terrestrial powers of daemons or Gods. These things, therefore, as being a hart of sacrifices, are not falsely asserted; but they do not comprehend the whole of the power of sacrifice, and all the goods it contains, which extend to every thing divine.

Chap. X.

WE, however, admit all these assertions; physical essences, indeed, being coexcited as in one animal, according to aptitude or sympathy, as in another respect being subjects, and following and being subservient to the cause of the efficacy of sacrifices; but daemons, and terrene or mundane divine powers, being primarily familiarized to our order; nevertheless, we must say, that the most perfect and leading cause of the efficacy of sacrifices is to be conjoined to demiurgic and the most perfect powers. But since these comprehend in themselves all the causes of sacrifice, we say that all the effective causes of it are at once coexcited together with these. And from all these a common utility is imparted to the whole of generation; sometimes through cities and people, or all various nations, or circumscriptions more or less extended than these; but at other times through houses, or an individual, these causes impart good with an unenvying and exuberant will, unaccompanied with passion; conferring their benefits with an impassive intellect, according to adaptation and alliance; one friendship at the same time which connectedly contains all things, producing this bond through a certain ineffable communion.

For these assertions are much more true, and more characteristic of the essence and power of the Gods, than what you suspect to be the case, *viz.*

"that the Gods are especially allured by the vapours produced in the sacrifices of animals." For if daemons are invested with a certain body, which some think is nourished by sacrifices, yet this body is immutable and impassive, luciform and unindigent; so that neither does any thing flow from it, nor is it in want of any influx externally introduced. And if some one should admit that there is this influx, yet since the world and the air contained in it have a never failing abundance of exhalations from terrene places, an efflux of this kind being equally diffused on all sides, what use can there be of sacrifices to daemons? But neither do the influxions equally and commensurately fill the place of the effluxions, so as that neither excess should at any time predominate, nor deficiency be produced, but that there should be a perfect equality and similitude of the bodies of daemons, and this invariably the same. For the Demiurgus of the universe has not provided abundant nutriment, and which may be easily obtained, for all the animals in the earth and the sea, but has made the beings superior to us to be in want of it; nor has he imparted to other animals a native abundance of what is daily requisite, but given to daemons nutriment which is adscititious and procured by us men; so that if we through indolence, or some other pretext, should neglect an offering of this kind, the bodies of daemons would be in want of food, and would participate of incommensuration and disorder. Why, therefore, do not the authors of these assertions subvert the whole order of things, so as to make us to be in a better and more powerful class of beings? For if we supply daemons with nutriment, we shall much more be the causes of their existence. For every thing receives nutriment and perfection from that by which it was generated. And this, indeed, may be seen in the visible generations of things; but it may also be surveyed in the heavens and the earth. For terrestrial are nourished by celestial natures. But this becomes most eminently manifest in invisible causes. For soul, indeed, is perfected by intellect; but nature by soul. And other things are in a similar manner nourished by their causes. If, therefore, it is impossible that we should be the primordial causes of daemons, it is, for the same reason, impossible that we should be the causes of their nutriment.

Chap. XI.

IT appears to me, also, that the present question errs in another respect. For it is ignorant that the offering of sacrifices through fire has the power of consuming and destroying the matter of them in a greater degree; that it assimilates this matter to itself, but is not itself assimilated to the matter; and that it elevates to divine, celestial, and immaterial fire, but does not tend downwards to matter and generation. For if the enjoyment of the vapours from matter allured daemons, it would be requisite that the matter should be pure and entire; since thus there would be a more abundant efflux from it to its participants. But now all the matter is enkindled and consumed, and is changed into the purity and tenuity of fire; which is itself a clear indication of the contrary to what you assert. For superior beings [i.e. daemons] are impassive, and they are delighted to amputate matter through fire, and render us impassive. They likewise assimilate whatever is in us to the Gods, in the same manner as fire [1] assimilates all solid and resisting substances to luminous and attenuated bodies. And they elevate us through sacrifices and the sacrifice fire to the fire of the Gods, in the same manner as fire elevates to fire, and draws upward gravitating and resisting substances to divine and celestial natures.

[1] It is well observed by Ficinus, in lib. i. Ennead. ii. Plotin. "that the fire which is enkindled by us is more similar to the heavens than other terrestrial substances. Hence it participates of light, which is something incorporeal, is the most powerful of all things, is as it were vital, is perpetually moved, divides all things, without being itself divided, absorbs all things in itself, and avoids any foreign mixture: and lastly, when the fuel of it is consumed, it suddenly flies back again to the celestial fire, which is every where latent."

Chap. XII.

FOR, in short, the vehicle [1] which is subservient to daemons neither consists of matter, nor of the elements, nor of any other of the bodies known to us. What perfect supply of food, therefore, can there be from one essence to another [specifically different]? Or what enjoyment can accede from foreign to foreign natures? There cannot be any. But much more, as the Gods by the fire of lightning divide matter, and separate from it things which are essentially immaterial, but which are vanquished and bound by it, and render them impassive from being passive; thus also the fire that is with us, imitating the energy of divine fire, destroys every thing which is material in sacrifices, purifies the things which are offered, liberates them from the bonds of matter, and renders them, through purity of nature, adapted to the communion of the Gods. It likewise liberates [2] us after the same manner from the bonds of generation, assimilates us to the Gods, causes us to be adapted to their friendship, and conducts our material nature to an immaterial essence.

[1] For this vehicle is luciform, and consists of pure, immaterial, unburning, and vivific fire. See the fifth book of my translation of Proclus on the Timaeus.
[2] Proclus in Tim. lib. v. observes concerning the telestic art, or the art which operates through mystic ceremonies, "that, as the oracles teach, it obliterates through divine fire all the stains produced by generation." Η τελεστικη δια του θειου πυρος αφανιζει τας εκ της γενεσεως απασας κηλιδας, ως τα λογια διδασκει. Hence another Chaldean oracle says, τω πυρι γαρ βροτος εμπελασας θεοθεν φαος εξιν. i.e. "The mortal who approaches to fire will have a light from divinity-." Hercules, as we also learn from Proclus, was an example of this telestic purification. For he says, Ηρακλης δια τελεστικης καθηπαμενος, και των αχραντων καρπων μετασχων, τελειας ετυχε εις τους θεους απακαταστασεωσ, in Plat.Polit. p. 382 i, e. " Hercules being purified

119

through the telestic art, and participating of undefiled fruits, obtained a perfect restoration to the Gods."

Chap. XIII.

SUBVERTING, therefore, in this manner the common absurd opinions concerning sacrifices, we shall introduce in their place true conceptions about them; omitting the particular discussion of each species of sacrifice, which the peculiar and distinct consideration of sacrifices requires, because this pertains to another inquiry, and because, at the same time, every one who is intelligent may be able to accomplish this from what has been already said, and from one thing may extend his reasoning power to many, and may easily know what is omitted from what has been discussed. And I, indeed, think that these things have been sufficiently explained, both in other respects and because the explanation pays attention in a becoming manner to the purity of the Gods. Because, however, it may perhaps appear to others to be incredible, and not sufficiently manifest, and the veracity of it may be suspected, as not exciting the discursive energy of reason, I wish to consider these things a little more fully; and, if possible, to add arguments more evident than those which have been adduced.

Chap. XIV.

WE shall begin, however, the elucidation of this subject in the best possible manner, if we demonstrate that the sacred law of sacrifices is connected with the order of the Gods. In the first place, therefore, we say, that of the Gods some are material, but others immaterial. And the material, indeed, are those that comprehend matter in themselves, and adorn it; but the immaterial are those that are perfectly exempt from, and transcend, matter. But, according to the sacrific art, it is requisite to begin sacred operations from the material Gods: for the ascent to the immaterial Gods will not otherwise be effected. The material Gods, therefore, have a certain communion with matter, so far as they preside over it. Hence they have dominion over things which happen about matter, such as the division, percussion, repercussion, mutation, generation, and corruption of all material bodies. He, therefore, who wishes to worship these theurgically, in a manner adapted to them, and to the dominion which they are allotted, should, as they are material, employ a material mode of worship. For thus we shall be wholly led to a familiarity with them, and worship them in an allied and appropriate manner. Dead bodies, therefore, and things deprived of life, the slaying of animals, and the consumption of victims, and, in short, the mutation of the matter which is offered, pertain to these Gods, not by themselves, but on account of the matter over which they preside. For though they are in the most eminent degree separate from it, yet at the same time they are present with it. And though they comprehend matter in an immaterial power, yet they are coexistent with it. Things that are governed, also, are not foreign from their governors; and things which are subservient as instruments, are not unadapted to those that use them. Hence, it is foreign to the immaterial Gods, to offer matter to them through sacrifices, but this is most adapted to all the material Gods.

Chap. XV.

LET US then, in the next place, direct our attention to that which accords with what has been before said, and with our twofold condition of being. For there is a time when we become wholly soul, are out of the body, and sublimely revolve on high, in conjunction with all the immaterial Gods. And there is also a time when we are bound in the testaceous body, are detained by matter, and are of a corporeal - formed nature. Again, therefore, there will be a twofold mode of worship. For one mode, indeed, will be simple, incorporeal, and pure from all generation, and this mode pertains to undefiled souls. Put the other is filled with bodies, and every thing of a material nature, and is adapted to souls which are neither pure nor liberated from all generation. We must admit, therefore, that there are twofold species of sacrifices; one kind, indeed, pertaining to men who are entirely purified, which, as Heraclitus says, rarely happens to one man, or to a certain easily to be numbered few of mankind; but the other kind, being material and corporeal-formed, and consisting in mutation, is adapted to souls that are still detained by the body. Hence, to cities and people not yet liberated from genesiurgic fate and the impeding communion of bodies, if such a mode of sacrifice as this latter is not permitted, they will wander both from immaterial and material good. For they will not be able to receive the former, and to the latter they will not offer what is appropriate. At the same time, likewise, every one in sacrificing performs the sacrifice with reference to what he is, and not with reference to what he is not. It is not proper, therefore, that the sacrifice should transcend the proper measure of him by whom it is offered. The same thing will also be said by me concerning the connexion which appropriately coadapts the men who worship and the powers that are worshiped. For this connexion requires that a mode of worship should be chosen adapted to itself; *viz.* an immaterial connexion, a mode of worship immaterially mingled, and purely conjoining by pure incorporeal powers, incorporeal natures to themselves; but a corporeal-formed connexion, a corporeal-formed mode which depends on bodies, and is mingled with the essences that preside over bodies.

Chap. XVI.

F ARTHER still, therefore, we must not disdain to add what follows; that we frequently perform something to the Gods who are the inspective guardians of body, and to good daemons, for the sake of the necessary use of the body; as, for instance, when [by sacrifices] we purify it from ancient stains, or liberate it from diseases, and fill it with health, or remove from it heaviness and torpor, or procure for it any other good. In this case, therefore, we evidently must not busy ourselves with the body in an intellectual and incorporeal manner. For the body is not adapted to participate of modes of this kind; but, obtaining things which are allied to itself, it is meliorated and purified by bodies. The rites of sacrifices, therefore, will necessarily, for a purpose of this kind, be corporeal-formed; partly cutting off what is super-fluous in us; partly supplying us with that of which we are in want; and part-ly leading into symmetry and order such things in us as are immoderately disturbed. We also frequently engage in sacred operations, entreating supe-rior beings to grant us such things as are adapted to the wants of human life. And these are such as preserve the body in health, or pertain to those things which we procure for the sake of the body.

Chap. XVII.

W HAT, therefore, shall we derive from the Gods who are entirely ex-empt from all human generation, with respect to sterility, or abundance or any thing else pertaining to [the mortal] life? Nothing whatever. For it is not the province of those who are liberated from all things to meddle with gifts of this kind. But if some one should say that the perfectly immaterial com-prehend in themselves the material Gods, and that through this they also contain in themselves their gifts according to one first cause; such a one will also say, that in consequence of this an abundance of divine gifts descend from the immaterial Gods. It must not, however, be granted to any one to say that the immaterial Gods bestow these gifts by proximately interfering with the actions of human life. For such an administration of our affairs is partible, is accomplished with a certain conversion [to the subjects of its care], is not entirely separate from bodies, and is incapable of receiving a pure and unde-filed domination. Will not, therefore, that mode of sacrifice in works of this kind be most appropriate which is mingled with bodies, and adheres to gen-eration; and not that which is entirely immaterial and incorporeal? For the *pure* mode of sacrifice is perfectly transcendent and incommensurate [with our concerns]. But the mode which employs bodies, and the powers that subsist through bodies, is in the most eminent degree allied to human affairs. It is also capable of producing a certain prosperous condition of things, and of imparting symmetry and temperament to the mortal race.

Chap. XVIII.

ACCORDING to another division, therefore, the numerous herd [or the great mass] of men is arranged under nature, is governed by physical powers, looks downward to the works of nature, gives completion to the administration of Fate, and to things pertaining to Fate, because it belongs to the order of it, and always employs practical reasoning about such particulars alone as subsist according to nature. But there are a certain few who, by employing a certain supernatural power of intellect, are removed indeed from nature, but are conducted to a separate and unmingled intellect; and these, at the same time, become superior to physical powers. Others again, who are the media between these, tend to things which subsist between nature and a pure intellect. And of these, some indeed equally follow both nature and an immaculate intellect; others embrace a life which is mingled from both; and others are liberated from things subordinate, and betake themselves to such as are more excellent.

This division, therefore, being made, that which follows will most manifestly take place. For those who are governed by the nature of the universe, who lived conformably to this, and employ the powers of nature, these should embrace a mode of worship adapted to nature, and to the bodies that are moved by nature, and should choose for this purpose appropriate places, air, matter, the powers of matter, bodies, and the habits of bodies, qualities, and proper motions, the mutations of things in generation, and other things connected with these, both in other parts of piety and in that part of it which pertains to sacrifice. But those who live conformably to intellect alone, and to the life of intellect, and are liberated from the bonds of nature, these should exercise in all the parts of theurgy the intellectual and incorporeal mode of worship. And those who are the media between these, should labour differently in the paths of piety, conformably to the differences of this middle condition of life, either by embracing both modes of piety, or separating themselves from one of the modes [and adhering to the other], or receiving both these modes as the foundation of things of a more honourable nature. For without these they never can arrive at things supereminent. Or, in some other way, they should thus, in a becoming manner, labour in the paths of sancity.

Chap. XIX.

ON this subject, however, there is also the following division. Of divine essences and powers some have [a genesiurgic] soul and nature subject and ministrant to their fabrications, whenever they wish to use them. But others are entirely separate from soul and nature, I mean from a divine, and not only from a mundane and genesiurgic soul and nature. [1] And others are the media [2] between these, and afford to the extremes a communion with each other, either according to an exuberant participation of greater good, or according to an unimpeded reception of less good, or according to a concord which binds together both the extremes. When, therefore, we worship the Gods who reign over soul and nature, it is not foreign to these to offer to them physical powers, and bodies which are governed by nature. For all the works of nature are subservient to them, and contribute to their government. But when we undertake to honour those Gods who are essentially uniform, then it is requisite to venerate them with liberated honours. Hence, intellectual gifts are adapted to these, and things which pertain to an incorporeal life, together with the fruits of virtue and wisdom, and whatever perfect and total goods of the soul there may be. Moreover, to the Gods who subsist as media, and who are the leaders of goods of a middle nature, sometimes twofold gifts will be adapted, and sometimes such as have a communication with both these; or such as are separated from inferiors, and pertain to more elevated natures; or, in short, such as in one of the modes give completion to the medium.

[1] In the original, λεγω δε της θειας ψοχης τε και φυσεως, αλλ' ουχι της περικοσμιου τε και γενεσιουργου. But it appears to me that we should here read, conformably to the above translation, λεγω δε της θειας, ψοχης τε και φυσεως, αλλ' ουχι μονου της περικοσμιου τε και γενεσιουργου.

[2] These media consist of the order of Gods denominated αρχαι, or rulers, and of those called απολυτοι, or liberated; the former of which also are denominated *supermundane*, and the latter *supercelestial*, in consequence of existing immediately above the celestial Gods. See, concerning these media, the sixth book of my translation of Proclus on the Theology of Plato.

Chap. XX.

BEING impelled, therefore, from another principle, *viz.* from the world and the mundane Gods, from the arrangement of the four elements in the world, and the association of the elements according to [appropriate] measures, and also from the orderly circulation of bodies about centres, we shall have an easy ascent to the truth of the piety respecting sacrifices. For if we are in the world, are contained as parts in the universe, are primarily produced by it, and perfected by the total powers that are in it, and if we consist of its elements, and receive from it a certain portion of life and nature; if this be the case, it is not proper to pass beyond the world and the mundane orders. We must admit, therefore, that in each part of the world there is this visible body, and that there are also incorporeal powers, which are divided about bodies. Hence the law of religion distributes similars to similars, and thus extends from on high, through wholes, as far as to the last of things; assigning, indeed, incorporeals to incorporeals, but bodies to bodies, and this commensurately to the nature of each. If, however, some theurgist should participate of the supermundane Gods, which is the rarest of all things, he, indeed, in the worship of the Gods will transcend both bodies and matter; being united to the Gods by a supermundane power. But that which happens to one person with difficulty and late, and at the end of the sacerdotal office, ought not to be promulgated as common to all men; nor ought it to be made a thing common to those who are commencing theurgic operations, nor to those who have made a middle proficiency in it. For these, after a manner, pay a corporeal-formed attention to sanctity.

Chap. XXI.

I THINK, therefore, that all who are lovers of the contemplation of theurgic truth will acknowledge this, that the piety which pertains to divine natures ought not to be exercised towards them partially or imperfectly. Hence, since prior to the appearance of the Gods, all such powers as are presubjacent to them are moved, and when the Gods are about to descend to the earth, precede them as in a solemn procession; [1] he who does not distribute to all these powers that which is adapted to them, and does not honour each in an appropriate manner, will depart imperfect, and destitute of the participation of the Gods. But he who propitiates all of them, and offers to each acceptable gifts, and such as are to the utmost of his power adapted to them, will always remain secure and irreprehensible, giving completion in a proper manner to the perfect and entire receptacle of the divine choir. Since this, therefore, is the case, whether is it necessary that the mode of sanctity should be simple, and consist of a certain few things, or that it should be multiform and all-harmonic, and mingled, as I may say, from every thing contained in the world? If, indeed, the power which is invoked, and is excited in the performance of sacred rites, was simple, the mode of sacrifice should necessarily be simple. But if the multitude of powers which are excited when the Gods descend and are moved, is not to be comprehended by any one, except theurgists alone, who accurately know this through experience in sacred operations; if this be the case, they alone are capable of knowing what the perfection is of the sacrific art; and they also know that the omission, though of a few things, subverts the whole work of religion; just as in harmony, from the bursting of one chord, the whole becomes dissonant and incommensurate. [2] As, therefore, in the visible descents of the Gods, a manifest injury is sustained by those who leave some one of the more excellent genera unhonoured [3] thus also in the invisible appearances of the Gods in sacrifices, it is not proper to honour one of thein, and not honour another, but it is entirely requisite to honour each of them according to the order which he is allotted. Put he who leaves some one of them unhonoured, confounds the whole work of piety, and divulses the one and whole orderly distribution of it; not, in so doing, as some one may think, imperfectly receiving the Gods, but entirely subverting all the ceremonies of religion.

[1] Proclus on the First Alcibiades observes, "that about every God there is an innumerable multitude of daemons, who have the same appellations with their leaders. And that these are delighted when they are called by the names of Apollo or Jupiter, because they express in themselves the characteristic peculiarity of their leading Gods." In the same admirable commentary, also, he says, "that in the most holy of the mysteries [i.e. in the Eleusinian mysteries], prior to the appearance of divinity, the incursions of certain terrestrial daemons present themselves to the view, alluring the souls of the spectators from undefiled good to matter."

[2] It is beautifully observed by Simplicius on Epictetus, °that as if you take away letters from a sentence, or change them, the form of the sentence no longer remains, thus also in divine works or words, if any thing is deficient, or is changed, or is confused, divine illumination does not take place, but the indolence of him who does this dissolves the power of what is effected." Ωσπερ γαρ εαν στοιχεια του λογου αφελης, ἢ υπαλλαξῃς, ουκ επιγινεται το του λογου ειδος, ουτω και των θειων εργων ἢ λογων ει ελλειπει τι, ἢ υπηλλακται, ἢ συγκεχυται, ουκ επιγινεται η του θειου ελλαμφις, αλλα και εξυδαροι την γινομενων δυναμιν η του ποιουντος ραθυμια.

[3] Conformably to this, Servius, in his Annotations on the words

Diique, demque omnes --

in the sixth book of the Aeneid observes, "more pontificum, per quos ritu veteri in omnibus sacris post speciales Deos, quos ad ipsum sacrum, quod fiebat necesse erat invocari, generaliter omnia numina invocabantur." i.e. "This is spoken after the manner of the pontiffs, by whom, according to ancient rites, in all sacrifices, after the appropriate Gods whom it was necessary to invoke to the sacrifice, all the divinities were invoked in general." And in his Annotations on the seventh of the Aeneid he informs us, "that king OEneus offered a sacrifice of first fruits to all the divinities but Diana, who being enraged sent a boar [as a punishment for the neglect]." With respect to this anger, however, of Diana, it is necessary to observe with Proclus, "that the anger of the Gods does not refer any passion to them, but indicates our inaptitude to participate of them." Ο γαρ των θεων χολος, ουκ εις εκεινας αναπεμπει τι παθος, αλλα την ημων δεινυσι ανεπιτηδειοτητα της εκεινων μεθεξεωσ.

Chap. XXII.

WHAT then [it may be said], does not the summit of the sacrific art recur to the most principal one of the whole multitude of Gods, and at one and the same time worship the many essences and principles that are [rooted and concentred] in it? Entirely so, but this happens at the latest period, and to a very few, and we must be satisfied if it takes place when the sun of life is setting. Our present discussion, how ever, does not ordain laws for a man of this kind; for he is superior to all law; [1] but it promulgates a law such as that of which we are now speaking, to those who are in want of a certain divine legislation.† It says, therefore, that as the world has one coarrangement from many orders, thus also it is necessary that the consummation of sacrifices, being never failing and entire, should be conjoined to the whole order of more excellent natures. If, however, the world is multiform, and all perfect, and is united from many orders, it is also necessary that sacred operations should imitate its omniform variety through the whole of the powers which they employ. Hence, in a similar manner, since the things which surround us are all-various, it is not fit that we should be connected with the divine causes that preside over them, from a certain part which they contain. Nor is it proper that we should ascend imperfectly to the primordial causes of them.

[1] Plotinus was a man of this description, to whom, most probably, Iamblichus alludes in what he now says.

[2] In the original θυμου τινος: but it is doubtless requisite to read with Gale, θεσμου τινοσ. This I have translated *a certain divine legislation*, because we are informed by Proclus, in Platon. Theol. lib. iv. p. 206, " that θεσμοσ is connected with deity, and pertains more to intelligibles; but that νομος, which unfolds intellectual distribution, is adapted to the intellectual fathers." Ο γαρ θεσμος συμπλεκεται τω θεω, και προηκει μαλλον τοις νοητοις· ο δε νομος την νοεραν εμφαινων διανομην, οικειος εστι τοις νοεροις πατρασι.

Chap. XXIII.

THE various mode, therefore, of sanctity in sacred operations partly purifies and partly perfects some one of the things that are in us or about us. And some things, indeed, it restores to symmetry and order; but others it liberates from mortal-formed error. But it renders all things familiar and friendly to all the natures that are superior to us. Moreover, when divine causes, and human preparations which are assimilated to them conspire in one and the same, then the perfection of sacred operations imparts all the perfect and great benefits of sacrifice. It will not be amiss, also, to add such particulars as the following, in order to the accurate comprehension of these things. An exuberance of power is always present with the highest causes, and at the same time that this power transcends all things, it is equally present with all with unimpeded energy. Hence, conformably to this, the first illuminate the last of things, and immaterial are present with material natures immaterially. Nor should it be considered by any one as wonderful, if we say that there is a certain pure and divine matter. [1] For matter being generated by the father and demiurgus of wholes, receives a perfection adapted to itself, in order to its becoming the receptacle of the Gods. At the same time nothing prevents more excellent beings from being able to impart their light to subordinate natures. Neither, therefore, is matter separated from the participation of better causes; so that such matter as is perfect, pure, and boniform, is not unadapted to the reception of the Gods. For, since it is requisite that terrestrial natures should by no means be destitute of divine communion, the, earth also receives a certain divine portion from it, sufficient for the participation of the Gods. The theurgic art, therefore, perceiving this to be the case, and thus having discovered in common, appropriate receptacles, conformably to the peculiarity of each of the Gods, it frequently connects together stones, herbs, animals, aromatics, and other sacred, perfect, and deiform substances of the like kind; and afterwards, from all these, it produces an entire and pure receptacle. For it is not proper to despise all matter, but that alone which is foreign from the Gods. But that matter is to be chosen which is adapted to them, as being able to accord with the edifices of the Gods, the dedication of statues, and the sacred operations of sacrifices. For no otherwise can a participation of superior beings be obtained by places in the earth, or by men that dwell in it, unless a foundation of this kind is first established. *It is also requisite to be persuaded by arcane assertions, that a certain matter is imparted by the Gods, through blessed visions.* This matter, therefore, i s doubtless connascent with those by whom it is imparted. Hence, does it not follow that the sacrifice of a matter of this kind excites the Gods to present themselves to the view, immediately calls forth the participation of them, receives them when they accede, and perfectly unfolds them into light?

[1] "Perhaps," says Proclus, in MS. Comment. in Parmenid. "it is necessary that, as in souls, natures, and bodies, fabrication does not begin from the imperfect; so likewise in matter, prior to that which is formless, and which has an evanescent being, there is that which is in a certain respect form, and which is beheld in one boundary and permanency." This, therefore, will be the pure and divine matter of which Iamblichus is now speaking. Damascius also says, that matter is from the same order whence form is derived.

Chap. XXIV.

THE same things also may be learned from the distribution of the Gods according to places; and from this, and the partible dominion over each particular thing, it may be seen how many allotments, greater or less, superior beings are assigned according to their different orders. For it is evident, that to the Gods who preside over certain places, the things produced by them are most appropriately offered in sacrifice; and that what pertains to the governed is most adapted to be sacrificed to the governors. For always to makers their own works are particularly grateful; and to those who primarily produce certain things, such things are primarily acceptable. Whether, therefore, certain animals, or plants, or any other productions of the earth, are governed by superior beings, at one and the same time, they participate of their inspective care, and impart to us an indivisible communion with the Gods. Some things, therefore, of this kind, if they are carefully preserved, increase the familiarity of those that retain them with the Gods; and these are such as by remaining entire, preserve the communion between Gods and men. Of this kind are some of the animals in Egypt, and man, who is everywhere sacred. But some things, when consecrated, produce a more manifest familiarity; and these are such as by an analysis into the principle of the first elements, effect an alliance more sacredly adapted to superior causes. For the more perfect this alliance is, the more perfect always is the good which is imparted by it.

Chap. XXV.

IF, therefore, these things were human customs alone, and derived their authority through our legal institutions, it might be said that the worship of the Gods was the invention of our conceptions. Now, however, divinity is the leader of it, who is thus invoked by sacrifices, and who is surrounded by a numerous multitude of Gods and angels. Under him, likewise, a certain common presiding power, is allotted dominion according to each nation of the earth. And a peculiar presiding power is allotted to each temple. Of the sacrifices, also, which are performed to the Gods, the inspective guardian is a God; but an angel, of those which are performed to angels; and a demon, of such as are performed to daemons. After the same manner, also, in other sacred operations, the presiding power is allotted dominion over each, in a way allied to his proper genus. When, therefore, we offer sacrifices to the Gods, accompanied by the presiding Gods, who give completion to sacred operations, then at the same time, it is necessary in sacrifices to venerate the sacred law of divine sanctity; and at the same time, also, we ought to be confident, as sacrificing under the Gods who are the rulers of such works. We ought, likewise, to be very cautious, lest we should offer any gift unworthy of, or foreign from, the Gods. And, as the last admonition, we should in a manner entirely perfect, pay attention to all that surrounds us, and to the Gods, angels, and daemons that are distributed according to genera in the universe. And to all these, in a similar manner, an acceptable sacrifice should be offered; for thus alone sanctity can be preserved in a way worthy of the Gods who preside over it.

Chap. XXVI.

SINCE, however, prayers are not the smallest [but on the contrary a very great] part of sacrifices, especially give completion to them, and through these the whole operation of them is corroborated and effected; and since, besides this, they afford a common utility to religion, and produce an indissoluble and sacred communion with the Gods, it will not be improper to discuss a few particulars concerning prayer. For this is of itself a thing worthy to be known, and renders more perfect the science concerning the Gods. I say, therefore, that the *first* species of prayer is *collective*; and that it is also the leader of contact with, and a knowledge of, divinity. The *second* species *is the bond of concordant communication*, calling forth, prior to the energy of speech, the gifts imparted by the Gods, and perfecting the whole of our operations prior to our intellectual conceptions. And the *third* and most perfect species of prayer is *the seal of ineffable union with the divinities*, in whom it establishes all the power and authority of prayer; and thus causes the soul to repose in the Gods, as in a never failing port. But from these three terms, in which all the divine measures are contained, suppliant adoration not only conciliates to us the friendship of the Gods, but supernally extends to us three fruits, being as it were three Hesperian apples of gold. [1] The *first* of these pertains to *illumination*; the *second*, to a *communion of operation*; but through the energy of the *third*, we receive *a perfect plenitude of divine fire*. And sometimes, indeed, supplication *precedes*; like a precursor preparing the way before the sacrifice appears. But some times it *intercedes as a mediator*; and sometimes *accomplishes the end of sacrificing*. No operation, however, in sacred concerns, can succeed without the intervention of prayer. Lastly, the continual exercise of prayer nourishes the vigour of our intellect, and renders the receptacles of the soul far more capacious for the communications of the Gods. It likewise is the *divine key,* which opens to men the penetralia of the Gods; accustoms us to the splendid rivers of supernal light; in a short time perfects our inmost recesses, and disposes them for the ineffable embrace and contact of the Gods; and does not desist till it raises us to the summit of all. It also gradually and silently draws upward the manners of our soul, by divesting them of every thing foreign to a divine nature, and clothes us with the perfections of the Gods. Besides this, it produces an indissoluble communion and friendship with divinity, nourishes a divine love, and inflames the divine part of the soul. Whatever is of an opposing and contrary nature in the soul, it expiates and purifies; expels whatever is prone to generation, and retains any thing of the dregs of mortality in its etherial and splendid spirit; perfects a good hope and faith concerning the reception of divine light: and, in one word, renders those by whom it is employed the familiars and domestics of the Gods. If such, then, are the advantages of prayer, and such its connexion with sacrifice, does it not appear from hence that the end of sacrifice is a conjunction with the Demiurgus of the world? And the benefit of prayer is of the same extent with the good which is conferred by the demiurgic causes on the race of mortals. Again, from hence the *anagogic, perfective*, and *replenishing* power of prayer appears; likewise how it becomes efficacious and unific: and how it possesses a common bond imparted by the Gods. And, in the third and last place, it may easily be conceived from hence how prayer and sacrifice mutually corroborate and confer on each other a sacred and perfect power in divine concerns.

Hence, since it appears that there is a perfect conspiration and cooperation of the sacerdotal discipline with itself, and that the parts of it are more connascent than those of any animal, being entirely conjoined through one connexion; this being the case, it is not by any means proper to neglect this concord, nor to admit some of its parts and reject others; but it is fit that all of them should be exercised in a similar manner, and that those should be perfected through all of them who wish to be genuinely conjoined to the Gods. These things therefore, cannot subsist otherwise.

[1] This particular respecting the apples of gold is added from the version of Scutellius, who appears to have translated this work from a more perfect manuscript than

Section VI.

Chap. I.

IT is now, however, time for me to pass on to the next doubt which you propose, *viz. "Why it is requisite that the inspector [who presides over sacred rites] ought not to touch a dead body, though most sacred operations are performed through dead bodies?"* Again, therefore, that we may dissolve this doubt, we shall direct our attention to this apparent opposition; for there is not in reality any, but these things alone seem to subsist contrarily. For if the laws of sacred rites ordered that the same dead bodies should not be touched and should be touched, this would be a thing contrary to itself. But if they order that some dead bodies should be abstained from as impure, but that others which are consecrated should be touched, this is not attended with any contrariety. Farther still, it is not lawful to touch human bodies when the soul has left them, since a certain vestige, image, or representation of divine (276) life is extinguished in the body by death. But it is no longer unholy to touch other dead bodies, because they did not [when living] participate of a more divine life. To other Gods, therefore, who are pure from matter, our not touching dead bodies is adapted; but to those Gods who preside over animals, and are proximately connected with them, invocation through animals is properly made. According to this, therefore, no contrariety takes place.

Chap. II.

AFTER another manner, also, this doubt may be dissolved. For in men, indeed, who are detained in matter, bodies deprived of life produce a certain stain; because that which is not alive inserts a certain defilement in that which is living, in the same manner as the impure in that which is pure, and that which is in privation in that which is in habit; and also because that which is dead produces a certain pollution, through a physical aptitude to a worse condition, in consequence of having possessed the power of dying. Put a dead body cannot produce any defilement in a daemon who is perfectly incorporeal, and does not receive any corruption. For it is necessary that he should transcend a corruptible body, and not participate of any representation of corruption from it. And thus much in answer to the contrariety of the doubt.

Chap. III.

IN the next place we shall explain how divination is effected through sacred animals, such, for instance, as hawks. We must never say, therefore, that the Gods accede through bodies that are thus procured, being employed. For they do not preside over animals, either partibly, or proximately, or materially, or with a certain habitude towards them. But to daemons and these such as are very much divided, to different orders of whom different animals are allotted, and who proximately exercise a government of this kind, and do not obtain their proper dominion in a way perfectly independent and immaterial, such a contact with the organs of divination must be ascribed. Or, if some one is willing so to admit, a seat must be attributed to them, through which we may be able to associate with and employ them. It is necessary, therefore, to think that this seat should be pure from bodies. For there can be no communion whatever between the pure and its contrary; but it is reasonable to admit that this seat is conjoined with men, through the soul of animals. For this soul has a certain alliance to men, through homogeneity of life; but it is allied to daemons, because, being liberated from body, it has in a certain respect a separate subsistence. Hence, being a medium between both, it is subservient to its presiding daemon, but announces to those who are yet detained in body that which its prefect commands. And it imparts to both these a common bond with each other.

Chap. IV.

IT is necessary, however, to think that the soul which uses divination of this kind, not only becomes an auditor of the prediction, but also contributes in no small degree from itself to the consummation of it, and of what pertains to its operations. For this soul is coexcited and cooperates, and at the same time foreknows, through a certain necessary sympathy. Such a mode, therefore, of divination as this is entirely different from the divine and true mode, being alone able to predict respecting small and diurnal concerns, *viz.* respecting such as being placed in a divided nature, are borne along about generation, and which impart motions from themselves to those things that are able to receive them, and produce multiform passions in things which are naturally adapted to be copassive. Perfect foreknowledge, however, can never be effected through passion. For that which is itself especially immutable, immaterial, and entirely pure, is accustomed to apprehend the future; but that which is mingled with the most irrational and dark nature of a corporeal-formed and material essence is filled with abundant ignorance. An artificial apparatus, therefore, of this kind does not deserve to be called divination; nor is it proper to bestow much attention upon it, nor to believe in any other person who uses it, as if it possessed in itself a certain clear and known indication of truth. And thus much concerning divination of this kind.

Chap. V.

LET us, therefore, now discuss another species of doubts, the cause of which is occult, and which, as you say, is accompanied with *"violent threats."* But it is variously divided about the multitude of threats. *"For it threatens either to burst the heavens, or to unfold the secrets of Isis, or to point out the arcanum in the adytum,* [1] *or to stop Baris, or to scatter the members of Osiris to Typhon, or to do something else of the like kind."* Men do not, however, as you think, threaten by such words as these the sun or the moon, or any of the celestial Gods; for if they did, more dire absurdities would ensue than those which you lament. But, as we before observed, there is a certain genus of powers in the world which is partible, inconsiderate, and most irrational, and which receives reason from another, and is obedient to it; neither itself employing a proper intelligence, nor distinguishing what is true and false, or what is possible or impossible. A genus, therefore, of this kind, when threatenings are extended, is immediately coexcited and astonished, because, as it appears to me, it is naturally adapted to be led by representations, and to allure other things, through an astounded and innstable phantasy.

[1] The conjecture of Gale, that for ἤ το εν Αβυδῳ in this place, we should read ἤ το εν Αδυτῳ, is, I have no doubt, right. For the highest order of intelligibles is denominated by Orpheus *the adytum*, as we are informed by Proclus in Tim. By the arcanum in the adytum, therefore, is meant the deity who subsists at the extremity of the intelligible order (i.e. Phanes); and of whom it is said in the Chaldean Oracles, "that he remains in the paternal profundity, and in the adytum, near to the god-nourished silence."

Chap. VI.

THESE things also admit of another explanation of the following kind. The theurgist, through the power of arcane signatures, commands mundane natures, no longer as man, nor as employing a human soul; but as existing superior to them in the order of the Gods, he makes use of greater mandates than pertain to himself, so far as he is human. This, however, does not take place as if he effected every thing which he vehemently threatens to accomplish; but he teaches us by such a use of words the magnitude and quality of the power which he possesses through a union with the Gods, and which he obtains from the knowledge of arcane symbols. This, likewise, may be said, that the daemons who are distributed according; to parts, and who guard the parts of the universe, pay so much attention to the parts over which they preside, that they cannot endure a word contrary [to the safety of these], but they preserve the permanency of mundane natures immutable. They preserve this permanency, therefore, in an unchanged condition, because the order of the Gods remains invariably the same. Hence they cannot endure even to hear that threatened in which the aerial and terrestrial daemons have their existence.

Chap. VII.

OR this thing may likewise be explained as follows: Daemons preside with a guardian power over arcane mysteries, and this in so remarkable a degree, because the orderly distribution of things in the universe is primarily contained in daemons. For the parts of the universe remain in order, because the beneficent power of Osiris continues sacred and undefiled, and is not mingled with any opposing error and perturbation. The life of all things likewise remains pure and incorruptible, because the occult vivific beauties of the productive principles in Isis do not descend into body which is born along, [1] and is the object of sight. But all things continue immoveable and perpetual, because the course of the sun is never stopped. And all things remain perfect and entire, because the arcana in the adytum [2] are never disclosed. Hence, in those particulars in which the whole of things possesses its safety, I mean in arcana being always preserved occult, and in the ineffable essence of the Gods, never receiving a contrary condition; in these, terrestrial daemons cannot endure, even in words, to hear that they subsist otherwise than they do, or that they become profaned; and on this account threatening language has a certain power when employed against them. No one, however, threatens the Gods, nor is such a mode of invocation addressed to them. Hence with the Chaldeans, by whom words used to the Gods alone are preserved distinct and pure, no threats are employed. But the Egyptians, mingling daemoniacal words with divine signatures, sometimes employ threats. You have, therefore, an answer to these doubts, concise indeed, but I think sufficiently free from error.

[1] For εις το φαινομενεν και ορωμενον σωμα, I read εις το φερομενεν κ. τ. λ.
[2] Here too for Αβυδω I read Αδυτω.

Section VII.

Chap. I.

THE doubts also that follow in the next place require for their solution the assistance of the same divinely-wise -Muse. But I am desirous, previous to this, to unfold to you the peculiarity of the theology of the Egyptians. For they, imitating the nature of the universe, and the fabricative energy of the Gods, exhibit certain images through symbols of mystic, occult, and invisible intellections; just as nature, after a certain manner, expresses invisible reasons [or productive powers] through visible forms. -But the fabricative energy of the Gods delineates the truth of forms, through visible images. Hence the Egyptians, perceiving that all superior natures rejoice in the similitude to them of inferior beings, and thus wishing to fill the latter with good, through the greatest possible imitation of the former, very properly exhibit a mode of theologizing adapted to the mystic doctrine concealed in the symbols.

Chap. II.

HEAR, therefore, the intellectual interpretation of symbols, according to the conceptions of the Egyptians; at the same time removing from your imagination and your cars the image of things symbolical, but elevating yourself to intellectual truth. By "*mire,*" therefore, understand every thing corporeal-formed and material; or that which is nutritive and prolific; or such as the material species of nature is, which is borne along in conjunction with the unstable flux of matter; or a thin- of such a kind as that which the river of generation receives, and which subsides together with it; or the primordial cause of the elements, and of all the powers distributed about the elements, and which must be antecedently conceived to exist analogous to a foundation. Being, therefore, a thing of this kind, the God who is the cause of generation, of all nature, and of all the powers in the elements, as transcending these, and as being immaterial, incorporeal, and supernatural, unbegotten and impartible, wholly derived from himself, and concealed in himself,-this God precedes all things, and comprehends all things in himself, And because, indeed, he comprehends all things, and imparts himself to all mundane natures, he is from these unfolded into light. Because, however, he transcends all things, and is by himself expanded above them, on this account he presents himself to the view as separate, exempt, elevated, and expanded by himself above the powers and elements in the world. The following symbol, likewise, testifies the truth of this. For by the God "*sitting above the lotus,*" a transcendency and strength which by no means come into contact with the mire, are obscurely signified, and also indicate his intellectual and empyrean empire. For every thing belonging to the lotus is seen to be circular, *viz.* both the form of the leaves and the fruit; and circulation is alone allied to the motion of intellect, which energizes with invariable sameness, in one order, and according to one reason. But the God is established by himself, and above a dominion and energy of this kind, venerable and holy, superexpanded, and abiding in himself, which his being seated is intended to signify. When the God, also, is represented as "*sailing in a ship,*" [1] it exhibits to us the power which governs the world. As, therefore, the pilot being separate from the ship presides over the rudder of it, thus the sun having a separate subsistence, governs the helm of the whole world. And as the pilot directs all things from the stern, giving from himself a small principle of motion to the vessel; thus, also, by a much greater priority, the God indivisibly imparts supernally from the first principles of nature, the primordial causes of motions. These particulars, therefore, and still more than these, are indicated by the God sailing in a ship.

[1] Conformably to this, Martianus Capella also, in lib. ii. De Nuptiis Philol. &c. speaking of the still, says, "Ibi quandam navin, totius naturae cursus diversa cupiditate moderantem, cunctaque flammarum congestione plenissimam, et beatis circumactam mercibus conspicatur. Cui nautae septem, germani tamen, suique similes praesidebant in prora. Praesidebat in prora felis forma depicta, leonis in arbore, crocodili in extimo." For these animals, the cat, the lion, and the crocodile were peculiarly sacred to the sun. Martianus adds, " In eadem vero rate, fons quidem lucis aethereae, arcanisque fluoribus manans, in totius mundi lumina fundebatur." i.e. "In the same ship there was a fountain of etherial light flowing with arcane streams, which were poured into all the luminaries of the world." Porphyry, likewise, in his treatise De Antro Nymph. says, "that the Eyptians placed the sun and all daemons not connected with any thing solid or stable, but raised on a sailing vessel."

Chap. III.

SINCE, however, every part of the heavens, every sign of the zodiac, [1] all the motion of the heavens, every period of time according to which the world is moved, and all things contained in the wholes of the universe, receive the powers which descend from the sun, some of which are complicated with these wholes, but others transcend a commixture with them, the symbolical mode of signification represents these also, indicating *"that the sun is diversified according to the signs of the zodiac, and that every hour he changes his form."* At the same time, also, it indicates his immutable, stable, never failing, and at once collected communication of good to the whole world. But since the recipients of the impartible gift of the God are variously affected towards it, and receive multiform powers from the sun, according to their peculiar motions, hence the symbolical doctrine evinces through the multitude of the gifts, that the God is one, and exhibits his one power through multiform powers. Hence, likewise, it says that he is one and the same, but that the vicissitudes of his form, and his configurations, must be admitted to exist in the recipients. On this account it asserts "that he is changed every hour, according to the signs of the zodiac," in consequence of these being variously changed about the God, according to the many modes by which they receive him. The Egyptians use prayers to the sun, conformable to these assertions, not only in visions which are seen by the bodily eyes, but also in their more common supplications, all which have such a meaning as this, and are offered to the God conformably to a symbolic and mystic doctrine of this kind. Hence it would not be reasonable in any one to undertake a defence of them.

Chap. IV.

BUT the inquiries which follow in the next place, require a more abundant doctrine, in order to their elucidation. At the same time, however, it is necessary to discuss the truth concerning them with brevity. For you inquire "what efficacy there is in names that are not significant." [1] They are not, however, as you think, without signification; but let them be indeed unknown to us (though some of them are known to us, the explications of which we receive from the Gods), yet to the Gods all of them are significant, though not according to an effable mode; nor in such a way as that which is significant and indicative with men through imaginations; but either intellectually, conformably to the divine intellect which is in us; or ineffably, and in a way more excellent and simple, and conformably to the intellect which is united to the Gods. It is requisite, therefore, to take away all conceptions derived by an abstraction from sensibles, and all logical evolutions from divine names; [2] and likewise the connascent physical similitudes of language to things which exist in nature. But the intellectual and divine symbolical character of divine similitude must be admitted to have a subsistence in names. And, moreover, though it should be unknown to us, yet this very circumstance is that which is most venerable in it, for it is too excellent to be divided into knowledge. But in those names which we can scientifically analyze, [3] we possess a knowledge of the whole divine essence, power, and order, comprehended in the name. And farther still, we preserve in the soul collectively the mystic and arcane image of the Gods, and through this we elevate the soul to the Gods, and when elevated conjoin it as much as possible with them. But you ask, *"Why, of significant names, we prefer such as are Barbaric to our own?"* Of this, also, there is a mystic reason. For because the Gods have shown that the whole dialect of sacred nations, such as those of the Egyptians and Assyrians, is adapted to sacred concerns; on this account we ought to think it necessary that our conference with the Gods should be in a language allied to them. Because, likewise, such a mode of speech is the first and most ancient. And especially because those who first learned the names of the Gods, having mingled them with their own proper tongue, delivered them to us, that we might always preserve immoveable the sacred law of tradition, in a language peculiar and adapted to them. For if any other thing pertains to the Gods, it is evident that the eternal and immutable must be allied to them.

[1] Of this kind are the following names in Alexand. Trallian. lib. ii. Μευ, Θρευ, Μορ, Φορ, Τευζ, Ζα, Ζων, Θε, Λου, Χρι, Γε, Ζε, Ων, i.e. *Meu, Threu, Mor, Phor, Teux, Za, Zon, The, Lou, Chri, Ge, Ze, On.* By these names Alexander Trallianus says, the sun becomes fixed in the heavens. He adds, "Again behold the great name Ιαξ, (lege Ιαω) Αζυφ, Ζυων, Θρευξ, Βαϊν, Χωωκ, i.e. *Iao, Azuph, Zuon, Threux, Bain, Chook.*" Among the Lat-

137

ins, also, Cato, Varro, and Marcellus de Medicamentis Empiricis, there are examples of these names; the power and efficacy of which, as Gale observes, are testified by history, though it is not easy to explain the reason of their operation.

[2] Proclus, in commenting on the following words of Plato in the Timaeus, (see vol. i. p. 228, of my translation of his Commentary), *viz.* "Let, therefore, this universe be denominated by us *all heaven*, or *the world*, or whatever other appellation it may be especially adapted to receive," beautifully thus observes concerning the *divine* name of the world. "As of statues established by the telestic art, some things pertaining to them are manifest, but others are inwardly concealed, being symbolical of the presence of the Gods, and which are only known to the mystic artists themselves; after the same manner, the world being a statue of the intelligible, and perfected by the father, has indeed some things which are visible indications of its divinity; but others, which are the invisible impressions of the participation of being received by it from the father, who gave it perfection, in order that through these it may be eternally rooted in real being. *Heaven*, indeed, and *the world* are names significant of the powers in the universe; the latter, so far as it proceeds from the intelligible; but the former, so far as it is converted to it. It is, however, necessary to know that *the divine name* of its abiding power, and which is a symbol of the impression of the Demiurgus, according to which it does not proceed out of being, is ineffable and arcane, and known only to the Gods themselves. For there are names adapted to every order of things; those, indeed, that are adapted to divine natures being divine, to the objects of dianoia being dianoetic, and to the objects of opinion doxastic. This also Plato says in the Cratylus, where he embraces what is asserted by Homer on this subject, who admits that names of the same things are with the Gods different from those that subsist in the opinions of men,

Xanthus by God, by men Scamander call'd.   ILIAD XX. V. 74.
And,
Which the Gods Chalcis, men Cymindis call.   ILIAD Xiv. V. =91.

And in a similar manner in many other names. For as the knowledge of the Gods is different from that of partial souls, thus also the names of the one are different from those of the other; since divine names unfold the whole essence of the things named, but those of men only partially come into contact with them. Plato, therefore, knowing that this preexisted in the world, omits the divine and ineffable name itself, which is different from the apparent name, and with the greatest caution introduces it as a symbol of the divine impression which the world contains. For the words, *"or whatever other appellation "* and *"it may receive,"* are a latent hymn of the mundane name, as ineffable, and as allotted a divine essence, in order that it may be coordinate to what is signified by it. Hence, also, divine mundane names are delivered by Theurgists; some of which are called by them ineffable, but others effable; and some being significant of the invisible powers in the world, but others of the visible elements from which it derives its completion. Through these causes, therefore, as hypotheses, the mundane form, the demiurgic cause and paradigm, and the apparent and unapparent name of the world are delivered. And the former name, indeed, is dyadic, but the latter monadic. For the words *"whatever other"* are significant of oneness. You may also consider the *ineffable name* of the universe as significant of its abiding in the father; but the name *world*, as indicative of its progression; and *heaven* of its conversion. But through the three, you have the final cause, on account of which it is full of good; abiding ineffably, proceeding perfectly, and converting itself to *the good* as the antecedent object of desire."

138

Chap. V.

YOU object, however, *"that he who hears words looks to their significa-tion, so that it is sufficient the conception remains the same, whatever the words may be that are used."* But the thing is not such as you suspect it to be. For if names subsisted through compact [1] it would be of no consequence whether some were used instead of others. But if they are suspended from the nature of things, those names which are more adapted to it will also be more dear to the Gods. From this, therefore, it is evident that the language of sacred nations is very reasonably preferred to that of other men. To which may be added, that names do not entirely preserve the same meaning when translated into another language; but there are certain idioms in each nation which cannot be signified by language to another nation. And, in the next place, though it should be possible to translate them, yet they no longer pre-serve the same power when translated. Barbarous names, likewise, have much emphasis, great conciseness, and participate of less ambiguity, variety, and multitude. Hence, on all these accounts, they are adapted to more excel-lent natures. Take away, therefore, entirely those suspicions of yours which fall off from the truth, *viz. "if he who is invoked is either an Egyptian or uses the Egyptian language."* But rather think that as the Egyptians were the first of men [2] who were allotted the participation of the Gods, the Gods when invoked rejoice in the Egyptian rites. Again, however, if all these were the fraudulent devices of enchanters, how is it possible that things which are in the most eminent degree united to the Gods, which also conjoin us with them, and have powers all but equal to those of superior beings, should be phantastic devices, though without them no sacred operation can be effect-ed? But neither *"do these veils [by which arcana are concealed] originate from our passions, which rumour as cubes to a divine nature."* For beginning, not, from our passions, but, on the contrary, from things allied to the Gods, we make use of words adapted to them. *"Nor do we frame conceptions of a divine nature, contrary to its real mode of subsistence."* But conformably to the na-ture which it possesses, and to the truth concerning it, which those obtained who first established the laws of sacred religion, we persevere in our concep-tions of divinity. *For if any thing else in a religious legal institutions is adapted to the Gods, this must certainly be immutability. And it is necessary that an-cient prayers,* [3] *like sacred asyla, should be preserved invariably the same, neither taking any thing from them, nor adding any thing to them which is elsewhere derived.* For this is nearly the cause at present that both names and prayers have lost their efficacy, because they are continually changed through the innovation and illegality of the Greeks. For the Greeks are naturally studious of novelty, and are carried about every where by their volatility; neither possessing any stability themselves, nor preserving what they have received from others; but rapidly relinquishing this, they transform every thing through an unstable desire of discovering something new. But the Barbarians are stable in their manners, and firmly continue to employ the same words. Hence they are dear to the Gods, and proffer words which are grateful to them; but which it is not lawful for any man by any means to change. And thus much we have said in answer to you concerning names, which though they are inexplicable, and are called Barbaric, yet are adapted to sacred concerns.

[1] See the additional notes at the end of vol. v. of my translation of Plato, and also the notes to my translation of Aristotle de Interpretatione, in which the reader will find a treasury of recondite information concerning names, from Proclus and Ammonius.

[2] Most historians give the palm of antiquity to the Egyptians. And Lucian, in lib. De Syria Dea, says, "that the Egyptians are said to be the first among men that had a conception of the Gods, and a knowledge of sacred concerns. ------- They were also the first that had a knowledge of sacred names." Αιγυπτιοι πρωτοι ανθρωπων λεγονται θεων τε εννοιην λαβειν και ιρα εισασθαι ------- πρωτοι δε και ονοματα ιρα εγνωσαν. Conformably to this, also, an oracle of Apollo, quoted by Eusebius, says that the Egyptians were the first that disclosed by infinite actions the path that leads to the Gods. This oracle is as follows:

Αιτεινη γαρ οδος, μακαρων, τρηχειατε πολλον,
Χαλκοετοις τα πρωτα διοιγομενη πυλεωσιν.
Ατροπιτοι δε εασσιν αθεσφατοι εγγεγαυιαι,
Ας πρωτοι μεροπων επ' απειρονα πρηξιν εφηναν,
Οι το καλον πινοντες υδωρ Νειωτιδος αιης·
Πολλας και Φοινικες οδους μακαρων εδαησαν,
Ασσυριοι, Λυδοιτε, και Εβραιων (lege Χαλδαιων) γενος ανδρων.

i.e. "The path by which to deity we climb,
Is arduous, rough, ineffable, sublime;
And the strong massy gates, through which we pass
In our first course, are bound with chains of brass.
Those men the first who of Egyptian birth
Drank the fair water of Nilotic earth,
Disclosed by actions infinite this road,
And many paths to God Phcenicians show'd.
This road th' Assyrians pointed out to view,
And this the Lydians and Chaldeans knew."

For Εβραιων in this oracle I read Χαλδαιων, because I have no doubt that either Aristobulus the Jew, well known for interpolating the writings of the Heathens, or the wicked Eusebius, as he is called by the Emperor Julian, have fraudulently substituted the former word for the latter.

[3] Prayers of this kind are such as those of which Proclus speaks in Tim, p. FS, when he says, "The cathartic prayer is that which is offered for the purpose of averting diseases originating from pestilence, and other contagious distempers, such as we have

written in our temples." Καθαρτικαι δε (ευχαι), επι αποτροπαις λοιμικων νοσημοτων, ἤ παντοιων μολυσμων· οιας δε και εν τοις ιεροις εχομεν αναγεγραμμενας.

Section VIII.

Chap. I.

LEAVING, therefore, these particulars, you wish in the next place that I would unfold to you *"What the Egyptians conceive the first cause to be; whether intellect, or above intellect; whether alone, or subsisting with some other or others; whether incorporeal, or corporeal; and whether it is the same with the Demiurgus, or is prior to the Demiurgus? Likewise, whether all things are from one principle, or from many principles; whether they have a knowledge of matter, or of primary corporeal qualities; and whether they admit matter to be unbegotten, or to be generated?"* I, therefore, will in the first place relate to you the cause why in the books of the ancient writers of sacred concerns many and various opinions concerning these things are circulated, and also why among those that are still living, and are renowned for their wisdom, the opinion on this subject is not simple and one. I say then, that as there are many essences, and these differing from each other, the all-various multitude of the principles of these, and which have different orders, were delivered by different ancient priests, As Seleucus [1] narrates, therefore, Hermes described the principles that rank as wholes in two myriads [2] of books; or, as we are informed by Manetho, [3] he perfectly unfolded these principles in three myriads six thousand five hundred and twenty five volumes. But different ancient writers differently explained the partial principles of essences. It is necessary, however, by investigation to discover the truth about all these principles, and concisely to unfold it to you as much as possible. And, in the first place, hear concerning that which is the first subject of your inquiry.

[1] Porphyry, in lib. ii. De Abstinentia, mentions Seleucus the theologist, and Suidas says that Seleucus the Alexandrian wrote 100 books *concerning the Gods.*
[2] These books (βιβλιο) were most probably nothing more than short discourses, such as the treatises now are which are circulated as written by Hermes, and which, as Iamblichus informs us, contain Hermaic doctrines.
[3] A great priest, a scribe of the Adyta in Egypt, by birth a Sebanite, and an inhabitant of Heliopolis, as he relates of himself.

Chap. II.

PRIOR to truly existing beings and total principles [or principles that rank as wholes], there is one God, prior to [that deity who is generally believed to be] the first God and king, [1] immoveable, and abiding in the solitude of his own unity. For neither is the intelligible connected with him, nor any thing else; but he is established as the paradigm of the God who is the father of himself, is self begotten, is father alone, and is truly good. For he is something even greater and prior to this, is the fountain of all things, and the root of the first intelligible forms. But from this one deity, the God who is sufficient to himself, unfolds himself into light. For this divinity, also, is the principle and God of Gods, a monad from *the one*, prior to essence, and the principle of essence. For from him entity and essence are derived; and hence, also, he is denominated the principle of intelligibles. These, therefore, are the most ancient principles of all things, which Hermes arranges prior to the etherial, empyrean, and celestial Gods. He likewise delivered to us the history of the empyrean Gods in one hundred books; of the etherial in an equal number; and of the celestial in a thousand books.

[1] In the original, πρωτος κια του πρωτου θεου και βασιλεωσ, which Gale translates, prior etiam primo Deo, et rege [sole]. But the addition of sole in his translation is obviously most unappropriate and false: for Iamblichus is evidently speaking of a deity much superior to the sun.

Chap. III.

ACCORDING to another order, however, he arranges the God *Emeph* [1] prior to, and as the leader of, the celestial Gods. And he says that this God is an intellect, itself intellectually perceiving itself, and converting intellections to itself. But prior to this, he arranges the impartible one, which he says is the first paradigm, and which he denominates *Eicton*. In this, also, is contained that which is first intellective, and the first intelligible, and which is to be worshiped through silence alone. Besides these, also, other leaders preside over the fabrication of visible natures. For the demiurgic intellect, who is the curator of truth and wisdom, descending into generation, and leading the power of occult reasons into light, is called in the Egyptian tongue Amon; but in consequence of perfecting all things with veracity and artificially, he is called Ptha. The Greeks, however, assume Ptha for Vulcan, solely directing their attention to the artificial peculiarity of the God. So far, also, as he is effective of good he is called Osiris; and he has other appellations through other powers and energies. With the Egyptians, therefore, there is another domination of the whole elements in generation, and of the powers contained in them; four of these powers being male and four female, which they attribute to the sun. And there is, likewise, another government of the whole of nature about generation, which they assign to the moon. [2] But dividing the heavens into two, or four, or twelve, or six-and-thirty parts, or the doubles of these, they give to the parts a greater or less number of rulers. And over all these they place one ruler, who transcends all the rest. Thus, therefore, the doctrine of the Egyptians concerning principles, proceeding from on high as far as to the last of things, begins from one principle, and descends to a multitude which is governed by this one; and every where an indefinite nature is under the dominion of a certain definite measure, and of the supreme unical cause of all things. But God produced matter by dividing materiality from essentiality; [3] and this being vital, the Demiurgus receiving, fabricated from it the simple and impassive spheres. But he distributed in an orderly manner the last of it into generable and corruptible bodies.

[1] For Ημηφ here, Gale conjectures that we should read Κνηφ *Kneph*: for Plutarch says that the unbegotten *Kneph* was celebrated with an extraordinary degree of veneration by the Egyptian Thebans.
[2] Hence the moon is said by Proclus to be αυτοπτον της φυσεως αγαλμα, the self-visible statue or image of nature.
[3] Proclus in Tim. p. 117, cites what is here said as the doctrine of the Egyptians, and also cites for it the authority of Iamblichus. But his words are, και μην και η των Αιγυπτιων παραδοσις τα αυτα περι αυτης (της υλης) φησιν. ο γε τοι θειος Ιαμβλιχος ιστορησεν οτι και Ερμης εκ της ουσιοτητος της υλοτητα παραγεσθαι βουλεται. i.e. "More over the doctrine of the Egyptians asserts the same things concerning matter. For the divine Iamblichus relates that Hermes also produces matter from essentiality."

Chap. IV.

THESE things, therefore, having been accurately discussed, the solution of the doubts which you have met with in certain books will be manifest. *For the books which are circulated under the name of Hermes contain Hermaic opinions, though they frequently employ the language of the philosophers: for they were translated from the Egyptian tongue by men who were not unskilled in philosophy.* But Chaeremon, [1] and any others who have at all discussed the first causes of mundane natures, have unfolded the last rulers of these. And such as have written concerning the planets, the zodiac, the decans, horoscopes, and what are called powerful and leading planets, these have unfolded the partible distributions of the rulers. The particulars, also, contained in the Calendars comprehend a certain very small part of the Hermaic arrangements. And the causes of such things as pertain to the phases or occultations of the stars, or to the increments and decrements of the moon, are assigned by the Egyptians the last of all. The Egyptians, likewise, do not say that all things are physical. For they separate the life of the soul and the intellectual life from nature, not only in the universe, but also in us. And admitting intellect and reason to subsist by themselves, they say that generated essences were thus fabricated. Then, likewise arrange the Demiurgus as the primary father of things in generation; and they acknowledge the existence of a vital power, prior to the heavens, and subsisting in the heavens. They also establish a pure intellect above the world, and one impartible intellect in the whole world, and another which is distributed into all the spheres. And these things they do not survey by mere reason alone, but through the sacerdotal theurgy, they announce that they are able to ascend to more elevated and universal essences, and to those that are established above Fate, *viz.* to God and the Demiurgus; neither employing matter, nor assuming any other thing besides, except the observation of a suitable time.

[1] This is most probably the Chaeremon who is said by Porphyry, in lib. iv. De Abstinentia, "to be a lover of truth, an accurate writer, and very conversant with the Stoic philosophy" Τοιαυτα μεν τα κατ' Αιγυπτιους υπ' ανδρος φιλαληθους τε και ακριβους, εντε τοις Στωϊκοις πραγματικωτατα φιλοσοφησαντος μεμαρτυρημενα.

Chap. V.

THIS deific and anagogic path Hermes, indeed, narrated, but Bitys, the prophet of King Ammon, [1] explained it, having found it in the adyta of Sais [2] in Egypt, written in hieroglyphics; and the same prophet also delivered the name of God, which pervades through the whole world. [3] But there are, likewise, many other coarrangements of the same things; so that you do not appear to me to act rightly in referring all things with the Egyptians to physical causes. For there are, according to them, many principles and many essences; and also supermundane powers, which they worship through sacerdotal sanctimony. To me, therefore, these things appear to afford common auxiliaries to the solution of all the remaining inquiries. But since it is necessary not to leave any one of them uninvestigated, we shall add them to these problems, and examine them on all sides, in order that we may see where there is any thing futile in your opinions.

[1] This was the ninth king in the twenty-sixth dynasty of the Saitan kings.
[2] This city is mentioned by Plato in the Timaeus, who represents Critias as saying "that there is a certain region of Egypt, called Delta, about the summit of which the streams of the Nile are divided, and in which there is a province called Saitical." He adds, "of this province the greatest city is Sais, from which also King Amasis derived his origin. The city has a presiding divinity, whose name is, in the Egyptian tongue, Neith, but in the Greek Athena, or Minerva." It is singular that Gale, who is not deficient in philology, though but a smatterer in philosophy, should have omitted to remark in his notes this passage of Plato.
[3] Proclus, in MS. Comment. in Alcibiad. cites one of the Chaldean oracles, which says,
-------------- πορθμιον ουνομα το δ' εν απειροισ
Κοσμοις ενθρωσκον.
i.e. "There is a transmitting name which leaps into the infinite worlds." And in his MS. Scholia in Cratyl. he quotes another of these oracles, viz.
Αλλα εστιν ουναμο σεμνον ακοιμηντῳ στροφαγγι,
Κοσμοις ενθρωσκον, κραιπνην δια πατρος ενιπην.
i.e. "There is a venerable name with a sleepless revolution, leaping into the worlds through the rapid reproofs of the father."

Chap. VI.

YOU say, therefore, *"that according to many of the Egyptians, that which is in our power depends on the motion of the stars."* What the truth, however, is respecting this, it is necessary to unfold to you from the Hermaic conceptions. For man, as these writings say, has two souls. And one, indeed, is derived from the first intelligible, and participates of the power of the Demiurgus; but the other is imparted from the circulation of the celestial bodies, to which the soul that sees God returns. These things, therefore, thus subsisting, the soul that descends to its from the worlds follows the periods of the worlds; but that which is intelligibly present from the intelligible, transcends the genesiurgic motion, and through this a liberation from fate, and the ascent to the intelligible Gods, are effected. Such theurgy, likewise, as leads to an unbegotten nature is perfected conformably to a life of this kind.

Chap. VII.

HENCE that of which you are dubious is not true, *"that all things are bound with the indissoluble bonds of Necessity,"* which we call Fate. For the soul has a proper principle of circumduction to the intelligible, and of a separation from generated natures; and also of a contact with real being, and that which is divine. *"Nor must we ascribe fate to the Gods, whom we worship in temples and statues, as the dissolvers of fate."* For the Gods, indeed, dissolve fate; but the last natures which proceed from them, and are complicated with the generation of the world and with body, give completion to fate. Hence we very properly worship the Gods with all possible sanctity, and the observance of all religious rites, in order that they may liberate us from the evils impending from fate, as they alone rule over necessity through intellectual persuasion. But neither are all things comprehended [1] in the nature of fate, but there is another principle of the soul, which is superior to all nature and generation, and through which we are capable of being united to the Gods, of transcending, the mundane order, and of participating eternal life, and the energy of the supercelestial Gods. Through this principle, therefore, we are able to liberate ourselves from fate. For when the more excellent parts of us energize, and the soul is elevated to natures better than itself, [2] then it is entirely separated from things which detain it in generation, departs from subordinate natures, exchanges the present for another life, and gives itself to another order of things, entirely abandoning the former order with which it was connected.

[1] For εχεται in this place, I read περιεχεται.
[2] Gale, in his translation of this part, has entirely mistaken the meaning of Iamblichus, which he frequently does in other places. For the words of Iamblichus are, οταν γαρ δη τα βελτιονα των εν ημιν ενεργῃ, και προς τα κρειττονα αναγεται

αυτης η ψυχη; and the version of Gale is "quando enim pars nostri melior operari incipiat, et ad sui portionem meliorem recolligatur anima." For τα κρειττονα is not the better part of the soul; but when the better parts of the soul energize, the soul is then intimately converted to itself, and through this conversion is elevated to superior natures.

Chap. VIII.

WHAT then, is it not possible for a man to liberate himself [from fate] through the Gods that revolve in the heavens, and to consider the same as the leaders of fate, and yet as those that bind our lives with indissoluble bonds? Perhaps nothing prevents this from being the case. For if the Gods comprehend in themselves many essences and powers, there are also in them other immense differences and contrarieties. Moreover, this also may be said, that in each of the Gods, though such as are visible, there are certain intelligible principles through which a liberation to souls from mundane generation is effected. But if some one leaves only two genera of Gods, *viz.* the mundane and supermundane, the liberation to souls will be effected through the supermundane Gods. These things, therefore, are more accurately discussed in our treatise *Concerning the Gods*, in which it is shown who are the anagogic Gods, and according to what kind of powers they are so; how they liberate from fate, and through what sacred regressions; and what the order is of mundane nature, and how the most perfect intellectual energy rules over this. So that what you add from Homer, "that the Gods are flexible," it is not holy to assert. For the works of the sacred ceremonies of religion have long since been defined by pure and intellectual laws. Subordinate natures, also, are liberated through a greater order and power; and when we abandon inferior natures, we are transferred into a more excellent allotment. This, however, is not effected contrary to any original sacred law, so as to cause the Gods to be changed, through a sacred operation being afterwards performed; but from the first divinity sent souls hither, in order that they might again return to him. Neither, therefore, is any mutation produced through a reascent of this kind, nor do the descents and ascents of souls oppose each other. For as generation and this universe are suspended from an intellectual essence; thus, also, in the orderly distribution of souls, the liberation from generation accords with the care employed by them about generation.

Section IX.

Chap. I.

LET us now, therefore, to the utmost of our power, endeavour to discuss the manifold doubt concerning the peculiar daemon, and which also is sub-

ject to various objections. Since, however, to speak summarily, the consideration of the peculiar daemon is twofold, the one being theurgic, but the other
artificial; and the one drawing this daemon down from supernal causes, but
the other from the visible periods in generation; and the one making no use
whatever of the calculation of nativities, but the other meddling with methods of this kind; and the one worshiping this daemon in a way more universal and supernatural, but the other partibily conformable to nature; this being the case, you appear to me to have absurdly transferred a more perfect
sacred operation to one that is human, and in this to have exercised your inquiries.

Chap. II.

IN the next place, here also you appear to me to have cut off only a certain small part of the discussion concerning the peculiar demon. For since it
is usual with those who artificially operate about nature to invoke this daemon in an orderly manner from the decans, from the dispensators of influx-
es, from the signs of the zodiac, the stars, the sun and moon, from the greater
and lesser bear, from the whole elements, and from the world, this being the
case, you do not act rightly in assuming one, and that the smallest part of all
these, *viz.* the lord of the geniture, and making your inquiries about this
alone. Here, likewise, again from one of the things proposed to be considered, you inquire *"how the lord of the geniture gives the peculiar daemon, and
according to what kind of eflux, or life, or power, it descends to us from
him."* You also speak concerning the calculation of nativities, and
ask *"whether there is any reality in it or not;"* and likewise concerning the invention of the lord of the geniture, *"Whether it is impossible to be found, or
possible."* In what respect, however, do these things pertain to the domination of the daemon? For it is evident that our knowledge of the manner in
which he subsists, contributes nothing to his essence and the cause of his
existence. For in things which belong to the empire of nature, such as are
generated in the universe have a proper stability of their own essence,
though we should be ignorant how they are produced. In this way, therefore,
we reply in *common* to your doubts. But directing our attention *particularly*
to the subjects of your inquiry, we shall endeavour to give you solutions of
them.

Chap. III.

YOU say, then, *"that he is happy who having learned the scheme of his
nativity, and knowing his proper daemon, is thus liberated from fate."* To me,
however, you appear to assert these things in a way neither consonant to
themselves nor to truth. For if our proper daemon is distributed to us from

the scheme of our nativity, and from thence we are able to discover him, how can we *be liberated from fate*, through a knowledge of the daemon imparted to us by fate? But if, as you sav, we are truly liberated from necessity through this daemon, how is he allotted to us by fate? Thus, therefore, what is now said by you opposes what you before asserted; and is also discordant with truth. For the proper daemon of every one does not entirely accede from the scheme of the peculiar nativity; but his origin is more ancient than this, which we shall hereafter discuss. To which may be added, that if the descending daemon was to be alone surveyed from hence, he will not be happy who obtains the knowledge of his genesiurgic daemon. And who would [willingly] receive this daemon as his leader to a liberation from fate, if he was given to him for this purpose, that he might accomplish the distributions of fate? Farther still, this appears to me to be only a certain and the last part of the theory pertaining to this daemon; and that the whole theory of his essence is omitted by a method of this kind. But these things, indeed, though they are falsely asserted, yet at the same time are not utterly foreign from the purpose. The doubts, however, adduced by you in the next place, concerning *"the enumeration of the canons and the genethlialogical science,"* as they are inscrutable, are not attended with any ambiguity in the present discussion. For whether these arts are known or are incomprehensible, yet, at the same time, the efflux from the stars distributes to us the daemon, whether we know it or not. But divine divination is able to teach us concerning the stars, in a way which is most true, and [when we are in possession of this] we are not entirely in want of the enumeration of canons, or of the divining art.

Chap. IV.

IF, however, it be necessary, dismissing these particulars, to speak what appears to me to be the truth, you do not rightly infer *"that a knowledge of this mathamatical science [1] cannot be obtained, because there is much dissonance concerning it, or because Chaeremon, or some other, has written against it."* For if this reason were admitted, all things will be incomprehensible. For all sciences have ten thousand controvertists, and the doubts with which they are attended are innumerable. As, therefore, we are accustomed to say in opposition to the contentious, that contraries in things that are true are naturally discordant, and that it is not falsities alone that are hostile to each other; thus, also, we say respecting this mathematical science, that it is indeed true; but that those who wander from the scope of it, being ignorant of the truth, contradict it. This, however happens not in this science alone, but likewise in all the sciences, which are imparted by the Gods to men. For time always proceeding the divine mode of knowledge becomes evanescent, through being frequently mingled and contaminated with much of what is mortal. This divine mode is indeed [in astrology also], and a certain clear indication of truth, though it is but small, is at the same time preserved in it.

For it places before our eyes manifest signs of the mensuration of the divine periods, when it predicts the eclipses of the sun and moon, and the concursions [2] of the moon with the fixed stars, and when the experience of the sight is seen to accord with the prediction. *Moreover, the observations of the celestial bodies through the whole of time,* [3] *both by the Chaldeans and by us, testify that this science is true.* Indications, also, more known than these might be adduced, if the present discussion was precedaneously about these particulars. But as they are superfluous, and do not pertain to the knowledge of the peculiar daemon, I shall, as it is fit so to do, omit them, and pass on to things more appropriate than these.

[1] *viz.* The science of calculating nativities.
[2] i.e. The joint risings and settings.
[3] i.e. Through a period of 300,000 years; and Procl. in Tim. lib. iv. p. 277, informs us that the Chaldeans had observations of the stars which embraced whole mundane periods. What Proclus likewise asserts of the Chaldeans is confirmed by Cicero in his first book on Divination, who says that they had records of the stars for the space of 370,000 years; and by Diodorus Siculus, Bibl. lib. xi. p. 118, who says that their observations comprehended the space of 473,000 years.

Chap. V.

YOU say then, in your epistle, *"that the discovery of the lord or lords of the geniture, if there are more than one in a nativity, can scarcely be obtained, and by astrologers themselves is confessed to be unattainable; and yet they say that the peculiar daemon is from thence to be known."* But how can astrologers confess that the knowledge of the lord of the geniture is not to be obtained by them, when they deliver clear methods for the discovery of it, and teach us rules by which we may discover the doubts; some, indeed, giving us five, [1] others more and others less than five rules? Omitting this, however, let us direct our attention to a thing of greater consequence, viz, the accidents pertaining to both these. For if it is possible to discover the lord of the geniture, the daemon imparted by him will be known; but if this knowledge is unattainable, we shall be ignorant of the lord of the geniture according to this hypothesis, and yet, nevertheless, he will have an existence, and also the daemon imparted by him. What therefore hinders, but that the discovery of him may be difficult through prediction from the nativity, and yet through sacred divination, or theurgy, there may be a great abundance of scientific knowledge on this subject? In short, the daemon is not alone imparted by the lord of the geniture, but there are many other principles of it more universal [2] than this. And farther still, a method of this kind introduces a certain artificial and human disquisition concerning the peculiar daemon. Hence, in these doubts of yours there is nothing sane.

[1] "We say," says Hephestion, "that a star is the lord of the geniture, which has five conditions of the lord of the nativity in the horoscope; viz if that star receives the luminaries in their proper boundaries, in their proper house, in their proper altitude, and in the proper triangle." He also adds, "and if besides it has contact, effluxion, and configuration." See likewise Porphyry in Ptolemaeum, p. 191.
[2] According to the Egyptians every one received his proper daemon at the hour of his birth; nor did they ascend any higher, in order to obtain a knowledge of it. For they alone considered the horoscope. See Porphyry apud Stobaeum, p. 201, and Hermes in Revolut. cap. iv.

Chap. VI.

IF, however, it be requisite to unfold to you the truth concerning the peculiar daemon, we must say that he is not distributed to us from one part of the heavens, or from some one of the visible elements; but that from the whole world, the all various life contained in it, and the all various body through which the soul descends into generation, a certain peculiar portion is distributed to each of the parts in us, according to a peculiar prefecture. This daemon, therefore, is established in the paradigm before the soul descends into generation; and when the soul has received him as its leader, the daemon immediately presides over the soul, gives completion to its lives, and binds it to body when it descends. He likewise governs the common animal of the soul, directs its peculiar life, and imparts to us the principles of all our thoughts and reasonings. We also perform such things as he suggests to our intellect, and he continues to govern us till, through sacerdotal theurgy, we obtain a God for the inspective guardian and leader of the soul. For then the daemon either yields or delivers his government to a more excellent nature, or is subjected to him, as contributing to his guardianship, or in some other way is ministrant to him as to his lord.

Chap. VII.

FROM these things, therefore, it is easy to answer your next question. For the peculiar daemon does not rule over one of the parts in us, but, in short, over all the parts at once, and extends to every principle within us, in the same manner as he was distributed to us from the total orders in the universe. For that which it appears to you proper to add as an indication *"that daemons preside over the parts of our body, so that one is the guardian of health, another of the form of the body, and another of the corporeal habits, and that there is one daemon who presides in common over all these;"* this you should consider as an argument that there is one demon who is the guardian and governor of every thing that is in us. You must not, therefore, distribute one daemon to the body, but another to the soul, and another to intellect: for it is absurd that the animal should be one, but the daemon that presides over it multiform. For every where the natures that govern are more simple than the natures that are governed. And it will be still more absurd if the many daemons that rule over the parts are not connascent, but separated from each other. But you also make contrariety among them. For you speak as if *"some of them, were good, but others bad."* Evil daemons, however, have no where a ruling allotment, nor are they oppositely divided to such as are good with equal authority and power.

Chap. VIII.

AFTERWARDS, abandoning these particulars, you pass on to the opinion of philosophy. But you subvert the whole hypothesis concerning the peculiar demon. For if [as you say] *"this daemon is a part of the soul,"* such, for instance, as the intellectual part, *"and he is happy who is in possession of a wise intellect,"* there will no longer be any other more excellent or daemoniacal order, presiding over, as transcending the human soul. But certain parts of the soul, or a certain divided power, will have dominion over many of the forms of life that arc in us; and will rule over these, not connascently, but as naturally exempt, and as transcending the whole of our composition.

Chap. IX.

AFTER this, therefore, you also mention another disquisition concerning the peculiar daemon, which represents *"some as worshiping two, but others three, daemons of this kind."* The whole of this, however, is erroneous. For it is a false mode of proceeding to divide the causes that preside over us, and not refer them to one; since this wanders from the union which has dominion over all things. The opinion, likewise, which distributes this daemon into body, and the government of body, draws down his domination to a certain most minute part. So that what necessity is there for those who embrace this opinion to direct their attention to sacred operations, the first principle of them being futile? There is, therefore, of each of us one peculiar presiding demon; but it is not proper to think that this daemon is common to all men; nor again, that he is common, but is peculiarly present with each individual. For division, according to species and difference of matter, do not receive the communion and sameness of things essentially incorporeal. *"Why then [you say] is the peculiar daemon invoked by a common mode by all men?"* Because the invocation of him is effected through one God, who is the lord of daemons; who from the first defined to every one his peculiar daemon; and who, in sacred operations, unfolds to every one his proper daemon, according to his own proper will. For always in the theurgic order secondary are invoked through primary natures. Among daemons, therefore, one common leader of the cosmocrators about generation sends to each of us his peculiar daemon.

Hence, when the peculiar daemon is present with each of us, he then unfolds the worship which is proper to be paid to him and his name, and likewise delivers the proper mode of invoking him.

Chap. X.

AND this order is adapted to daemons; one part of it being allied to those that are invoked; another being derived from more ancient causes; and the third part effecting a common completion from both the others. Do not, therefore, assimilate divine invocations to such as are human, nor those that are ineffable to those that are effable; nor compare those that are prior to every boundary, and every indefinite mode, to those that are defined by men, or to indefinite actions. For our concerns have nothing in common with theirs, whose genus and whole order transcend and govern the whole of our essence and nature. But here, especially, the greatest errors happen to men, when from human imbecility they infer any thing concerning the domination of daemons, and from things which are small, of no worth, and distributed into parts, form a conjecture of great, excellent, and perfect natures. And thus much in answer to you concerning the peculiar daemon, in addition to what has been before said.

Section X.

Chap. I.

IT now remains, in the last place, that we should speak concerning felicity, about which you make various inquiries, first of all proposing objections, afterwards doubting, and then interrogating. Adducing, therefore, all that is said by you, we shall answer it appropriately. You inquire, then, *"whether there is not some other latent way to felicity."* But how, in that path which recedes from the Gods, is it probable there can be an ascent to felicity? For if the essence and perfection of all good are comprehended in the Gods, and the first and ancient power of them is with us priests, and if by those who similarly adhere to more excellent natures, and genuinely obtain a union with them, the beginning and end of all good is earnestly pursued; if this be the case, here the contemplation of truth, and the possession whole of intellectual science are to be found.* And a knowledge of the Gods is accompanied with a conversion to, and the knowledge of, ourselves.

[1] In the original ενταυθα δη ουν και η της αληθειας παρεστι θεα, και η της νοερας επιστεμες. But instead of η της νοερας απιστημησ, which appears to me to be defective, I read η κτησις της νοερας επιστημης.

Chap. II.

HENCE you in vain doubt, *"that it is not proper to look to human opinions."* For what leisure can he have whose intellect is directed to the Gods to look downward to the praises of men? Nor do you rightly doubt in what follows, viz. *"that the soul devises great things from casual circumstances."* For what principle of fictions can there be in truly existing beings? Is it not the phantastic power in us which is the maker of images? *But the phantasy is never excited when the intellectual life energizes perfectly.* And is not truth essentially coexistent with the Gods? Is it not, likewise, concordantly established in intelligibles? It is in vain, therefore, that things of this kind are disseminated by you and others. But neither do those things for which certain futile and arrogant men calumniate the worshipers of the Gods, the like to which have been asserted by you, at all pertain to true theology and theurgy. And if certain things of this kind germinate in the sciences of divine concerns, as in other arts evil arts blossom forth; these are doubtless more contrary to such sciences than to any thing else. For evil is more hostile to good than to that which is not good.

Chap. III.

I WISH, in the next place, to reply to such assertions as calumniate divine prediction. For you compare with it *"certain other methods which are conversant with the prediction of future events."* To me, however, it does not appear to be any thing honourable if a certain natural aptitude is ingenerated in us to the indication of the future, just as in animals there is a foreknowledge of earthquakes, or winds, or tempests. For an innate presage of this kind is the consequence of acuteness of sensation, or sympathy, or some other conjoint motion of the physical powers, and is not attended with any thing venerable and supernatural. Nor if some one, by human reasoning, or artificial observation, conjectures from signs those things of which the signs are indicative (as physicians foreknow that a fever will take place from the systole and torpor of the pulse), neither does he appear to me to possess any thing honourable and good. For he conjectures after a human manner, and concludes from our reasoning power about things which are acknowledged to be effected naturally, and forms a judgment not very remote from the corporeal-formed order. Hence, if there is in us a certain natural presentiment of the future, in the same manner as in all other animals, this power is clearly seen to energize; this presentiment does not in reality possess any thing which is most blessed. For what is there among the things which are implanted in us by nature in the realms of generation that is a genuine, perfect, and eternal good?

Chap. IV.

DIVINE divination, therefore, which is conjoined with the Gods, alone truly imparts to us a divine life; since it participates of [divine] fore-knowledge, and divine intellections, and renders us in reality divine. It like-wise causes us to be genuine participants of *the good*, because the most blessed intellectual perception of the Gods is filled with all good. Hence those who possess this divination *"do not,"* as you conjecture, *"foresee future events, and are nevertheless happy."* For all divine foreknowledge is boniform. Nor *"do they foresee, indeed, what is future, but do not know how to use this knowledge properly."* For, together with the foreknowledge, they receive the beautiful itself, and true and appropriate order: and utility is also present with it. For the Gods, in conjunction with it, deliver a transcendent power of defence against the inconveniences which accede from nature. And when it is necessary to exercise virtue, and the ignorance of future events contributes to this, then the Gods conceal what will be for the sake of rendering the soul better. But when the ignorance of what is future does not at all contribute to this, and foreknowledge is advantageous to souls, for the sake of their salva-tion and reascent [to divinity], then the Gods insert the foreknowledge which pertains to divination in the penetralia of the essences of souls.

Chap. V.

BUT why am I prolix about these particulars? For I have abundantly shown, in what has been before said, the transcendency of divine above hu-man divination. It is better, therefore, in compliance with your request, *"to point out to you the way to felicity, and show you in what the essence of it is placed."* For from this the truth will be discovered, and at the same time all the doubts may be easily dissolved. I say, therefore, that the more divine [1] intelligible man, who was formerly united to the Gods by the vision of them, afterwards entered into another soul, which is coadapted to the human form, and through this became fettered with the bonds of necessity and fate. Hence it is requisite to consider how he may be liberated from these bonds. There, is, therefore, no other dissolution of them than the knowledge of the Gods. For to know scientifically the good is the idea of felicity; just as the oblivion of good, and deception about evil, happen to be the idea of evil. The former, therefore, is present with divinity; but the latter, which is an inferior destiny, is inseparable from the mortal nature. And the former, indeed, measures the essences of intelligibles [2] by sacred ways; but the latter, abandoning prin-ciples, gives itself up to the measurement of the idea of body. The former is a knowledge of the father; but the latter is a departure from him, and an obliv-ion of the God who is a superessential father, and sufficient to himself. The former, likewise, preserves the true life of the soul, and leads it back to its father; but the latter draws down the generation-ruling [3] man, as far as to that which is never permanent, but is always flowing. You must understand, therefore, that this is the first path to felicity, affording to souls an intellectual plenitude of divine union. But the sacerdotal and theurgic gift of felicity is called, indeed, the gate to the Demiurgus of wholes, or the seat, or palace, of the good. In the first place, likewise, it possesses a power of purifying the soul, much more perfect than the power which purifies the body; afterwards it causes a coaptation of the reasoning power to the participation and vision of the good, and a liberation from every thing of a contrary nature; and, in the last place, produces a union with the Gods, who are the givers of every good.

[1] For θεωτος here, I read θεωτερος.
[2] In the original, by a strange mistake, των θνητων is inserted here instead of των νοητων, which is obviously the true reading. The version of Gale also has *intelligibilium*.
[3] i.e. Man, considered as a rational soul, connected with the irrational life; for this man has dominion in the realms of generation.

Chap. VI.

MOREOVER, after it has conjoined the soul to the several parts of the universe, and to the total divine powers which pass through it; then it leads the soul to, and deposits it in, the whole Demiurgus, and causes it to be independent of all matter, and to be counited with the eternal reason alone. But my meaning is, that it peculiarly connects the soul with the self-begotten and self-moved God, and with the all-sustaining, intellectual, and all-adorning powers of the God, and likewise with that power of him which elevates to truth, and with his self-perfect, effective, and other demiurgic powers; so that the theurgic soul becomes perfectly established in the energies and demiurgic intellections of these powers. Then, also, it inserts the soul in the whole demiurgic God. And this is the end with the Egyptians of the sacerdotal elevation of the soul to divinity.

Chap. VII.

MOREOVER, respect to *the good,* likewise, they conceive that one kind is divine, and this is the God who is prior to the intelligible; but that the other is human, and is a union with the former. And these two kinds of good Bitys has unfolded from the Hermaic books. This part, therefore, is not, as you suspect, omitted by the Egyptians, but is divinely delivered by them. Nor do *"theurgists disturb the divine intellect about trifling concerns;"* but they consult it about things which pertain to the purification, liberation, and salvation of the soul. Neither do they studiously employ themselves in things which are indeed difficult, yet useless to mankind; but, on the contrary, they direct their attention to things which are of all others most beneficial to the soul. Nor, in the last place, are *"they deceived by a certain fraudulent daemon,"* who, having vanquished a fallacious and daemoniacal nature, ascend to an intelligible and divine essence.

Chap. VIII.

AND thus we have answered, to the utmost of our ability, your inquiries concerning divination and theurgy. It remains, therefore, at the end of this discussion, that I should beseech the Gods to afford me an immutable guard of true conceptions, to insert in me truth eternally, and to supply me abundantly with the participation of more perfect conceptions of the Gods, in which the most blessed end of our good is posited, and the confirmation of our concordant friendship with each other.

Additional Notes

Page 12. *Anebo.* Porphyry in his Life of Plotinus, and also in the second book of his Treatise on Abstinence from Animals, informs us that he was familiar with a certain Egyptian priest, who, as Gale conjectures, is probably the priest to whom Porphyry nosy writes. The diction, indeed, as Gale observes, denotes that the person to whom this Epistle is addressed was a very great prophet, who, nevertheless, is afterwards said to be a priest. This, however, is not any thing novel or incongruous. For by Apuleius in Metamorph. lib. xi. the Egyptian Zaclas is said to be *propheta primarius et sacerdos, a chief prophet and priest.*

Page 18. *Hermes the God who presides over language.* The Egyptians celebrated two Hermes, the former of which is here signified by Iamblichus. This deity is the source of *invention*, and hence he is said to be the son of Maia; because *search*, which is implied by *Maia*, leads *invention* into light. He bestows too *mathesis* on souls, by unfolding the will of his father Jupiter; and this he accomplishes as the angel or messenger of Jupiter. Proclus in MS. Comment. in Alcibiad. observes, "that this deity is the inspective guardian of *gymnastic exercises*; and hence *hermae*, or carved statues of Mercury, were placed in the Palaestrae; of music, and hence he is honoured as *the lyrist* λυραιος among the celestial constellations; and of *disciplines*, because the invention of geometry, reasoning, and discourse is referred to this God. He presides, therefore, over every species of erudition, leading us to an intelligible essence from this mortal abode, governing the different herds of souls, and dispersing the sleep and oblivion with which they are oppressed. He is likewise the supplier of recollection, the end of which is a genuine intellectual apprehension of divine natures."

P. 20. *The ancient pillars of erzues.* These pillars, according to Amm. Marcellinus, lib. xxii. were concealed prior to the deluge in certain caverns, which were called συριγγεσ, syringes, not far from the Egyptian Thebes. The second Hermes interpreted these pillars, and his interpretation formed many volumes, as Iamblichus informs us in Section viii. of this work. These pillars are mentioned by Laertius in his Life of Democritus; by Dio Chrysostom in Orat. 4g; by Achilles Tatius on Aratus; and by others of the ancients.

P. 24. *There is, therefore, the good itself which is beyond essence, and there is that good which subsists according to essence.* There are three orders of good; *viz.* that which is imparticipable and superessential; that which is imparticipable and essential; and that which is essential and participable. Of these, the last is such as our nature contains; *the good* which ranks among forms is essential; and that which is beyond essence is superessential. Or we say that the good which subsists in us may be considered as a habit, in consequence of subsisting in a subject; the next to this ranks as essence, and a part of essence, I mean *the good* which ranks among forms; and *the good* which is beyond essence, is neither a habit, nor a part. With respect to *the good,* also, which subsists according to essence, it must be observed, that since forms are twofold, some alone distinguishing the *essences* of the things fashioned by form, but others their *perfections*, the genus of essence, same and different, and the form of animal, horse, and man, and every thing of this kind, give distinction to essence and subjects; but the form of *the good*, the beautiful, and the just, and in like manner the form of virtue, of health, strength, and every thing of a similar nature, are perfective of the beings to which they belong: and of some, essence is the leader, but of others the good. For, as Plato says, every thing except *the one*, must necessarily participate of essence; and whatever preserves, gives perfection to, or defends any being, must be good. Hence, since these two are leaders, the one of forms which give subsistence to things, and the other of such as are the sources of their perfection; it is necessary that one of these should be subordinate to the other; I mean that *the good* which is allotted a coordination among forms that are the sources of perfection, should be subordinate to essence, which ranks among causes, whence subsistence originates, if *the good* is being, and a certain being. For it is either the same with, or different from, essence, which the Elean guest or stranger in the Sophista of Plato shows to be the genus of being. And if the good is the same with essence, an absurdity must ensue: for being and well-being are not the same. But if *the good* is something different from essence, it must necessarily participate of essence, in consequence of essence being the genus of all forms. But if genera are more ancient than forms, the good which ranks among forms, and is posterior to their genus, will not be the superessential good which reigns over intelligibles; but this must be asserted of that good, under which this and every form is arranged, which possesses being, and which is the leader of the other genera of being.

P. 24. *But the other medium, which is suspended from the Gods, though it is far inferior to them, is that of daemons.* In addition to what is said in this work by Iamblichus concerning daemons, the following information about them from Olympiodorus, in his MS. Scholia on the Phaedo of Plato, is well worthy the attention of the philosophical reader:

"Since there are in the universe things which subsist differently at different times, and since there are also natures which are conjoined with the superessential unities, it is necessary that there should be a certain middle genus, which is neither immediately suspended from deity, nor subsists differently at different times, according to better and worse, but which is always perfect, and does not depart from its proper virtue; and is immutable indeed, but is not conjoined with the superessential [which is the characteristic of deity]. The whole of this genus is daemoniacal There are, also, different genera of daemons: for they are placed under the mundane Gods. The highest of these subsists according to the one of the Gods, and is called an unific and divine genus of daemons. The next subsists according to the intellect which is suspended from deity, and is called intellectual. The third subsists according to soul, and is called rational. The fourth, according to nature, and is denominated physical. The fifth according to body, which is called corporeal-formed. And the sixth according to matter, and this is denominated material." Olympiodorus adds, "or after another manner it may be said, that some of these are celestial, others etherial, others aerial, others aquatic, others terrestrial, and others subterranean. With respect to this division also, it is

158

evident that it is derived from the parts of the universe. But irrational daemons originate from the aerial governors, whence, also, the Chaldean Oracle says,

Ηεριων ελατηρα κυνων χθονιων τε και υγρων,

i.e. "being the charioteer of the aerial, terrestrial, and aquatic dogs." Our guardian (daeemons, however, belong to that order of daemons which is arranged under the Gods that preside over the ascent and descent of souls. For a more copious account of daemons see the notes on the First Alcibiades in vol, i. of my translation of Plato.

One and the best solution will be obtained by surveying the mode of divine allotment.

The manner in which divine allotments subsist is admirably unfolded by Proclus in Tim. as follows: "Since, according to a division of the universe into two parts, we have distributed allotments into the celestial and sublunary, there can be no doubt what the former are, and whether they possess an invariable sameness of subsistence. But the sublunary allotments are deservedly a subject of admiration, whether they are said to be perpetual or not. For since all things in generation are continually changing and flowing, how can the allotments of the providential rulers of them be said to be perpetual? For things in generation are not perpetual. But if their allotments are not perpetual, how is it possible to suppose that divine government can subsist differently at different times? For an allotment is neither a certain separate energy of the Gods, so that sublunary natures changing, we might say that it is exempt, and remains immutable, nor is it that which is governed alone, so that no absurdity would follow from admitting that an allotment is in a flowing condition, and is conversant with all various mutations; but it is a providential inspection, and unrestrained government of divinity over sublunary concerns. Such being the doubts with which this subject is attended, the following appears to be a solution of the difficulty.

"We must say, then, that it is not proper to consider all the natures that are in generation, and generation itself, as alone consisting of things mutable and flowing, but that there is also something immutable in these, and which is naturally adapted to remain perpetually the same. For the interval which receives and comprehends in itself all the parts of the world, and which has an arrangement through all bodies, is immoveable, lest, being moved, it should require another place, and thus should proceed front one receptacle to another, *ad infinitum*. The etherial vehicles, also, of divine souls, with which they are circularly invested, and which imitate the lives in the heavens, have a perpetual essence, and are eternally suspended from these divine souls themselves, being g full of prolific powers, and performing a circular motion, according to a certain secundary revolution of the celestial orbs. And, in the third place, the wholeness (ολοτησ) of the elements has a permanent subsistence, though the parts are all-variously corrupted. For it is necessary that every form in the universe should be neverfailing, in order that the universe may be perfect, and that, being generated from an immoveable cause, it may be immoveable in its essence. *But every wholeness is a form, or rather it is that which it is said to be through the participation of one allperfect form.*

"And here we may see the orderly progression of the nature of bodies. For the interval of the universe is immoveable according to every kind of motion. But the

159

vehicles of divine souls alone receive a mutation according to place; for such a motion as this is most remote from essential mutation. And the wholeness of the elements admits in its parts the other motions of bodies, but the whole remains perfectly immutable. The celestial allotments also, which proximately divide the interval of the universe, codistribute likewise the heavens themselves. But those in the sublunary region are primarily, indeed, allotted the parts which are in the interval of the universe, but afterwards they make a distribution according to the definite vehicles of souls. And, in the third place, they remain perpetually the same, according g to the total parts of generation. The allotments of the Gods, therefore, do not change, nor do they subsist differently at different times; for they have not their subsistence proximately in that which may be changed.

"How, therefore, do the illuminations of the Gods accede to these? How are the dissolutions of sacred rites effected? And how is the same place at different times under the influence of different spirits? May it not be said, that since the Gods have perpetual allotments, and divide the earth according to divine numbers, similarly to the sections of the heavens, the parts of the earth also are illuminated, so far as they participate of aptitude. But the circulation of the heavenly bodies, through the figures which they possess, produce this aptitude; divine illumination at the same time imparting a power more excellent than the nature which is present with these parts of the earth. This aptitude is also effected by nature herself as a whole, inserting divine impressions in each of the illuminated parts, through which they spontaneously participate of the Gods. For as these parts depend on the Gods, nature inserts in such of them as are different, different images of the divinities. Times too cooperate in producing this aptitude, according to which other things, also, are governed; the proper temperature of the air likewise; and, in short, every thing by which we are surrounded contributes to the increase and diminution of this aptitude. When, therefore, conformably to a concurrence of these many causes, an aptitude to the participation of the Gods is ingenerated in some one of the natures which are disposed to be Changed, then a certain divinity is unfolded into light, which, prior to this, was concealed through the inaptitude of the recipients; possessing, indeed, his appropriate allotment eternally, and always extending the participation of himself, similarly to illuminations from the sun, but not being always participated by sublunary natures, in consequence of their inaptitude to such participation. For as with respect to partial souls such as ours, which at different times embrace different lives, some of them, indeed, choose lives accommodated to their appropriate Gods, but others foreign lives, through oblivion of the divinities to whom they belong; thus, also, with respect to sacred places, some are adapted to the power which there receives its allotment, but others are suspended from a different order. And on this account, as the Athenian guest in Plato says, some places are more fortunate, but others more unfortunate.

"The divine Iamblichus, however, doubts how the Gods are said to be allotted certain places according to definite times, as, by Plato in the Timaeus, Minerva is said to have been first allotted the guardianship of Athens, and afterwards of Sais. For if their allotment commenced from a certain time, it will also at a certain time cease. For every thing which is measured by time is of this kind. And farther still, was the place which at a certain time they are allotted, without a

160

presiding deity prior to this allotment, or was it under the government of other Gods? For if it was without a presiding deity, how is it to be admitted that a certain part of the universe was once entirely destitute of divinity? How can any place remain without the guardianship of superior beings? And if any place is sufficient to the preservation of itself, how does it afterwards become the allotment of some one of the Gods? But if it should be said, that it is afterwards under the government of another God, of whom it becomes the allotment, this also is absurd. For the second God does not divulse the government and allotment of the former, nor do the Gods alternately occupy the places of each other, nor daemons change their allotments. Such being the doubts on this subject, he solves them by saying, that the allotments of the Gods remain perpetually unchanged, but that the participants of them at onetime, indeed, enjoy the beneficent influence of the presiding powers, but at another are deprived of it. He adds, that *these are the mutations measured by time, which sacred institutes frequently call the birthday of the Gods.*

P. 31. *Which also, the art of divine works perceiving, &c.* This art of divine works is called *theurgy*, in which Pythagoras was initiated among the Syrians, as we are informed by Iamblichus in his Life of that philosopher. (See p. 9 of my translation of that work.) Proclus also was skilled in this art, as may be seen in the Life of him by Marinus. Psellus, in his MS. treatise on Daemons, says, as we have before observed, "that magic formed the last part of the sacerdotal science"; in which place by magic he doubtless means that kind of it which is denominated theurgy. And that theurgy was employed by the ancients in their mysteries, I have fully proved in my treatise on the Eleusinian and Bacchic Mysteries. [*] This theurgy, too, is doubtless the same as the magic of Zoroaster, which Plato in the First Alcibiades says, consisted in the worship of the Gods; on which passage the following account of theurgy by Proclus was, I have no doubt, originally part of a commentary. For the MS. Commentary of Proclus, which is extant on this dialogue, does not extend to more than a third part of it; and this Dissertation on Theurgy, which is only extant in Latin, was published by Ficinus the translator, immediately after his Excerpta, from this Commentary. So that it seems highly probable that the manuscript from which Ficinus translated his Excerpta, was much more perfect than that which has been preserved to us, in consequence of containing this account of the theurgy of the ancients.

"In the same manner as lovers gradually advance from that beauty which is apparent in sensible forms, to that which is divine; so the ancient priests, when they considered that there is a certain alliance and sympathy in natural things to each other, and of things manifest to occult powers, and discovered that all things subsist in all, they fabricated a sacred science from this mutual sympathy and similarity. Thus they recognised things supreme in such as are subordinate, and the subordinate in the Supreme: in the celestial regions, terrene properties subsisting in a causal and celestial manner; and in earth celestial properties, but according to a terrene condition. For how shall we account for those plants called heliotropes, that is, attendants on the sun, moving in correspondence with the revolution of its orb, but selenitropes, or attendants on the moon, turning in exact conformity to her motion? It is because all things pray, and hymn the leaders of their respective orders; but some intellectually, and others rationally;

some in a natural, and others after a sensible, manner. Hence the sunflower, as far as it is able, moves in a circular dance towards the sun; so that if any one could hear the pulsation made by its circuit in the air, he would perceive something composed by a sound of this kind, in honour of its king, such as a plant is capable of framing. Hence, too, we may behold the sun and moon in the earth, but according to a terrene quality; but in the celestial regions, all plants, and stones, and animals, possessing an intellectual life according to a celestial nature. Now the ancients, having contemplated this mutual sympathy of things, applied for occult purposes, both celestial and terrene natures, by means of which, through a certain similitude, they deduced divine virtues into this inferior abode. For, indeed, similitude itself is a sufficient cause of binding things together in union and consent. Thus, if a piece of paper is heated, and afterwards placed near a lamp, though it does not touch the fire, the paper will be suddenly inflamed, and the flame will descend from the superior to the inferior parts. This heated paper we may compare to a certain relation of inferiors to superiors; and its approximation to the lamp, to the opportune use of things according to time, place, and matter. But the procession of fire into the paper, aptly represents the presence of divine light to that nature which is capable of its reception. Lastly, the inflammation of the paper may be compared to the deification of mortals, and to the illumination of material natures, which are afterwards carried upwards, like the enkindled paper, from a certain participation of divine seed.

"Again, the lotus, before the rising of the sun, folds its leaves into itself, but gradually expands them on its rising: unfolding them in proportion to the sun's ascent to the zenith; but as gradually contracting them as that luminary descends to the west. Hence this plant, by the expansion and contraction of its leaves, appears no less to honour the sun, than men by the gesture of their eyelids, and the motion of their lips. But this imitation and certain participation of supernal light is not only visible in plants, which possess nothing more than a vestige of life, but likewise in particular stones. Thus the sun-stone, by its golden rays, imitates those of the sun; but the stone called the eye of heaven, or of the sun, has a figure similar to the pupil of an eye, and a ray shines from the middle of the pupil. Thus, too, the lunar stone, which has a figure similar to the moon when horned, by a certain change of itself, follows the lunar motion. Lastly, the stone called helioselenus, i.e. of the sun and moon, imitates, after a manner, the congress of those luminaries, which it images by its colour. So that all things are full of divine natures; terrestrial natures receiving the plenitude of such as are celestial, but celestial of supercelestial essences; [**] while every order of things proceeds gradually, in a beautiful descent, from the highest to the lowest. For whatever particulars are collected into one above the order of things, are afterwards dilated in descending, various souls being distributed under their various ruling divinities.

"In the next place, there are many solar animals, such as lions and cocks, which participate, according to their nature, of a certain solar divinity; whence it is wonderful how much inferiors yield to superiors in the same order, though they do not yield in magnitude and power. Hence it is said, that a cock is very much feared, and, as it were, reverenced, by a lion; the reason of which we cannot assign from matter or sense, but from the contemplation alone of a supernal order. For thus we shall find that the presence of the solar virtue accords more with a cock than with a lion. This will be evident from considering that the cock, as it were, with certain hymns, applauds and calls to the rising sun, when he bends his course to us from the antipodes; and that solar angels sometimes appear in forms of this kind, who, though they are without shape, yet present themselves to us, who are connected with shape, in some sensible form. Sometimes, too, there are daemons with a leonine front, who when a cock is placed before them, unless they are of a solar order, suddenly disappear; and this because those natures which have an inferior rank in the same order always reverence their superiors; just as many, on beholding the images of divine men, are accustomed, from the very view, to be fearful of perpetrating any thing base.

"In fine, some things turn round correspondent to the revolutions of the sun, as the plants which we have mentioned, and others after a manner imitate the solar rays, as the palm and the date; some the fiery nature of the sun, as the laurel; and others a different property. For, indeed, we may perceive that the properties which are collected in the sun, are every where distributed to subsequent natures constituted in a solar order, that is, to angels, daemons, souls, animals, plants, and stones. Hence the authors of the ancient priesthood discovered from things apparent the worship of superior powers, while they mingled some things and purified others. They mingled many things indeed together, because they saw that some simple substances possessed a divine property (though not taken singly) sufficient to call down that particular power, of which they were participants. Hence, by the mingling of many things together, they attracted upon us a supernal influx; and by the composition of one thing from many, they produced an assimilation to that one which is above many; and composed statues from the mixture of various substances conspiring in sympathy and consent. Besides this, they collected composite odours, by a divine art, into one, comprehending a multitude of powers, and symbolizing with the unity of a divine essence; considering that division debilitates each of these, but that mingling them together restores them to the idea of their exemplar.

"But sometimes one herb, or one stone, is sufficient to a divine operation. Thus a thistle is sufficient to procure the sudden appearance of some superior power; but a laurel, raccinum (or a thorny kind of sprig), the land and sea onion, the coral, the diamond, and the jasper, operate as a safeguard. The heart of a mole is subservient to divination, but sulphur and marine water to purification. Hence the ancient priests, by the mutual relation and sympathy of things to each other, collected their virtues into one, but expelled them by repugnancy and antipathy; purifying when it was requisite with sulphur and bitumen, and sprinkling with marine water. For sulphur purifies, from the sharpness of its odour; but marine water on account of its fiery portion. Besides this, in the worship of the Gods, they offered animals, and other substances congruous to their nature; and received, in the first place, the powers of daemons, as proximate to natural substances and operations; and by these natural substances they convoked into their presence those powers to which they approached. Afterwards they proceeded from daemons to the powers and energies of the Gods; partly, indeed, from daemoniacal instruction, but partly by their own industry, interpreting appropriate symbols, and ascending to a proper intelligence of the Gods. And lastly, laying aside natural substances and their operations, they received themselves into the communion and fellowship of thc Gods."

The Emperor Julian alludes to this theurgical art, in the following extract from his Arguments against the Christians, preserved by Cyril. Το γαρ εν θεων εις ανθρωπους αφικνουμενον πνευμα σπανιακις μεν και εν ολιγοις γινεται, και ουτε παντα ανδρα τουτου μετασχειν ρᾳδιον, ουτε εν παντι καιρῳ. τουτη και το παρ' Εβραιοις επελιπεν, ουκουν ουδε παρ'Αιγυπτιοις εις τουτο σωζεται. Φαινεται δε και τα αυτοφυν χρηστηρια τιας των χρονων εικοντα περιοδοις. ὅ δε φιλανθρωπος ημων δεσποτης και πατηρ Ζευς εννοησας, ως αν μη πανταπασι της προς τους θεους αποστερηθωμεν κοινωνιας δεδωκεν ημιν δια των ιρων τεχνων επισκεψιν, υφ' ης προς τας χρειας εξομεν την αποχρωσαν βόηθειαν. i.e. " For the inspiration which arrives to men from the Gods is rare, and exists but in a few. Nor is it easy for every man to partake of this, nor at every time. This has ceased among the Hebrews, nor is it preserved to the present time among the Egyptians. Spontaneous oracles, also, are seen to yield to temporal periods. This, however, our philanthropic lord and father Jupiter understanding, that we might not be entirely deprived of communion with the Gods, has given us observation through sacred arts, by which we have at hand sufficient assistance." For the cause why, at stated times, sacred arts, oracles, and inspiration fail, see the additional notes to my translation of Iamblichus's Life of Pythagoras.

[*] See the second edition of this work in Nos. XV. and XVI. of the Pamphleteer.
[**] i.e. Of natures which are not connected with body.

P. 32. *The participant of the rational soul becomes the cause of suffering to the composite.* See my translation of Plotinus on the Impassivity of Incorporeal Natures, in which this is beautifully and profoundly demonstrated. Proclus, also, in Tim. lib, v. p. 340, admirably observes, that the motion of the nutritive power, and the percussions of sense, are the causes of the perturbation of the soul; but that we must not fancy that the soul suffers any thing through these. "For as if," says he, "some one standing on the margin of a river should behold the image and form of himself in the floating stream, he indeed will preserve his face unchanged; but the stream, being all-variously moved, will change the image, so that at different times it will appear to him different, oblique and erect, and perhaps divulsed and continuous. Let us suppose too, that such a one, through being unaccustomed to the spectacle, should think that it was himself that suffered this distortion, in consequence of surveying his shadow in the water, and thus thinking, should be afflicted and disturbed, astonished and impeded. After the same manner, the soul beholding the image of herself in body, borne along in the river of generation, and variously disposed at different times, through inward passions and external impulses, is indeed herself impassive, but thinks that she suffers; and being ignorant of, and mistaking her image for, herself, is disturbed, astonished, and perplexed."

P. 41. *Since, however, the order of all the Gods is profoundly united.--For the very existence in them, whatever it may be, is the one of their nature.*
The Gods are self-perfect superessential unities, so far as they are Gods. For the principal subsistence of every thing is according to the summit of its essence, and this in the Gods is *theone*, through which they are profoundly united to each oth-

er and to *the one itself*; or the ineffable principle of things, from which they are ineffably unfolded into light. Concerning this union of them with each other, Proclus admirably observes as follows, 'in his MS. Commentary on the Parmenides of Plato. "All these unities are in, and are profoundly united to, each other, and their union is far greater than the communion and sameness which subsist in beings. For in the latter there is indeed a mutual mixture of forms, similitude, and friendship, and a participation of each other; but the union of the Gods, as being a union of unities, is much more uniform, ineffable, and transcendent: for here *all are in all*, which does not take place in forms or ideas; [*] and their unmingled purity, and the characteristic of each, in a manner far surpassing the diversity in ideas, preserves their natures unconfused, and distinguishes their peculiar powers. Hence, some of them are more universal, and others more particular; some of them are characterised by permanency, others by progression, and others by conversion, or regression. Some, again, are generative, others anagogic, or of an elevating nature, and others demiurgic; and universally, there are different characteristics of different Gods, the connective, perfective, demiurgic, assimilative, and such others as are celebrated posterior to these; so that all are in all, and yet each is at the same time separate and distinct.

"Indeed we obtain this knowledge of their union and characteristics from the natures by which they are participated. For, with respect to the visible Gods, we say that there is one soul of' the sun, and another of the earth, directing our attention to the visible bodies of these divinities, which possess much variety in their essence, powers, and dignity among wholes. As, therefore, we apprehend the difference of incorporeal essences from sensible inspection, in like manner from the variety of incorporeal essences, we are enabled to know something of the unmingled distinction of the first and superessential unities, and of the characteristics of each. For each unity has a multitude suspended from its nature, which is either intelligible alone; or intelligible, and at the same time intellectual; or intellectual alone; and this last is either participated, or not participated; and this again, is either supermundane, or mundane. And thus far does the progression of the unities extend." Shortly after he adds, "As trees by their extremities are rooted in the earth, and through this are earthly in every part, in the same manner' divine natures are rooted by their summits in *the one*, and each is a *unity* and *one*, through its unconfused union with *the one itself*." See more on this most important of all subjects in the notes to my translation of the Parmenides.

[*] For in these, all are in each, but not all in all.

P. 54. *For as in all other things, such as are principal, primarily begin from themselves, &c.*

Hence every God begins his own energy from himself, which Proclus thus demonstrates in Prop. 131 of his Elements of Theology. "For every God first exhibits the peculiarity of his presence with secondary natures in himself; because he imparts himself to other things also according to his own exuberant plenitude. For neither is deficiency adapted to the Gods, nor fulness alone. For every thing deficient is imperfect, and not being itself perfect, it is impossible it should make another thing to be perfect. But that which is full is alone sufficient to itself, and is not yet prepared to communicate. It is necessary, therefore, that the nature which fills other things, and which extends to other things the communications of itself, should be superplenary, or exuberantly full. Hence, if a divine nature fills all things from itself with the good which it contains in itself, it is exuberantly full. And if this be the case, establishing first in itself the peculiarity which it imparts to others, it will extend to them the communications of superplenary goodness.

P. 62. *It is requisite also to know what enthusiasm is, and how it is produced.* The following account of enthusiasm, and of the different kinds of mania mentioned by Plato in the Phaedrus, from the Schola of Hermeas on that dialogue, is extracted from the additional notes to my translation of Proclus on the Timaeus, and is given in this place for the sake of the Platonic English reader, who may not have that translation in his possession, as a valuable addition to what is here said by Iamblichus on this subject.

"Since Plato here delivers four kinds of mania, by which I mean enthusiasm, and possession or inspiration from the Gods, *viz.* the musical, the telestic, the prophetic, and the amatory, previous to the discussion of each, we must first speak about enthusiasm, and show to what part of the soul the enthusiastic energy pertains; whether each part of it possesses this energy; if all enthusiasm is from the Gods; and in what part of the soul it is ingenerated; or whether it subsists in something else more excellent than soul. Where, then, does that which is properly and primarily called enthusiasm subsist, and what is it? Of the rational soul there are two parts, one of which is *dianoia*, but the other *opinion*. Again, however, of dianoia, one part is said to be the lowest, and is properly dianoia, but another part of it is the highest, which is said to be the intellect of it, according to which the soul especially becomes intellectual, and which some call intellect in capacity. There is also another thing above this, which is the summit of the whole soul, and most allied to *the one*, which likewise wishes well to all things, and always gives itself up to the Gods, and is readily disposed to do whatever they please. This, too, is said to be *the one* of the soul, bears the image of the superessential one, and unites the whole soul. But that these things necessarily thus subsist, we may learn as follows: The rational soul derives its existence from all the causes prior to itself, i.e. from intellect and the Gods. But it subsists also from itself: for it perfects itself So far, therefore, as it subsists from the Gods, it possesses *the one*, which unites all its powers, and all the multitude of itself, and conjoins them to *the one itself*; and is the first recipient of the goods imparted by the Gods. It likewise makes all the essence of the soul to be boniform, according to which it is connected with the Gods, and united to them. But so far as it subsists from intellect it possesses an intellectual nature, according to which it apprehends forms, by simple projections, or intuitions, and not discursively; and is conjoined to the intellect which is above itself. And so far as it constitutes itself, it possesses the dianoetic power, according to which it generates sciences and certain theorems, energizes discursively, and collects conclusions from propositions. For that it constitutes or gives subsistence to itself, is evident from its imparting perfection to itself; since that which leads itself to perfection, and imparts to itself well-being, will much more impart to itself existence. For well-being is a greater thing than being. If, therefore, the soul imparts that which is

166

greater to itself, it will much more impart that which is less. Hence that which is primarily, properly, and truly enthusiasm from the Gods, is effected according to this one of the soul, which is above dianoia, and above the intellect of the soul; which one is at another time in a relaxed and dormant state. This one, likewise, becoming illuminated [by the Gods], all the life of the soul is illuminated, and also intellect, dianoia, and the irrational part, and the resemblance of enthusiasm is transmitted as far as to the body itself.

"Other enthusiasms, therefore, are produced about other parts of the soul, [*] certain daemons exciting them, [†] or the Gods also, though not without the intervention of daemons. For dianoia is said to energize enthusiastically, when it discovers sciences and theorems in a very short space of time, and in a greater degree than other men. Opinion, likewise, and the phantasy, are said thus to energize when they discover arts, and accomplish admirable works, such, for instance, as Phidias effected in the formation of statues, and another in another art, as also Homer says [**] of him who made the belt of Hercules, 'that he neither did nor would artificially produce such another.' Anger, likewise, is said to energize enthusiastically-, when in battle it energizes supernaturally.

Like Mars, when brandishing his spear, he raged. [††]

But if some one, yielding to desire, should eat of that which reason forbids, and through this should unexpectedly become well, you may say that desire also, in this instance, energized enthusiastically, though obscurely; so that enthusiasm is likewise produced about the other parts of the soul. Enthusiasm, however, properly so called, is when this one of the soul, which is above intellect, is excited to the Gods, and is from thence inspired. But at different times it is possessed about the aptitudes of itself, be different Gods; and is more or less possessed when intellect or dianoia is that which is moved. As, therefore, when we inquire what philosophy is, we do not always accurately define it, but frequently, front an improper use of the word, call mathematics or physics philosophy and science; we do the like also with respect to enthusiasm. For though it should be the phantasy which is excited, we are accustomed to call the excitation enthusiasm. Moreover, those who ascribe enthusiasm to the temperatures of bodies, or the excellent temperament of the air, or the ascendency of exhalations, or the aptitudes of times and places, or the agency of the bodies that revolve in the heavens, speak rather of the cooperating and material causes of the thing than of the causes of it properly so called. You have, therefore, for the producing cause of enthusiasm, the Gods; for the material cause, the enthusiastically energizing soul itself, or the external symbols; for the formal cause, the inspiration of the Gods about the me of the soul; and for the final cause, good.

"If, however, the Gods always wish the soul what is good, why does not the soul always energize enthusiastically? May we not say, that the Gods indeed always wish the soul what is good, but they are also willing that the order of the universe should prevail, and that the soul, through many causes, is not always adapted to enthusiasm, on which account it does not always enthusiastically energize? But some say that the telestic art extends as far as to the sublunary region. If, therefore, they mean that no one of the superlunary and celestial natures energizes in the sublunary region, they evidently assert what is absurd. But if they mean that the Telestae, or mystic operators, are not able to energize above the lunar sphere, w e say, that if all the allotments of souls are sublunary, their assertion will be true; but if there are also allotments of souls above the moon, as there are (for some are the attendants of the sun, others of the moon, and others of Saturn, since the Demiurgus disseminated some of them into the earth, others into the moon, and others elsewhere), this being the case, it will be possible for the soul to energize above the moon. For what the whole order of things imparts to the soul for a very extended period of time, this the soul is also able to impart to itself for a short space of time, when assisted by the Gods through the telestic art. For the soul can never energize above its own allotment, but can energize to the extent of it. Thus, for instance, if the allotment of the soul was as far as to philosophy, the soul would be able, though it should not choose a philosophic but some other life, to energize in that life somewhat philosophically. There are also said to be certain supermundane souls. And thus we have shown how the soul energizes enthusiastically.

But how are statues said to have an enthusiastic energy? May we not say, that a statue being inanimate, does not itself energize about divinity, but the telestic art, purifying the matter of which the statue consists, and placing round it certain characters and symbols, in the first place renders it, through these means, animated, and causes it to receive a certain life from the world; and, in the next place, after this, it prepares the statue to be illuminated by a divine nature, through which it always delivers oracles, as long as it is properly adapted. For the statue, when it has been rendered perfect by the telestic art, remains afterwards [endued with a prophetic power] till it becomes entirely unadapted to divine illumination; but he who receives the inspiring influence of the Gods receives it only at certain times, and not always. But the cause of this is, that the soul, when filled with deity, energizes about it. Hence, in consequence of energizing above its own power, it becomes weary. For it would be a God, and similar to the souls of the stars, if it did not become weary. But the statue, conformably to its participations, remains illuminated. Hence the inaptitude of it entirely proceeds into privation, unless it is again, *de novo*, perfected and animated by the mystic operator. We have sufficiently shown, therefore, that enthusiasm, properly so called, is effected about *the one* of the soul, and that it is an illumination of divinity.

"In the next place, let us discuss the order and the use of the four manias, and show why the philosopher makes mention of these alone. Is it because there are no other than these, or because these were sufficient for his purpose? That there are, therefore, many other divine inspirations and manias Plato himself indicates as he proceeds, and prior to this, he makes mention of the inspiration from the Nymphs. But there are also inspirations from Pan, from the mother of the Gods, and from the Corybantes, which are elsewhere mentioned by Plato. Here, however, he alone delivers these four manias; in the first place, because these alone are sufficient to the soul, in the attainment of its proper apocatastasis, as we shall afterwards show; and in the next place, because he delivers the proximate steps of ascent to the soul. For the gifts of the Gods to all beings are many and incomprehensible. But now he delivers to us the energies of the Gods which are extended to souls. He delivers, however, these four manias, not as if one of them was not sufficient, and especially the amatory, to lead back the soul to its pristine felicity; but at present the series and regular gradation of them, and the orderly perfection of the soul, are unfolded. As, therefore, it is possible for the tyrannic life, when suddenly changed, to become aristocratic, through employing strenuous promptitude and a divine allotment, but the gradual ascent is from a tyrannic to a democratic, and from this to an oligarchic life, afterwards to a timocratic, and at last to an aristocratic life, but the descent and lapse are vice versa; thus also here, the soul being about to ascend, and be restored to its former felicity, is in the first place possessed with the musical mania, afterwards with the telestic, then with the prophetic, and, in the last place, with the amatory mania. These inspirations, however, conspire with, and are in want of, each other; so abundant is their communion. For the telestic requires the prophetic [***] mania; since the latter [†††] interprets many things pertaining to the former. And again, the prophetic requires the telestic mania. For the telestic mania perfects and establishes oracular predictions. Farther still, the prophetic uses the poetic and musical mania. For prophets, as I may, say, always speak in verse. And again, the musical uses the prophetic mania spontaneously, as Plato says. But what occasion is there to speak about the amatory and musical manias? For nearly the same persons exercise both these, as, for instance, Sappho, Anacreon, and the like, in consequence of these not being able to subsist without each other. But it is very evident that the amatory mania contributes to all these, since it is subservient to enthusiasm of every kind: for no enthusiasm can be effected without amatory inspiration. And you may see how Orpheus appears to have applied himself to all these, as being in want of, and adhering to, each other. For we learn that he was most telestic, and most prophetic, and was excited by Apollo; and besides this, that he was most poetic, on which account he is said to have been the son of Calliope. He was likewise most amatory, as he himself acknowledges to Musaeus, extending to him divine goods, and rendering him perfect. Hence he appears to have been possessed with all the manias, and this by a necessary consequence. For there is an abundant union, conspiration, and alliance with each other, of the Gods who preside over these manias, *viz.* of the Muses, Bacchus, Apollo, and Love.

"It remains, therefore, that we should unfold the nature of each of the manias, previously observing that those which are internal, and originate from the soul itself, and give perfection to it, are of one kind; but the external energies of them, and which preserve the outward man, and our nature, are of another. The four external, however, are analogous to the four internal manias. Let us consider, therefore, in the first place, the internal, and which alone originate from the soul itself, and let us see what they effect in the soul. In order, likewise, that this may become manifest, and also their arrangement, let us survey from on hi-h, the descent, as Plato says, and defluxion of the wings of the soul. From the beginning, therefore, and at first, the soul was united to the Gods, and its unity to their one. But afterwards the soul departing from this divine union descended into intellect, and no longer possessed real beings unitedly, and in one, but apprehended and surveyed them by simple projections, and, as it were, contacts of its intellect. In the next place, departing from intellect, and descending into reasoning and dianoia, it no longer apprehended real beings by simple intuitions, but syllogisti-

169

cally and transitively, proceeding from one thin; to another, from propositions to conclusions. Afterwards, abandoning, truc reasoning, and the dissolving peculiarity, it descended into generation, and became filled with much irrationality and perturbation. It is necessary, therefore, that it should recur to its proper principles and again return to the place from whence it came. To this ascent and apocatastasis, however, these four manias contribute. And the musical mania, indeed, leads to symphony and harmony, the agitated and disturbed nature of the parts of the soul, which were hurried away to indefiniteness and inaptitude, and were filled with abundant tumult. But the telestic mania causes the soul to be perfect and entire, and prepares it to energize intellectually. For the musical mania alone harmonizes and represses the parts of the soul; but the telestic causes the whole of it to energize, and prepares it to become entire, so that the intellectual part of it may energize. For the soul, by descending into the realms of generation, resembles a thin, broken and relaxed. And the circle of *the same*, or the intellectual part of it, is fettered; but the circle of *the different*, or the doxastic part, sustains many fractures and turnings. Hence, the soul energizes partially, and not according to the whole of itself. The Dionysiacal inspiration, therefore, after the parts of the soul are coharmonized, renders it perfect, and causes it to energize according to the whole of itself, and to live intellectually. But the Apolloniacal mania converts and coexcites all the multiplied powers, and the whole of the soul, to the one of it. Hence Apollo is denominated as elevating the soul from multitude to the one. And the remaining mania, the amatory, receiving the soul united, conjoins this one of the soul to the Gods, and to intelligible beauty. As the givers, therefore, of these manias are transcendently united, and are in each other, the gifts also on this account participate of, and communicate with, each other, and the recipient, which is the soul, possesses an adaptation to all the gifts. This, therefore, is the order, and these are the energies and powers within the soul itself, of these four manias.

"But let us also consider their external energies on man, and what they outwardly effect about us. The musical mania, therefore, causes us to speak in verse, and to act and be moved rhythmically, and to sing in metre, the splendid deeds of divine men, and their virtues and pursuits; and, through these, to discipline our life, in the same manner as the inward manias coharmonize our soul. But the telestic mania, expelling every thin- foreign, contaminating, and noxious, preserves our life perfect and innoxious, and banishing an insane and diabolical phantasy, causes us to be sane, entire, and perfect, just as the internal telestic mania makes the soul to be perfect and entire. Again, the prophetic mania contracts into one the extension and infinity of time, and sees, as in one present now, all things, the past, the future, and the existing time. Hence it predicts what will be, which it sees as present to itself. It causes us, therefore, to pass through life in an irreprehensible manner; just as the internal prophetic mania contracts and elevates all the multiplied and many powers and lives of the soul to the one, in order that it may in a greater degree be preserved and connected. But the amatory mania converts young persons to us, and causes them to become our friends, being instructive of youth, and leading them from sensible beauty to our psychical beauty, and from this sending them to intelligible beauty; in the same manner as the internal amatory mania conjoins *the one*of the soul to the Gods.

"All the above-mentioned manias, therefore, are superior to the prudent and temperate energies of the soul. Nevertheless, there is a mania which is coordinate with temperance, and which we say has in a certain respect a prerogative above [****] it. For certain inspirations are produced, according to the middle and also according to the doxastic reasons of the soul, conformably to which artists effect certain things, and discover theorems beyond expectation, as Asclepius, for instance, in medicine, and Hercules in the practic [††††] life."

Afterwards, in commenting on what Plato says of the mania from the Muses, ii:. "that it adorns the infinite deeds of the ancients," Hermeas observes, "that the inward energy in the soul of the poetic mania, by applying itself to superior and intelligible natures, imparts to subordinate natures harmony and order; but that the external divinely inspired poetry celebrates the deeds of the ancients, and instructs both its contemporaries and posterity, extending its energies every where." But Plato says, "that he who without the divinely-inspired mania of the Muses expects to become a divine poet, will, by thus fancying, become himself imperfect, and his poetry will be vanquished and concealed by the poetry which is the progeny of mania." Hermeas adds, "For what similitude is there between the poetry of Chxrilus and Callimachus, and that of Homer and Pindar? For the divinely-inspired poets, as being filled from the Muses, always invoke them, and extend to them all that they say." For a fuller and most admirable account of the poetic mania, and of the different species of poetry by Proclus, see the notes on the tenth book of the Republic, in my translation of Plato, and also the Introduction to my translation of the Rhetoric, Poetic, and Nicomachean Ethics of Aristotle.

From what is here said by Hermeas about enthusiasm, the intelligent reader will easily see that none of the Roman poets, whose works have been transmitted to us, possessed that which is primarily, properly, and truly enthusiasm, or that highest species of it in which the one of the soul is illuminated by a divine nature, and through transcendent, similitude is united to it. As to Virgil, indeed, the prince of these poets, though he invokes the Muse in the beginning of the Aeneid, yet his invocation of her is but a partial and secondary thing. For he only calls on her to unfold to him the causes that involved a man of such remarkable piety as Aeneas in so many misfortunes:

Musa, mihi causa memora, &c.

And, confiding in his own genius, he begins his poem without soliciting supernal inspiration,

Arma, virumque cano, &c.

To which may be added, that this placing himself before the Muse, resembles the *ego et meus rex* of Wolsey. On the contrary, divinely-inspired poets, as Hermeas well observes, knock, as it were, at the gates of the Muses, and thus being filled from thence exclaim,

Εσπετε νυν μοι Μουσαι

And,

Μηνιν αειδε θεα ---

And,

Ανδρα μοι εννεπε Μουσα.

For being always extended to them, they dispose the whole of what they afterwards say as derived from their inspiring influence. With an arrogance too, peculiar to the Romans, who, as a certain Greek poet [*****] says, were a people
Beyond measure proud.
Ile associates himself, in his fourth Eclogue, with the Muses, as their equal:
Sicelides Musae, paulo majora canamus.
Which reminds me of what Suetonius relates of Caligula, that he would place himself between the statues of Castor and Pollux, and confer privately with Jupiter Capitolinus, fancying that he was intimate with, and of equal divinity with, these divinities. And as to the poets that have lived since the fall of the Roman empire, it would be ridiculous to suppose that they possessed this highest enthusiasm, as they did not believe in the existence of the sources from whence it is alone genuinely derived.

[*] By an unaccountable mistake here του σωματοα is inserted instead of της ψυχησ; but the mistake is not noticed by the German editor of these Scholia.
[†] And in consequence of this mistake, for αυτο in this place, we must read αυτα..
[**] Odyss. xi. 612.
[††] Iliad xv, 005.
[***] For μουσικησ here, it is necessary to read μανττικησ.
[†††] And for μαντικην read μαντικη.
[****] For υπο here, it is necessary to read υπερ.
[††††] The German editor of these Scholia, instead of πρακτικη, which is the true reading in this place, and which he found in the manuscript, absurdly substitutes for it πυκτικη, as if Hercules was a pugilist. See my translation of the Dissertation of Maximus Tyrius, on the Practic and Theoretic Life.
[*****] Vid. Olympiodor. in Aristot. Meteor.

P. 74. *The attentive power of the soul.* This is that part or power of the rational soul which primarily apprehends the operations of the senses. For the rational soul not oly has intellect in capacity, the dianoetic power, will, and choice, but another power, which is called by the best of the Greek interpreters of Aristotle, as well as by Iamblichus, Το το προσεδτικον, *the attentive.* This power investigates and perceives whatever is transacted in man; and says, I understand, I think, I opine, I am angry, I desire. And, in short, this attentive part of the rational soul passes through all the rational, irrational, vegetable, or physical powers. If, therefore, it is requisite it should pass through all these powers, it will also proceed through the senses, and say, I see, I hear; for it is the peculiarity of that which apprehends energies thus to speak. Hence if it is the attentive power which says these things, it is this power which apprehends the energy of sensibles; for it is necessary that the nature which apprehends all things should be one, since man also is one. For if one part of it should apprehend *these*, and another *those* things, it is just, as Aristotle says, as if you should perceive *this* thing, and *I* that. It is necessary, therefore, that the attentive power should be one indivisible thing.

P. 82. *For the human soul is on all sides darkened by the body, which he who denominates the river of Negligence, or the water of Oblivion, &c ------ will not by such appellations sufficiently express its turpitude.* "The whole of generation, as well as the human body," says Proclus in Tim. lib. v. p. 339, "may be called a river, through its rapid, impetuous, and unstable flux. Thus also in the Republic, Plato calls the whole genesiurgic nature the river of Lethe; in which are contained, as Empedocles says, Oblivion, and the meadow of Ate; the voracity of matter, and the light hating world, as the Gods say; and the winding streams under which many are drawn down, as the Chaldean oracles assert."

P. 119. *But there are a certain few who by employing a certain supernatural power of intellect, are removed from nature, &c.* The class to which these few belong is beautifully unfolded, as follows, by Plotinus, in the beginning of his Treatise on Intellect, Ideas, and real Being. "Since all men from their birth employ sense prior to intellect, and are necessarily first conversant with sensibles, some proceeding no farther, pass through life, considering these as the first and last of things, and apprehending that whatever is painful among these is evil, and whatever is pleasant is good; thus thinking it sufficient to pursue the one and avoid the other. Those, too, among them who pretend to a greater share of reason than others, esteem this to be wisdom, being affected in a manner similar to more heavy birds, who collecting many things from the earth, and being oppressed with the weight, are unable to fly on high, though they have received wings for this purpose from nature. But others are in a small degree elevated from things subordinate, the more excellent part of the soul recalling them from pleasure to a more worthy pursuit. As they are, however, unable to look on him, and as not possessing any thing else which can afford them rest, they betake themselves, together with the name of virtue, to actions and the election of things inferior, from which they at first endeavoured to raise themselves, though in vain. *In the third class is the race of divine men*, who, through a more excellent power, and with piercing eyes, acutely perceive supernal light, to the vision of which they raise themselves above the clouds and darkness, as it were, of this lower world, and there abiding despise every thing in these regions of sense; being no otherwise delighted with the place which is truly and properly their own, than he who after many wanderings is at length restored to his lawful country." See my translation of the whole of this treatise.

P. 131. *By mire, therefore, understand everything corporeal-formed and material.* "Matter," says Simplicius in his Commentary on the first book of Aristotle's Physics, "is nothing else than the mutation of sensibles, with respect to intelligibles, deviating from thence, and carried downwards to non-being. Those things, indeed, which are the properties of sensibles are irrational, corporeal, distributed into parts, and passing into bulk and divulsion, through an ultimate progression into generation, *viz.* into matter; for matter is always truly the last sediment. Hence, also, the Egyptians call the dregs of the first life, which they symbolically denominate water, matter, being as it were a certain mire. And matter is, as it were, the receptacle of generated and sensible natures, not subsisting s any definite form, but as the state or condition of subsistence; just as the impartible, the immaterial, true being, and things of this kind, are the constitution of an intelligible nature; all forms, indeed, subsisting both in sensibles and intelligibles, but in the former materially, and in the latter immaterially; *viz.* in the one impartibly and truly, but in the other partibly and shadowy. Hence every form is in sensibles distributed according to material interval."

P. 135. *Through the innovation and illegality of the Greeks.* Iamblichus says, that through this innovation and illegality, both names and prayers have at present lost their efficacy. For during his time, and for some centuries prior to it, the genuine religion of the Greeks was rapidly declining, through their novelty and volatility, of which he here complains. Hence the Emperor Julian, in the fragments of his treatise against the Christians, preserved by Ciryl, says, speaking of the Christians, "If any one wishes to consider the truth respecting you, he will find that your impiety consists of the Judaic audacity, and the *indolence* and *confusion of the heathens*. For deriving from both, not that which is most beautiful, but the worst, you have fabricated a web of evils. Hence, from the innovation of the Hebrews, you have seized blasphemy towards the venerable Gods; but from our religion you have cast aside reverence to every nature more excellent than man, and the love of paternal institutes." Το γαρ αληθες ει τις υπερ υμων εθελοι σκοπειν, ευρησει της υμετεραν ασεβειαν, εκ τε της Ιουδαϊκης τολμης και της παρα τοις εθνεσιν αδιαφοριας και χυδαιτητος συγκειμενην. εξ αμφιον γαρ ουτι το καλλεστον αλλα το χειρον ελκυσαντες, παρυφην κακων ειργασασθε. ----- Απο μεν ουν της Εβραιων καινοτομιας το βλασφημειν τιμωμενους θεους ηρπασατε· απο δε της παρ ημιν θρησκειας το μεν ευλαβες τε ομου προς απασαν την κρειττονα φυσιν, και των πατριων αγαπητικον, απολελοιπατε.

P. 137. *Prior to truly existing beings, and total principles, &c.* Of the two most ancient principles of all things mentioned in this chapter, as celebrated by Hermes, the first corresponds to the one itself of Plato, and the second to being itself, or superessential being, the summit of the intelligible triad; which two principles are beautifully unfolded by Proclus in the second and third books of his treatise on the Theology of Plato.

P. 138. *He arranges the God Eneph prior to, and as the leader of; the celestial Gods.* ---*But prior to this he arranges the impartible one, which he says is the first paradigm, and which he denominates Eicton.* It appears to me that the former of these two divinities is the same with Saturn, who is the summit of the intellectual order of Gods; and that the latter is *the animal itself* of Plato, or the Phanes of Orpheus, who subsists at the extremity of the intelligible triad. For the God Eneph is said by Iamblichus to be an intellect intellectually perceiving itself, and converting intellections to itself; and these are the characteristics of Saturn. And the God Eicton is said to be the first paradigm, and this is also asserted of Phanes.

P. 139. *For the books which are circulated under the name of Hermes, contain Hermaic opinions, though they frequently employ the language of the philosophers: for they were translated from the Egyptian tongue by men who were not unskilled in philosophy.* A few only of these books are now extant, but what is here said by Iamblichus sufficiently proves their authenticity, and that they contain the genuine doctrines of Hermes. They have doubtless, however, been occasionally interpolated by some of the early Christians, though not to that extent which modern critics, and that mitred sophist Warburton, suppose.

P. 139. *And such as have written concerning the planets.* The twelve parts, mentioned in the preceding chapter, into which the Egyptians divide the heavens, are the twelve signs of the zodiac. But the thirty-six parts are the twelve houses of the planets, divided into three other portions, which they call decans. Ptolemy, however, in his Quadripartite, subverts this doctrine of the Egyptians.

Concerning these decans, see Scaliger ad Manilium, Kircher ii. parte Oedipi, and Salmasius de Annis climactericis. Gale also gives the following extract from Hermes relative to the decans, which had not been before published, and which he derived from a MS. copy of Stobaeus in the possession of Vossius. i.e. "We say, O son, that the body [of the universe] is comprehensive of all things. Conceive, therefore, this to be as it were of a circular form------- But under the circle of this body the thirty-six decans are arranged, as the media of the whole circle of the zodiac.------- These, likewise, must be understood to preside as guardians over every thing in the world, connecting and containing all things-------and preserving the established order of all things--------Farther still, understand, O Tat, that these decans are impassive to the things which the other stars suffer. For neither being detained, do they stop their course, nor being impeded do they recede, nor are they, like the other stars, concealed as with veil by the light of the sun. But being liberated above all things, they comprehend the universe as the guardians and accurate inspectors of it, in the Nycthemeron [or the space of night and day].------- They also possess, with respect to us, the greatest power."

P. 142. *So that what you add from Homer, "that the Gods are flexible," It is not holy to assert.* The words of Homer are στρεπτοι δε τε και θεοι αυτοι, and are to be found in Iliad ix. v. 493. But when Iamblichus says, it is not holy to assert the Gods are flexible, he means that it is not holy according to the literal signification of the words; divine flexibility indicating nothing more than this, that those who through depravity were before unadapted to receive the illuminations of the Gods, and in consequence of this were subject to the power of avenging daemons; when afterwards they obtain pardon of their guilt through prayers and sacrifices, and through methods of this kind apply a remedy to their vices, again become partakers of the goodness of the Gods. So that divine flexibility is a resumption of the participation of divine light and goodness by those who through inaptitude were before deprived of it.

P. 146. *Daemons preside over the parts of our body.* Proclus in the fragments of his Ten Doubts concerning Providence, preserved by Fabricius in the eighth vol. of his Bibliotheca Graeca, observes, "That the Gods, with an exempt transcendency, extend their providence to all things, but that daemons, dividing their superessential subsistence, receive the guardianship of different herds of animals, distributing the providence of the Gods, as Plato says, as far as to the most ultimate division. Hence some of them preside over men, others over lions or other animals, and others over plants; and still more partially, some are the inspective guardians of the eye, others of the heart, and others of the liver." He adds, "all things, however, are full of Gods, some of whom exert their providential energies immediately, but others through daemons as media: not that the Gods are incapable of being present to all things, but that ultimate are themselves unable to participate primary natures." Hence it must be said that there is one principal daemon, who is the guardian and governor of every thing that is in us, and many daemons subordinate to him, who preside over our parts.

P. 150. *Hence it is requisite to consider how he may be liberated from these bonds.* "The one salvation of the soul herself," says Proclus in Tim. lib. v. p. 330, "which is extended by the Demiurgus, and which liberates her from the circle of generation, from abundant wanderings, and an inefficacious life, is her return to the intellectual form, and a flight from every thing which naturally adheres to us from generation. For it is necessary that the soul, which is hurled like seed into the realms of generation, should lay aside the stubble and bark, as it were, which she obtained from being disseminated into these fluctuating realms and that purifying herself from every thing circumjacent, she should become an intellectual flower and fruit, delighting in an intellectual life, instead of doxastic nutriment, and pursuing the uniform and simple energy of the period of sameness, instead of the abundantly wandering motion of the period which is characterized by difference. For she contains each of these circles, and twofold powers. And of her horses one is good, but the other the contrary [as is said in the Phaedrus]. And one of these leads her to generation, but the other from generation to true being. The one also leads her round the genesiurgic, but the other round the intellectual circle. For the period of the same and the similar elevates to intellect, and an intelligible nature, and to the first and most excellent habit. But this habit is that according to which the soul being winged governs the whole world, becoming assimilated to the Gods themselves. And this is the universal form of life in the soul, just as that is the partial form, when she falls into the last body, and becomes something belonging to an individual, instead of belonging to the universe. The middle of these, also, is the partial universal, when she lives in conjunction with her middle vehicle, as a citizen of generation. Dismissing, therefore, her first habit, which subsists according to an alliance to the whole of generation, and laying aside the irrational nature which connects her with generation, likewise governing her irrational part by reason, and extending opinion to intellect, she will be circularly led to a happy life from the wanderings about the regions of sense; which life those that are initiated by Orpheus in the mysteries of Bacchus and Proserpine, pray that they may obtain, together with the allotments of the [celestial] sphere, and a cessation of evil. But if our soul necessarily lives well, when living according to the circle of sameness, much more must this be the case with divine souls. It is, however, possible for our soul to live according to the circle of sameness, when purified, as Plato says. Cathartic virtue, therefore, alone must be called the salvation of souls; since this cuts off; and vehemently obliterates, material natures, and the passions which adhere to us from generation; separates the soul and leads it to intellect; and causes it to leave on earth the vehicles with which it is invested. For souls in descending receive from the elements different vehicles, aerial, aquatic, and terrestrial; and thus at last enter into this gross bulk. For how, without a medium, could they proceed into this body from immaterial spirits?"

Lightning Source UK Ltd.
Milton Keynes UK
UKHW012026240919
350378UK00001B/127/P